Not just another book—it's like a manual that puts the process and details of building a youth ministry at your fingertips. I recommend *Purpose-Driven™ Youth Ministry* to any youth worker who is serious about achieving long-term results.

Paul Fleischmann, Executive Director,
National Network of Youth Ministries

The focus of a purpose-driven church has had a wonderful impact on our church. The same principles have reshaped our youth program. Doug offers hands-on practical insights for igniting young people!

Max Lucado, Author, Pastor

An excellent resource that effectively handles the tension of strategy versus ideas of implementation. Doug clearly grasps disciple-making in the local church, and you will find this resource a valuable tool for you and your leaders. It will assist the new youth worker as well as stretch the veteran leader to new levels. I highly commend this resource.

Dr. Dann Spader, Executive Director, Sonlife Ministries

I believe *PDYM* will be the standard by which all youth ministry programs are judged for years to come. It is solid enough for the college or seminary classroom and practical enough for the novice.

Chap Clark, Ph.D., Associate Professor of
Youth and Family Ministries, Fuller Theological Seminary

PDYM is exciting, logical, jam-packed with creativity and fresh ideas—and complete!

Susie Shellenberger, *Brio* magazine, Focus on the Family

Doug Fields provides a refreshingly practical framework for youth ministry, which is not only effective but thoroughly biblical.

Wayne Rice, Director,
Understand Your Teenager Seminars, Co-founder, Youth Specialties

In my thirty years of professional youth ministry, I have not seen a leadership resource as valuable as *PDYM*. It is both rich in philosophy as well as practical, transferable ideas and illustrations. I heartily recommend it.

Dennis Rogers, Youth Ministry Consultant, Georgia Baptist Convention

If I had to take only one book to partner with the Bible in serving as a foundation for effective local youth ministry, this would be the one.

Larry Mitchell, Youth Ministry Department, Indiana Wesleyan University

Few life experiences can cause a youth minister to radically shift directions in his or her ministry. Reading *PDYM* can—and will.

Richard Ross, Youth Ministry Consultant for the Sunday School Board

Doug Fields has crafted this book to help you define the purpose that God has called you to, and to ensure that every program you initiate is directly linked to your purpose.

Ron Luce, President, Teen Mania Ministries

Doug Fields has created a handbook and filled it with tools that will apply to every youth ministry . . . from five to five hundred. This is a must read!

Barry St. Clair, Founder/Executive Director, Reach Out Ministries

A smart youth worker will read this book. A brilliant youth worker will digest this book. And a wise youth worker will share this book with his or her youth ministry team.

Tic Long, President, Youth Specialties

PDYM reflects on the purposes of youth work rather than the "how to." This book returns to the basics. I plan to use it in my classes.

Jay Kesler, President, Taylor University

PDYM should be in every serious youth leader's and pastor's library!

Bill Muir, Senior Vice President, Youth for Christ, USA

PDYM may be the most influential youth ministry book written to date. It is filled with powerful insights, yet with practical hands-on tools to help you advance God's kingdom where you do ministry. Doug Fields has hit a grand slam.

Chuck Wysong, Director of Youth Ministry, North Park Seminary

Finally, a youth ministry book that moves beyond familiar jargon and gives substance, strategies, and a plan of attack.

Dr. David Olshine, Chairman of Youth Ministries,
Columbia International University

Doug Fields has given us principles that, when applied, will change kids' hearts and, in turn, the collective heart of today's youth culture. If you think you're already ministering with purpose, use this book as an evaluation tool.

Walt Mueller, President, Center for Parent/Youth Understanding

PDYM is an excellent tool to help you develop a youth ministry with substance. Doug's nine components will be a wonderful guide in the development of your own unique youth program.

Chris Liebrum, Youth Ministry Consultant,
Baptist General Convention of Texas

PDYM meets a largely unaddressed area in youth ministry literature today—the area of building a strong transferable philosophy that is both biblical and practical.

Gordon L. Coulter, Assistant Professor
of Christian Education, Azuza Pacific University

Doug has a grip on what it takes to build an effective student ministry. He's a youth ministry strategist and a man of God.

Dan Webster, President, Authentic Leadership, Inc.

PDYM rings with authenticity and conviction that is born out of the real-life experiences of Doug Fields's own life and ministry. Because of Doug's work, we're going to begin to see more youth ministry being driven, not by pride or pressure or problems or programs, but by the power of a Bible-centered purpose.

Duffy Robbins, Associate Professor of
Youth Ministry, Eastern College

PDYM will quickly become a standard work in the field ... read, quoted, and implemented. Doug walks his talk and he invites us here to walk with him.

Len Kageler, Associate Professor of Youth Ministry, Nyack College

All youth workers will be forced to examine the foundations of their youth ministry as they turn these pages. This will bring the balance and focus to the next generation of youth ministry that we so desperately need!

Robert Oglesby, Director of the Center for
Adolescent Studies, Abilene Christian University

Anyone who has a vision to effectively reach adolescents for Christ should read this book.

Steve Gerali, D.Phil., Chair, Department of
Youth Ministry and Adolescent Studies, Judson College

Once in a decade a book is written that will shape the direction of youth work for a coming generation. Doug Fields has written that book. Doug has the experience and expertise to lead us into the twenty-first century with a practical strategy to help all of us be more effective youth workers.

Jim Burns, Ph.D., President, National Institute of Youth Ministry

Thank you, Doug, for writing such a stimulating, eye-opening, and spiritually challenging book. *PDYM* will now be "must reading" in every youth ministry course that I teach.

Dewey Bertolini, Associate Professor of
Youth Ministry and Bible Chaplain, Western Baptist College

PDYM is a foundational book that is practical. It's easy to comprehend and gets your creative juices going.

Les Christie, Associate Professor of Youth Ministry,
San Jose Christian College

Doug Fields is a top leader in the field of youth ministry. He understands what it means to be purpose driven and establish essential values for student ministry. Further, his clear communication skills allow him to provide practical applications that will take your ministry to the next level. I highly recommend this book.

Bo Boshers, Executive Director,
Student Impact, Willow Creek Community Church

PDYM is a long overdue wake-up call for the youth ministry world.

Rich Van Pelt, President, Alongside Ministries

Doug Fields brings all his years of effective student ministry together in nine practical, biblical, and usable foundational principles that any youth worker can apply.

Dr. Ken Garland, Associate Professor of Christian Education,
Biola University, Talbot Theological Seminary

Doug Fields provides a response that is philosophically sound, yet practical for any youth ministry setting. *PDYM* offers principles and strategies that make it a valuable tool in the classroom and the ministry of every serious youth leader.

Doug Randlett, Executive Director, Center for Youth Ministry, Liberty University

I found myself agreeing with Doug on every page. I especially appreciated Doug's personal vulnerability and his emphasis on applying the clear principles of God's Word.

Dave Veerman, Partner, Livingstone Corporation, youth ministry author

Doug Fields has written the textbook on youth ministry. Luckily, it doesn't read like a textbook, it reads like a letter from a close friend. This book is packed with learnable concepts that do more than educate, they stimulate. *PDYM* is not one man's idea about youth ministry, it is a description of youth ministry the way it ought to be.

Mike Yaconelli, Co-founder, Youth Specialties

PDYM combines practice, principles, and theory with the end result being an incredible youth ministry book. Doug's personal commitment and experience in youth ministry will encourage the volunteer, student, and professional to reach this generation for Christ.

Helen Musick, Instructor of Youth Ministry, Asbury Seminary

Doug Fields has finally released the "why" book. This text will help youth ministers do fewer purposeless activities and more life-challenging discipleship. I will use it here at the seminary to help leaders gear up for a lifetime of ministry.

Allen Jackson, Professor of Youth Education,
New Orleans Baptist Theological Seminary

PDYM feeds timeless vision, values, and tips to youth workers who are hungry to see students' lives changed by Christ.

Kara Eckmann, Youth Pastor, Author of *The Word on the Old Testament*

The best, most comprehensive book on youth minstry I've ever read. A must read for any cutting-edge youth worker.

Billy Beacham, President, Student Discipleship Ministries

The credibility of this book comes from its unique combination of biblical principles and the real church world. Doug is actually a youth pastor who works with kids, parents, volunteers, and church custodians on a daily basis. These bedrock principles work equally well in a large or small church setting.

Dr. Marv Penner, Chairman, Youth Ministries Development,
Briercrest Schools Director, Canadian Center for Adolescent Research

Move the other books off the shelf. This is the most comprehensive, practical, and balanced book you'll ever need for developing your youth ministry. This book will set the standard for any effective youth ministry as we move into the twenty-first century.

Lanny Donoho, President, Youth Ministry Resources

PDYM is a call for the death of fly-by-the-seat-of-your-pants youth ministry. I especially appreciate Doug's emphasis on developing spiritual habits with students, not simply running them through a discipleship program.

Tim Smith, Author, *8 Habits of an Effective Youth Worker*

Doug cuts through the fat and gets straight to what is biblically important in youth ministry.

Miles McPherson, President, Miles Ahead Ministries

This book is filled with powerful principles, wise counsel, practical insights, and helpful tools. I believe a rookie or seasoned veteran of youth work will benefit from reading it.

Lynn Ziegenfuss, Director of Training, Youth for Christ/USA

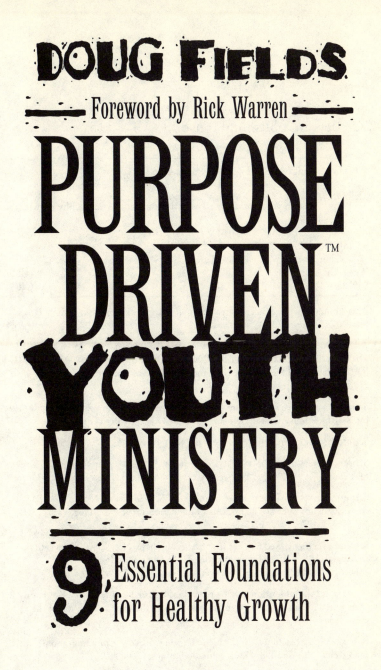

DOUG FIELDS

Foreword by Rick Warren

PURPOSE DRIVEN™ YOUTH MINISTRY

9 Essential Foundations for Healthy Growth

ZondervanPublishingHouse

Grand Rapids, Michigan

A Division of HarperCollinsPublishers

Purpose-Driven™ Youth Ministry
Copyright © 1998 by Doug Fields

Requests for information should be addressed to:

🏛 ZondervanPublishingHouse
Grand Rapids, Michigan 49530

Library of Congress Cataloging-in-Publication Data

Fields, Doug, 1962–
    Purpose-driven youth ministry : 9 essential foundations for healthy growth /
Doug Fields.
      p.   cm.
    ISBN 0–310–21253–7
    1. Church work with youth. I. Title.
BV4447.F543   1998   97–40916
259'.23—dc21   CIP

This edition is printed on acid-free paper and meets the American National
Standards Institute Z39.48 standard.

Published in association with the literary agency of Alive Communications, Inc.,
1465 Kelly Johnson Blvd. #320, Colorado Springs, CO 80920

Interior design by Pam Eicher and Sue Vandenberg Koppenol

Printed in the United States of America

---

00 01 02 /❖ DC/ 26 25 24 23 22 21 20 19 18 17 16

To the scores of committed youth workers who love learning.
You crave information about how to care for the students
God has entrusted to you.
You search untiringly for ways to reach those
who don't yet know Christ.
You are the reason for this book.
Thank you for loving God and students!

Contents

Foreword

You hold in your hand a virtual seminary degree in youth ministry. It describes the vision, values, strategy, and structure behind one of the most effective student ministries in America. I don't know anyone who does youth ministry better than Doug Fields—and his secrets are all here in this book.

Before joining the pastoral team of Saddleback Valley Community Church, Doug was already a nationally known authority in youth ministry. I was so impressed by his personal integrity, his love for God and for kids, and his willingness to keep learning in spite of his success that I asked him to join the Saddleback team. Since then I've watched this veteran pastor build a student ministry that has transformed the lives of literally thousands of teenagers. My own children have been powerfully impacted by Doug's purpose-driven youth ministry.

If you're looking for fads, gimmicks, or quick fixes for your youth program, this is the wrong book. On the other hand, if you're interested in building a solid, biblical, balanced foundation for reaching and discipling youth year after year, then you've come to the right place.

The essence of the purpose-driven paradigm is a strategy and structure that ensures equal emphasis to all five New Testament purposes of the church. Most churches, and most youth ministries, tend to overemphasize one of the purposes (evangelism, worship, fellowship, discipleship, or ministry) to the neglect of the others. This creates imbalance. But, as Saddleback and many other purpose-driven churches have proven, balance creates health and health causes growth. This book is about building a healthy youth ministry.

Since the publication of *The Purpose-Driven™ Church*, we have been overwhelmed with reports from churches that have been revitalized by applying its principles. That book is now used as a textbook in scores of seminaries and Christian colleges, and as a result we have received many requests for help in transitioning specific ministries, such as student work, to being purpose-driven. This volume is the answer to hundreds of letters we have received from youth ministers.

Purpose-Driven™ Youth Ministry is a book to be studied, not just read. To get the most out of it, I encourage you to purchase a copy for each of your youth staff and study it with them, one chapter at a time, as many have already done with *The Purpose-Driven Church*. Discuss the implications of each chapter for your church and create a list of action steps you intend to take.

I honor you for purchasing this book. It shows that you are a learner. All leaders are learners, and the moment you stop learning, you stop leading. Fortunately, there is plenty to learn in this book, even for the veteran youth minister. You'll learn how to build a balanced, purpose-driven ministry; how to program on purpose; how to recruit and train staff on purpose; and even how to purposefully maintain your personal life while ministering to students.

I believe the greatest days of the church are ahead of us. This is a wonderful time to be ministering to youth. Many of the concepts I used in building Saddleback Church were ones I discovered and developed when I was a minister to youth years ago. Student ministry is a great place to experiment with ideas that can bless the entire church.

So go for it! Take risks! Experiment with different methods, but stay focused and purpose driven! My prayer is that God will use this book to enable you, as he did King David, to "serve God's purpose in your generation" (see Acts 13:36).

We'd love to hear from you.

Rick Warren
Senior Pastor, Saddleback Valley Community Church

Acknowledgments

Although my name appears on the cover of this book as the author, those closest to me know that it never would have been written without the extraordinary godly men and women who have invested in me over the years. I thank God for giving me supportive friendships.

I want to thank the three pastors for whom I have worked, great men who have each taken an interest in me, mentored me, cared for me, and allowed me the privilege of sharing in ministry with them: Jim Burns, Tim Timmons, and Rick Warren. Each in his own way has shaped my life through my association and friendship with him.

I also want to thank my friends at Youth Specialties who have inspired and challenged me during the many years we have been together. Special thanks goes to Tic Long, who believed enough in me as a young youth worker to give me a platform to test my gifts. I am, indeed, a richer person for these relationships with my Youth Specialties friends. Also, thank you, Chap Clark and Marv Penner, for sharing your wisdom about family ministry.

My current staff at Saddleback Church—Lynne Ellis, Aaron Gutridge, Ted Lowe, and Matt McGill—are not only some of my dearest friends, but their partnership in ministry clearly impacts these pages. I particularly want to thank Matt for the extra time and effort he cheerfully devoted to this project.

I wouldn't have found the voice to write *Purpose-Driven*™ *Youth Ministry* without the deep friendships and commitments from other youth worker friends who have added to my depth and breadth as a youth minister: Johnny Baker, Barry Bland, Carol

Cooper, Eddie James, Kurt Johnston, Mike Katzenberger, Amanda Korte, Jeff Maguire, Scott Rachels, Katie Sadler, and especially Keith Page, who played an instrumental role in my early youth ministry years.

I also want to express my loving thanks to the dozens of youth workers who read drafts of my manuscript and gave me valuable insight into better communicating these principles. One special friend, Katie Brazelton, poured her life into this book with me. Not only did she edit chapters, she challenged my thinking, pushing me towards clarity, and encouraged along the way. She was God's gift to me through this project. Sincere thanks goes to Greg Lafferty for wrestling chapter 18 to the ground with me, to Wendy Dalzell for typing the manuscript, Gaye Lyon, Mark Rayburn, and Dave Lovejoy for graphic support, Linda Kaye for being my organized assistant and long-time friend, and Forrest Reinhart for going far beyond the call of friendship and pouring countless hours into this work. This is a better book because of all of these people.

My most heartfelt appreciation goes to my precious wife, Cathy, and my children, Torie, Cody, and Cassie, who are a constant source of laughter and rejuvenation. I love you! The sacrifices you four endured to make this book possible were only surpassed by your love for God and me. *Our* book is done! May we delight in having faithfully served God, and may we be blessed by hearing the reports of fruitful youth ministries!

Introduction

Imagine a sports dynasty for a minute—pick your favorite. Its success can't be attributed to one component; several factors combine to produce success. A true dynasty is stronger than its one great player. It must also have supportive key players, a motivating head coach, experienced assistant coaches, a position in the free agency market, a risk-taking owner, a productive front office, and a strong farm system (or luck with the draft). Average sports fans don't consider all of these factors when they watch their favorite team play. Instead, they focus on the team's best player and falsely assume that the team's success is due to that great player.

Unfortunately, many in the church view youth ministry with that same mentality. They look for the one great player (youth worker) who can save the franchise (the youth ministry) and develop a winning team (volunteers) that will attract the fans (students). Once a great player is identified (either hired clergy or volunteer layperson), the owners (church board, selection committee, senior pastor) settle into other pressing affairs within the organization (church). This type of scenario usually results in a suicide mission for the "star" player. He or she charges in with enthusiasm and practices (works) endless hours trying to achieve success (lots of students and programs) to please the owners. But to please everyone the player has to run (often knowing not where) so hard and so fast for so long that he or she eventually tires and becomes injured (burns out) and has to be replaced (quits or is fired). At this point the owners get involved and look for another great player to bring the team out of the dumps. The cycle starts all over with no foundation to build on because the last great player felt the burden to win by her- or himself.

The Nine Components of a
Purpose-Driven Youth Ministry

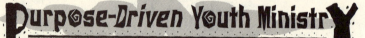

PERSEVERANCE   **9**
Knowing how to stay focused, remain fresh—and stay alive!

PARTICIPATING LEADERS   **8**
Knowing how to bring others on board to help fulfill the purposes

PARENTS   **7**
Teaming up with the family for a stronger youth ministry

PLANNED VALUES   **6**
Identifying the beliefs and styles that will help support the purposes

PROCESS   **5**
Showing how you intend to move your audience toward spiritual maturity

PROGRAMS   **4**
Creating programs to fulfill the purposes and reach the potential audiences

POTENTIAL AUDIENCE   **3**
Identifying your students and their receptivity to your purposes

PURPOSE   **2**
Knowing why your ministry exists, writing it out, and putting leadership behind it

Power of God   **1**
Helping passionate leaders with pure hearts to rely on God

My goal for this book is to coach you through a plan to build a healthy youth ministry that isn't dependent on one great youth worker and won't be destroyed when that person leaves the church. I hope that you will use my experiences and observations and my conversations with hundreds of youth workers to infuse your youth ministry with knowledge that will help to make it healthy. Where there is health, there is eventual growth.

A healthy youth ministry is a purpose-driven youth ministry (PDYM). But having a purpose-driven youth ministry does not simply mean that you have a purpose behind everything you do. It means that you pursue and reflect the purposes that were commanded by Jesus and manifested in the early church: the Great Commandment and the Great Commission. You'll recognize the five purposes as

1. evangelism
2. worship
3. fellowship
4. discipleship
5. ministry

A purpose-driven youth ministry will have programs and structures that reflect these purposes. In the chapters that follow, nine essential components are used to develop a blueprint for building a healthy youth ministry. The five eternal purposes form the central component around which the others are constructed. These nine components, which all start with *p* for easy retention, are

1. power of God
2. purpose
3. potential audience
4. programs
5. process
6. planned values
7. parents
8. participating leaders
9. perseverance

If you follow the blueprint, you will discover a holistic strategy that works. PDYM is not a cookie-cutter approach that promotes "do it my way because it's the only way." The PDYM model is *a* model; it is not *the* model. There are many ways to do youth ministry, and good youth workers look at other effective models to stimulate their thinking and learn from them how to be more competent ministers. If you are embarrassed to learn from another person or ministry, you have a pride problem (Prov. 13:10). God honors the motives of the humble and teachable but is pained by the hearts of the proud.

Purpose-driven youth ministry is not derived from a way youth ministry *was* done or *should be* done, but from how it *is being* done. I'm in the trenches every day as a youth worker, trying to strengthen these nine components in my church. For almost twenty years I've been living with the weighty responsibility of developing a youth ministry that equips students rather than a youth ministry that coordinates events. I don't want to direct programs; I want to disciple students. Throughout these years I have experienced a wide array of successes and failures in my attempts to build a healthy youth ministry. This book is part of an ongoing journey to honor God through my commitment to both church and students.

This book is for leaders of youth ministries with only a few students as well as those with hundreds. And it is geared for volunteers just starting out as well as for seminary-trained veterans with twenty years of youth ministry experience. How can this be possible? It is possible because the nine components rely on your ability to take the transferable principles and apply them to your youth ministry context. Your leadership style, education, and practical experience will become important as you interpret the principles and determine how to use them to strengthen your ministry. Don't try to do this alone! Read this book with a team who is committed to pursuing a spiritually healthy ministry. Then use the questions, "Making It Personal", at the end of each chapter to spur each other on to new levels of personal and group growth.

Here is a brief overview of the nine components.

Component 1
THE POWER OF GOD
working through passionate leaders with pure hearts

Healthy youth ministry begins when we take seriously the power of God for our own spiritual lives. A direct connection exists between a leader's spiritual vitality and a healthy youth ministry. Today's youth ministry training often overemphasizes *how to do the work of God* and neglects *how to be a person of God.*

Component 2
PURPOSE
discovering why your ministry exists and following it up with communication and leadership

---

Too often youth ministry consists of the get-in-there-and-get-some-programs-going mentality. This section stresses the importance of designing a blueprint for your youth ministry based on the five New Testament purposes that a healthy church maintains.

Discovery of the purposes is just the beginning. Real health begins with your ability to communicate the purposes, and it continues as you learn how to put leadership behind them so that people will have an exciting direction and an image of growth.

Component 3
POTENTIAL AUDIENCE
identifying which students are the target for the purposes

It is not uncommon for a youth ministry to establish programs for students who don't exist or to create programs without regard for students who are at all different commitment levels. This section will explain how to identify the differences in your students' spiritual commitments so that your programs will be more effective in fulfilling the five New Testament purposes.

Component 4
PROGRAMS
deciding what programs will reach your potential audience and help fulfill God's purposes

Programs are a means of reaching students at different levels and fulfilling the five purposes of the church. The equation for putting a program together should be as follows:

Purpose + Potential Audience = Program

This detailed section will help you focus on building healthy order or purposes, evangelism, fellowship, discipleship, ministry, and worship into your youth ministry and into students' lives.

Component 5
PROCESS
displaying your programs so you can help students move toward spiritual maturity

Process enables students to see where they are in your ministry's spiritual growth plan. A process may be diagrammed as a funnel, a baseball diamond, a pyramid, or anything else that acts as a framework for the purposes and programs.

Component 6
PLANNED VALUES
defining what values will strengthen your ministry and enhance your purposes

All people have values, attitudes, styles, and beliefs that influence their lives. A healthy youth ministry identifies its key values and uses them to strengthen its ministry. By the time you finish reading about this component, you will be aware that

- purposes reveal *why* your ministry exists;
- potential audience defines *who* you plan to target;

- programs outline *how* you attempt to reach your target and fulfill a purpose;
- process communicates *where* you want students to go for spiritual growth;
- planned values show *what* is important to your ministry; and,
- the power of God determines *when* growth is going to happen.

At this point the book shifts emphasis from programming to people. The next three components focus on parents, volunteers, and you.

Component 7
PARENTS
teaming up with the family
for a stronger youth ministry and church

Youth ministry cannot be healthy if it is isolated from the family. Careful attention to strategy is needed to maximize the valuable role parents play as partners in helping their kids reach their spiritual potential. While neither students nor parents inherently want total integration, there are some deliberate ways to build a family-friendly youth ministry.

Component 8
PARTICIPATING LEADERS
finding volunteers and developing them
into ministers who fulfill the purposes

Healthy youth ministry is built on the strong leadership of adult volunteers who express their passion by caring and taking time from their busy lives to build relationships with students and help them grow in their faith. Health begins to emerge when adult leaders move from chaperoning events to becoming leaders.

Component 9
PERSEVERANCE
learning how to survive the overwhelming responsibilities, discipline problems, and the adventure of change

---

Youth ministry is tough, as evidenced by the high degree of youth worker turnover. This section focuses on managing time, dealing with problem students, contending with church politics, and making wise changes before these issues lead to burnout. These survival chapters have grown out of years of experience and are rich in passion to help you *run to win* the race of youth ministry.

Warning: While reading this book, you may at times feel overwhelmed by the extensive amount of material to be absorbed and applied. Following the tips listed here will alleviate your anxiety:

1. Look for the transferable principle behind every idea. You may read a specific idea and say, "I can't do that!" You can, however, transfer the general principle into your youth ministry setting.

2. Recognize that your time, help, and resources will be different than mine. Your ability to transfer principles will vary depending on your available *time,* your ability to get *help,* and the strength of your *resources.*

3. PDYM is a team approach. I minister with a team of people, and we share our joys and frustrations. The principles and the leadership may originate with me as the point person, but the application is a team process.

4. Don't compare your youth ministry to ours or anyone else's. Comparing isn't productive—you'll either feel bad ("We're worse") or arrogant ("We're better"). You will always lose when you compare what you know about yourself with what you don't know about me. You can't see all of the mistakes I've made that helped me to discover what I know today. Take note: Other ministries always look better from a distance.

5. Don't feel guilty about the things you're not doing. You will see many ideas and principles in this book that I wasn't acting

on twenty years ago or even five years ago. As you process this material, take what will work and adapt it to your setting.

6. A healthy youth ministry will take time to build. Rome wasn't built in a day and neither will be your youth ministry. Be patient, realistic, and strategic about which principles are assigned top priority. It may take two years to begin seeing the health you desire. Take your time, build wisely, rely on God's wisdom, and don't be afraid to get help from others.

7. Developing a purpose-driven youth ministry will challenge you. The principles in this book may not be easy for you to immediately grasp and implement. You may need to mark certain sections and discuss them with other youth leaders. The more you revisit a chapter and think through the principles, the better you will understand and apply them.

Although there are several youth ministry books available, I am not aware of any that are as comprehensive and as practical as this one. Many of the outstanding youth ministry books I've read are rich in theory but fall short in practice; many provide a few pieces of the puzzle but leave the rest for readers to figure out on their own. You will find this book both philosophical and practical. It is intended to leave you with transferable principles that can be applied to any youth group regardless of size, denomination, facilities, resources, or existing leadership.

Blessings,
Doug Fields

COMPONENT ONE

THE POWER
OF GOD

ONE

Healthy Youth Ministries Have Spiritually Healthy Leaders

My friend Ted read this first chapter and said, "Doug, you can't start your book this way; there aren't enough program ideas." My friend Lissa, on the other hand, read the same chapter and said, "Powerful beginning! Every youth worker should be required to read this material before ever starting youth ministry." Why the difference in responses?

Ted is twenty-two years old and just starting out in youth ministry. He believes a hyped-up, flashy youth ministry with slick logos, fancy calendars, big programs, and creative ideas paves the route to a healthy youth ministry.

Lissa is a forty-two-year-old, experienced youth worker who once walked in Ted's shoes. She understands the seduction of an enticing youth ministry idea. For several years she placed hype above health in her leadership. Youth ministry ideas were more important than intimacy with God. Programs out-prioritized prayer. She allowed her heart to become hard and later described herself as a spiritual liar rather than a spiritual leader.

Lissa is not alone. I also walked down that path. I, too, was always looking for creative ideas and fancy programs to make my youth ministry flashy. I've since learned, as has Lissa, that a healthy youth ministry doesn't begin with ideas, but with spiritual leaders.

When a church (or youth ministry point person) primarily values hype, there is little need for spiritual leadership. A non-Christian could become a "successful" youth worker at that kind of church by increasing activities, launching new ideas, and boosting attendance. With a little investigation, you probably wouldn't find any measurable difference between this type of youth ministry and a local non-Christian service club. Both use hype to attract.

This first chapter challenges you (and your church and youth ministry team) to develop a youth ministry in which the leaders rely on God's power. This is the essential and foundational ingredient for building a spiritual legacy of long-term health. In the long run, health is more attractive than hype.

My Journey from Hype to Health

I started youth ministry in 1979 as a volunteer for the junior high ministry at my home church. I loved it! Although I had no idea what I was doing, I knew God was using me and my energy to connect with students and care for them. Within my first year the junior high director left our church and I became the point person by default. (I was the only other volunteer!) One year later I still didn't know what I was doing, but I was sure busy doing it. I had our junior high group participating in everything I could find. If a flyer came to our church promoting an activity for junior high students, we went. I'd get a sample curriculum from a conference I attended and use it for Sunday school as soon as I returned. I was too busy and having too much fun to recognize or admit that I really had no idea how to build a healthy youth ministry or even that I was supposed to build anything. The ministry was nothing more than adolescent baby-sitting with some occasional Bible study. But since the students were entertained and attendance was up, everyone seemed to think we were a healthy youth ministry.

After being a volunteer for two years, I was offered a paid youth ministry position in 1981 as an intern with an established youth ministry professional. I was thrilled to get paid to do what I loved. I jumped at the opportunity and continued to do more youth ministry while I finished college and seminary. My life never slowed down. In addition to heavy school loads, I coached school teams for better access to the local campus. I planned camps, spoke to any group that would listen, and went to every youth ministry training available. My life was youth ministry, and I had become an expert at going, doing, and achieving.

In 1985 my youth ministry mentor handed me the leadership of what was considered to be a successful youth ministry. While I was thrilled, I was also driven by the need to prove I could "be the man." This pushed me to do more and to look for the bigger and better in everything I did (hype). I was out of the house almost every night of the week. While all of the activities and excitement assured that no one questioned my work ethic, I questioned everything. In the midst of all that was happening, I couldn't shake the emptiness of all I was doing. I was distant from the Lord and my heart was slowly hardening. No one knew of my weakening disciplines because everything looked good on the outside. I could "talk the game" as it related to my spirituality. I had become the poster child for Proverbs 26:23: "Smooth words may hide a wicked heart, just as a pretty glaze covers a common clay pot" (NLT).

As my inner life was hardening, my outer world of youth ministry was beginning to show cracks. Three main problems haunted me and left me continually frustrated: I couldn't create attractive programs like those of other churches, I wasn't sure that I was the right person for youth ministry, and I could never do enough to please everyone.

I was too arrogant to think these problems would get the best of me and too insecure to ask for help. But within a year of my new pastoral reign, God used these looming problems to soften my heart and teach me what I desperately needed to know if I was going to continue in the ministry. I wish I could have learned these lessons from a book, but to be honest, I don't think I would have slowed down long enough to learn from others even if they had written about it.

Instead, I was driven to an authentic dependence on the power of God to change my life and impact my youth ministry.

Problem 1: I Couldn't Create Attractive Programs Like Those of Other Churches

In my continual search for new ideas, the ultimate catch became the program that would please parents, bring students out in droves, and help students grow spiritually. I needed a power-house program that would move us from the minors to the majors. Not knowing any better, I studied the big league youth ministries and hoped that what they were doing would provide my answer. I tried to implement their programs into my youth ministry setting, but I didn't understand that there were too many variables to be copied and taken into my youth ministry context.

I was too immature to look for transferable principles that might help. Instead, I wanted an instant program to bring quick success. What I learned was that copying someone else's program always led to failure. Some program ideas worked for a while, but they didn't have the same strength in my setting that they had in the other churches.

> Copying someone else's program
> always led to failure.

I thought that if youth ministry was about designing programs and I couldn't get programs to work, then maybe I shouldn't do youth ministry. I was depending on other ministries to provide my answers instead of depending on God to show me his plan for a healthy ministry. I was always comparing myself to other youth workers who made incredible programming appear so simple. My inability to create superb programs was fueled by my comparisons, and my self-doubt skyrocketed. I became convinced that I didn't have the knowledge and skills to do youth ministry well.

Problem 2: Perhaps I Wasn't the Right Person for Youth Ministry

During my first years in youth ministry, I remember standing in front of junior high students and basking in their looks of anticipation. I was young, fun, energetic, and well-liked. Their faces said, "This is going to be good." But only a few years later, when things weren't going as well, I saw a different look—one that said, "This better be good." Because I lacked knowledge and skills, I thought the students didn't like me anymore. Their enthusiasm waned, attendance dropped, volunteers found other church ministries to which they could devote their time, and our programs changed every time I spied on another youth ministry. Parents as well as church elders questioned what was happening, and I accepted all the problems as my fault. I constantly looked over my shoulder to see if other people were thinking what I was thinking—that maybe I wasn't the right person for youth ministry despite my having the necessary goods.

Even though I worked exhausting hours, the job wasn't getting done the way everyone seemed to want. Previously unspoken expectations surfaced, and they fueled my workaholic personality to fix everything, even though I couldn't specifically identify the problems. My desire for doing ministry had long moved from pleasing God to appeasing people. I wanted to be liked by everyone, and that desire moved me to my third major problem.

Problem 3: I Could Never Do Enough to Please Everyone

The critical breaking moment came in the wake of an attempt to boost sagging attendance numbers. I organized an evangelistic camp with the requirement that the only way students could attend was if they brought an unchurched friend. To my amazement, our students responded to the challenge. The power of God moved that weekend, and the majority of the unchurched students returned from camp with a new and meaningful relationship with Jesus Christ. It was the greatest camp I had ever experienced.

On the Monday following camp, I went into the church office eager to share the news with the church staff and hear the praise reports that I anticipated had been coming in all morning. As I approached the church office, my insecurity and pride mixed to create a fantasy in which I envisioned the staff awaiting my arrival and lining the entrance for congratulations and a chorus of "How Great Thou Art."

My fantasy bubble popped when the church administrator immediately asked, "Did you know our megaphone was busted this weekend and the church vans weren't returned to their proper parking spots?" I didn't know how to respond. I was speechless (which was a small miracle). This wasn't the greeting I had expected. In my state of shock, I stuttered something about reparking the vans and buying a new megaphone. Then I hung my head and walked to my office. As I sat at my desk, I thought, "Does resignation have one *s* or two?" Just then I received a phone call from a student's mother. I assumed that she was calling to thank me for her son's life-changing weekend. Instead, she said, "Doug, I have some problems with your leadership at camp this weekend." She went on to explain that the only story she had heard from her son was how the boys were lying around in their underwear one night passing gas on lit matches and laughing at the appearance of flames. She continued to chastise me for how irresponsible and dangerous that was—saying the boys could actually explode. (All I could think of was what a great video that would make!) I guess she thought it was one of our planned events as opposed to a random act of teenage silliness. Either way, I became the object of her anger.

I had been in the office for ten minutes, and already I had had two negative conversations regarding one of my best weekends of ministry. I left the office immediately. As I drove home, I couldn't contain my emotions and began to weep (not the watery-eye cry, but the body-convulsing cry). I thought about all of the time, energy, and emotion that had gone into the weekend. I mentally replayed the intense conversations, the numerous tough leadership decisions, and the faces of the many students who had become excited about Christ. In tears, I arrogantly concluded that after all of the work I had done this treatment was undeserved.

It was at this point, sitting in my car on the side of the road, that I felt the supernatural presence of God. I wish I could say there was an audible instruction; there wasn't. But I felt God impress on my heart as I had never experienced before. I sensed God saying, "Doug, you'll never be able to do enough to please everyone. Focus on me. Rest in me. Abide in me. When your heart is turned toward me, we can work together and do some good things." That was it. That was the moment that revolutionized my ministry! My three youth ministry problems were solved by this one soul-shaking experience. The answer was not in programs or in feeling liked or in pleasing everyone. The answer was in becoming the right person for youth ministry. I had left God out of the equation and had been doing youth ministry, using my own power. My heart had become hard, and I was spending all my time *doing* the work of God without *being* a man of God.

> I was spending all my time doing the work of God without being a person of God.

Not only did God work in the lives of students through that camp, but he also used it to do his work in me. My focus and dependence had been foolishly centered on my own ability to perform (*to do*). Now I understood that if I stayed dependent and focused on God, he would empower me *to be* his servant and thus accomplish his purposes in my ministry.

How Does One Become a Youth Worker Who Depends on God?

Many youth workers I talk to can relate to feeling inadequate about their gifts, their call into youth ministry, and their performance as leaders. Hope for these struggles can be found by focusing on God and his Word. The solution to my three problems changed my life and ministry, and drives me to increase my dependence on God's power and to develop my abilities as a spiritual leader.

Answer 1: Recognize God's Power Through Personal Humility

When my pride pushed me to create extravagant programs, God taught me humility. Through my broken-heart experience, I realized that, ultimately, programs don't work—God works. God doesn't need a program in order to work. He doesn't even need me. This realization brought humility when I finally admitted my very small part in God's work. When good things happen I need to recognize that they happen because of God's power and not my own.

> **God doesn't need a program in order to work. He doesn't even need me.**

If you are someone who soaks up credit for success, humility may be a foreign quality. When you take credit for success, it is easy to lose sight of God's power. I never plan to take credit for God's work, but I have often found myself making a subtle shift in thought from the youth ministry being God's work to it being a result of my skills and efforts. I hate to admit it, but there have been many times when I've patted myself on the back when God deserved the credit. Sadly, I haven't taken the blame when things were going bad. Almost without exception, when things were rough I pleaded for God to strengthen "his" work.

When lives are changed, when attendance increases, when good things happen, we need to recognize God's power and give praise and credit to him. Paul shared this advice in 1 Corinthians 1:31: "Let him who boasts boast in the Lord." You and I have nothing to do with the actual transformation of an earthly life to an eternal life—that is God's work. We may point students in the right direction, and we may even have the privilege of being God's spokespersons, but in no way should we ever take credit away from God. If we brag, we need to brag about God. It is truly humbling to think about the awesome privilege and responsibility of being used by God.

Answer 2: Submit Your Abilities to God and Allow His Power to Work Through Who You Are

When feeling inadequate as a youth minister and questioning my call, I have had to practice submission. I regularly submit to God all that I am and all that I have to offer because I don't have the knowledge, the natural energy, and the ability to relate to teenagers like I did twenty years ago. Every week when I'm with teenagers I'm reminded that I'm not young anymore (I'm the age of their parents).

Do you ever feel like a boring adult? I do! Students may ask for a ride home from church, and I say, "Sure, but do you mind sitting in my child's car seat?" You see, I have diapers and bottles all over the place, and that's not cool. Once they are in my car, they hit my preset radio stations thinking they are going to find a music station. Not in my car! I listen to news (about as wild as I get is talk radio). I try to be relevant by listening to some of their music. Every so often I turn on MTV until I get a headache from all the camera gyrations. I don't know the latest bands, and when students play their music for me, I don't like it (mostly because I can't understand the words).

In addition to feeling irrelevant, I have less energy than I once did. I hate overnighters! I can't always be on the go. I have to honestly admit that I don't have the same set of abilities I had a decade ago. I'm also learning that's not all bad.

By submitting my abilities to God's power, I can rest in the same truth that the apostle Paul communicated about his weakness when God told him in 2 Corinthians 12:9, "'My grace is sufficient for you, for my power is made perfect in weakness.'" Paul's response was, "Therefore I will boast all the more gladly about my weaknesses, so that Christ's power may rest on me."

This submission keeps me from depression. I admit that I can't keep up with teenage culture and that I'm not as hip anymore. When I submit my life and my abilities to God for the work of youth ministry, I can rest on the promise that God's power is available to me, "for to be sure, [Jesus Christ] was crucified in weakness, yet he lives by God's power. Likewise, we are weak in him, yet by God's power we will live with him to serve [others]" (2 Cor. 13:4).

Allow your abilities to be ignited by the divine power that is revealed in a believer's life. Rejoice that your presence and your words give the power of God another opportunity to be communicated to students whom God loves. Remember what Paul said about his lack of verbal skills in 1 Corinthians 2:4–5: "My message and my preaching were not with wise and persuasive words, but with a demonstration of the Spirit's power, so that your faith might not rest on men's wisdom, but on God's power." When I think about the truth of God working through my weaknesses, it thrills my soul and keeps me going.

> **Rejoice that your presence and your words give the power of God another opportunity to be communicated to students whom God loves.**

Answer 3: Focus on Being a Person of God Before Doing the Work of God

Instead of trying to please others, I have learned to live my life for an audience of One. Doing God's work isn't as important as being God's person. Since I tend to be a people-pleaser, I need a continual reminder that God is more concerned about my spiritual health than about my youth ministry hype.

In the church, *doing* can become an illusion that requires more attention than our *being*. Jesus has a warning for people who are more concerned about doing than being: "Not everyone who says to me, 'Lord, Lord,' will enter the kingdom of heaven, but only he who does the will of my Father who is in heaven. Many will say to me on that day, 'Lord, Lord, did we not prophesy in your name, and in your name drive out demons and perform many miracles?' Then I will tell them plainly, 'I never knew you. Away from me, you evildoers!'" (Matt. 7:21–23).

Can you envision standing before God and listing all the things you've done? "God, I spoke for you; I put on retreats for you; I volunteered for several years; I even did lock-ins for you. Do you want me to continue with my list? I made great videos; I read *Purpose-Driven Youth Ministry* for you; I even loved the senior pastor's kids. And I did it all for you!" I am not suggesting that you question your salvation, but I am encouraging you to think through your doing by laughing at how ludicrous any such list would be in the eyes of God.

The following sentence is worth the price of this book if you can apply it to your life: "You can never do enough." This time insert your name in the blank and imagine me as a friend telling you this face to face. "I want you to know an important truth that will save you a lot of pain, heartache, and time if you can understand it: _____, you can never do enough. There is always more to be done. Youth ministry never stops! Don't allow doing the work of God to come at the expense of being God's person."

Strengthen your youth ministry by placing a higher priority on being than doing. I've seen spiritual integrity play such an important role in youth ministry that I can honestly say that I would rather have one godly volunteer than ten skilled volunteers who don't rely on God. I make this no secret. Adults in our ministry understand that I value their spiritual maturity much more than their ministry. Don't get me wrong—I want volunteers doing ministry, but not at the expense of their spiritual growth. The power of God working in the lives of leaders is the foundation of a healthy youth ministry.

"Olley, Olley Oxen, Free, Free, Free"

Too many youth workers are knowingly or unknowingly trapped in a futile game of ministry hide and seek. They do ministry by hiding behind a hyped-up program, desperately seeking for the next idea to pump up their ministry. If this describes you, my prayer is that you hear the voice of God calling out "Olley, olley oxen, free, free, free." God is compassionately calling us back home where we are free to be safe and secure in our relationship with him. It is here that we can put first things first by developing our own spiritual lives and focusing on growing in Christ.

Proverbs 5:21–23 reminds us that no matter how much we do for God or how busy we are in youth ministry, we can't fool God about our inner life: "For a man's ways are in full view of the LORD, and he examines all his paths. The evil deeds of a wicked man ensnare him; the cords of his sin hold him fast. He will die for lack of discipline, led astray by his own great folly."

The students in your youth ministry don't need your clever ideas and great programming skills. They need a living model— a man or woman of God who is passionate about his or her faith. Your passion will be contagious. Students will want what you have. Your faith will help you develop a strong foundation for a healthy youth ministry.

Jesus communicated this same principle to his followers when he said in Luke 6:47–49, "I will show you what he is like who comes to me and hears my words and puts them into practice. He is like a man building a house, who dug down deep and laid the foundation on rock. When a flood came, the torrent struck that house but could not shake it, because it was well built. But the one who hears my words and does not put them into practice is like a man who built a house on the ground without a foundation. The moment the torrent struck that house, it collapsed and its destruction was complete."

Youth ministry is tough! It is filled with different types of storms, and God's power is all you have to help you combat the downpours. No youth ministry idea or program can compete with

God's power working in and through you as he gives you a passion for students and you give him a pure heart. When you seek God you will see supernatural elements within your youth ministry that no flashy idea could ever produce. By relying on God and trusting in his power, you leave room for him to do his work. Pray that God will bring on the miracles as you read this book.

> No youth ministry idea or program can compete with God's power working in and through you as he gives you a passion for students and you give him a pure heart.

MAKING IT PERSONAL

For You to Digest

Whether you are a volunteer youth worker, an intern, a paid staff member, or a college student being called by God into youth ministry, remember that your church's youth ministry won't be healthy if your life isn't rooted in God and reliant on his power. Your spiritual walk is a vital part of your youth ministry's health equation.

Jesus made it clear that we bear fruit when we are connected to him (John 15:5). The apostle Paul understood spiritual growth, and he challenged his readers to evaluate their faith to ensure that they weren't just "going through the motions" (see 2 Cor. 13:5).

If you test yourself and find that you need help in your spiritual life, I encourage you to do whatever it takes to strengthen your godly foundation. The following actions have always helped me:

1. Admit your struggles to yourself.
2. Ask God for the power to discipline yourself for the purpose of godliness (1 Tim. 4:7 NASB).
3. Ask God for the courage to confess these struggles to a friend who cares deeply about you and who can help you.
4. Work with this friend on a spiritual restoration plan.

To Discuss

Your youth ministry will take a step toward health if you are willing to enter into dialogue about the material you are reading. Good leaders are avid learners, and they aren't afraid of discussion, even when it causes vulnerability. The questions at the end of each chapter serve as triggers to get your youth ministry team talking.

1. Do you have a youth ministry environment where spiritual growth is valued?
2. Do your students sense that the youth ministry leaders are men and women of God?
3. What role does prayer play in your ministry?
4. As a team, are you honestly concerned with students' spiritual health or the exhilaration from the hype of great programs?
5. How can you encourage spirituality among your leadership?
6. What will you do if you see a leader showing signs of a hard heart?
7. Where is God's power evident in your ministry?

COMPONENT TWO

PURPOSE

TWO

Discovering the Five Purposes for Your Youth Ministry

When I speak at youth worker conferences, the question I'm asked most often is "How do I grow my group?" Although this is an ambitious question, it is not the most important.

I respond, "First, tell me, why does your youth ministry exist?" That's the most important question. The answer, or more commonly, lack of an answer, usually gives a good indication of the group's growth capability. Any youth ministry is capable of growth when it is built on God's purposes for the church.

The material in this chapter will help you discover God's five purposes for a healthy ministry. These purposes are the vital components—the cornerstone—for constructing a youth ministry that enjoys long-term health and growth. The process of understanding God's purposes and applying them will slow down the get-in-there-and-get-some-programs-going mentality. While slowing

> **The process of understanding God's purposes and applying them will slow down the get-in-there-and-get-some-programs-going mentality.**

down to discover God's purposes, you will at the same time improve the health and quicken the growth rate of your ministry.

Far too many youth workers are busy doing programs, but they can't articulate the biblical purpose behind what they're doing. They're just doing. I recently met a veteran youth pastor (twenty-plus years) who bashfully admitted that he's never been able to tell you why he's been doing what he's been doing. He never slowed down enough to think about it. I know he's not alone. I estimate that less than ten percent of the youth leaders I talk to can explain the reason for their ministry's existence. Even fewer have communicated their purpose with a clear statement that others can embrace and follow. And it is a rare youth ministry that has the necessary leadership to drive and fulfill the purposes. In the absence of biblical purpose and leadership, there is little chance of developing a healthy youth ministry. On the other hand, I have seen an obvious relationship between spiritual and numerical growth in youth ministries that have discovered the following five purposes, defined them in a clear statement (chapter 3), and put leadership behind the purposes (chapter 4). When you do this, you will be able to lead with passion, direction, and confidence.

The Five Eternal Purposes of a Purpose-Driven Youth Ministry

The Purpose-Driven Church

My pastor, Rick Warren, has written a best-selling book called *The Purpose-Driven Church*,[1] in which six chapters are devoted to discovering the five purposes God has for your ministry—*evangelism, worship, fellowship, discipleship,* and *ministry.*

Rick didn't create these purposes; he studied the Scriptures and discovered them. And he has built a healthy church by expressing them. One of the great privileges of my life has been to work with Rick and see these purposes expressed through a strategy at Saddleback Church in southern California. He has helped to develop my thinking by drawing me back to God's Word as the source of our ministry's existence.

This chapter is a minor reflection of Rick's work, but it is enough to help you understand and get started in the process of discovering the five purposes. Rick's premise in *The Purpose-Driven Church* is that all churches are driven by either a verbal or nonverbal emphasis. A church may be driven by tradition, personality, finances, people, or programs, but none of these will build health in your church. A healthy church must be built on the five New Testament purposes. Rick writes:

> Strong churches are built on purpose! By focusing equally on all five of the New Testament purposes of the church, your church will develop the healthy balance that makes lasting growth possible. Proverbs 19:21 says, "Many are the plans in a man's heart, but it is the LORD's purpose that prevails." Plans, programs, and personalities don't last. But God's purposes *will* last. . . . Unless the driving force behind a church is biblical, the health and growth of the church will never be what God intended. Strong churches are not built on programs, personalities, or gimmicks. They are built on the eternal purposes of God.[2]

Healthy youth ministries are built on these same eternal purposes. Fortunately, God has already given them to us in the Bible. It is our job to uncover them, communicate them, and put leadership behind them.

You Don't Create the Five Purposes; You Discover Them

Many youth workers like to be innovative when it comes to their ministry. This is a good quality and will serve as a great asset when crafting a purpose statement. But when it comes to God's purposes for his church, the element of innovation doesn't rest with us. No purposes that we could create on our own would be more complete than the five God has already divinely created for us. Our programs can be negotiable—but evangelism, worship, fellowship, discipleship, and ministry aren't negotiable. Our programs and our style may reflect our personality and creativity, but God's purposes reflect his plan and love for the church.

Our programs and our style may reflect our personality and creativity, but God's purposes reflect his plan and love for the church.

A purpose-driven church is built around the five purposes found in two popular passages, the Great Commandment and the Great Commission. While the five purposes are described in several New Testament verses,[3] these two passages, relating the words of Jesus, summarize all the others.

Great Commandment: "Jesus replied: 'Love the Lord your God with all your heart and with all your soul and with all your mind.' This is the first and greatest commandment. And the second is like it: 'Love your neighbor as yourself.' All the Law and the Prophets hang on these two commandments" (Matt. 22:37–40).

Great Commission: "Therefore go and make disciples of all nations, baptizing them in the name of the Father and of the Son and of the Holy Spirit, and teaching them to obey everything I have commanded you. And surely I am with you always, to the very end of the age" (Matt. 28:19–20).

The five purposes are found in these two passages:

1. Worship: "Love the Lord your God with all your heart"
2. Ministry: "Love your neighbor as yourself "
3. Evangelism: "Go and make disciples"
4. Fellowship: "Baptizing them"[4]
5. Discipleship: "Teaching them to obey"

These are the five New Testament purposes that drive Saddleback Church and thousands of other churches that have discovered them. I hope you're thinking, "Hey, this isn't new; I've heard those before." Exactly. They've been around for two thousand years. What may be new to you is the impetus to lead a youth ministry designed to reflect and fulfill these five purposes. When the five purposes lay the foundation for why you do what you do, yours will become a purpose-driven youth ministry.

> **When the five purposes lay the foundation for why you do what you do, yours will become a purpose-driven youth ministry.**

You and I may differ on *how* we attempt to fulfill these five purposes (with programs), but there should never be any disagreement about *what* God has called us to do.

A Closer Look At the Five Purposes Within a Youth Ministry

Before going any further, let's look at a basic definition for each purpose.

The Purpose of Evangelism

Evangelism is sharing the good news of Jesus Christ with those who don't yet have a personal relationship with him. God has chosen to use his people to help consummate his plan for salvation. Jesus' last words remind us that we are called to be his witnesses (Acts 1:8).

Evangelism is a weakly expressed purpose in many youth ministries. It is difficult to fulfill on a program level, and it is threatening on a personal level. Adult leadership must model the purpose of evangelism if we want students to see the importance of this commission. As students grow in their faith, they must learn that evangelism is not only their responsibility as believers but also their privilege. When this purpose is evident in a youth ministry, substantial growth will take place. This growth won't depend on an evangelistic program but will happen because of evangelistic students.

> **Growth won't depend on an evangelistic program but will happen because of evangelistic students.**

Chapter 6 suggests practical ways to build evangelism into your youth ministry.

The Purpose of Worship

We define worship as celebrating God's presence and honoring him with our lifestyle. It is our reason for existence. In Romans 12:1 we are told, "Offer your bodies as living sacrifices, holy and pleasing to God—this is your spiritual act of worship." Everything we do in our youth ministry is done because we love God and desire to honor and worship him with our lifestyle.

In youth ministry we typically limit the definition of worship to singing praise songs. This is too narrow a definition. Worship is expressed in several ways, such as praying (Ps. 95:6), hearing the Word (John 17:17; Deut. 31:11), giving (1 Cor. 16:1–2), baptizing (Rom. 6:3–4), meditating (Hab. 2:20), and partaking of the Lord's Supper (1 Cor. 11:23–26).

Chapter 7 presents a unique example of how a worship service can reach both Christians and non-Christians.

The Purpose of Fellowship

After students become believers, usually through some avenue of personal or programmatic evangelism, they are welcomed into the fellowship of believers. Ephesians 2:19 says, "Consequently, you are no longer foreigners and aliens, but fellow citizens with God's people and members of God's household." God did not intend for Christians to live in isolation, but in fellowship with other believers and to be identified as the body of Christ. True fellowship happens when students are known, cared for, held accountable, and encouraged in their spiritual journey.

While evangelism may be weak in many youth ministries, fellowship is usually the strongest purpose. Often, fellowship is expressed so strongly that Christian students lose sight of evangelism and focus only on other believers, excluding the unbelieving world from their mission field. These youth ministries become youth groups, Christian cliques, or holy huddles dangerously apathetic toward the lost.

Chapter 8 is dedicated to helping you create a fellowship environment in which your students can be known, nurtured, held accountable, and encouraged.

The Purpose of Discipleship

Discipleship is the term regularly used to describe the building up or strengthening of believers in their quest to be like Christ. The Scriptures are filled with commands to mature and grow up in the faith. In Hebrews 6:1 we are exhorted, "Let us leave the elementary teachings about Christ and go on to maturity." Discipleship is a lifelong process that God uses to bring us to maturity in Christ.

In youth ministry, discipleship can be the most unrewarding and nebulous of the purposes since spiritual maturity is difficult to measure. This is especially true if you work specifically with junior high students. Two years in a teenager's life usually isn't enough time to observe maturation that occurs as a result of your discipling labor. Just when you think you're beginning to recognize spiritual fruit, junior highers graduate to high school.

Healthy discipleship flourishes under spiritual leaders who are willing to do the possible. They consistently plant seeds and water students' faith. All this is done with faith that God will do the impossible and bring growth. The apostle Paul reminds us of this process in 1 Corinthians 3:6–7: "I planted the seed, Apollos watered it, but God made it grow. So neither he who plants nor he who waters is anything, but only God, who makes things grow."

Chapter 9 presents a new and exciting way to aid the discipleship process without allowing students to become dependent on a program or a person for their spiritual maturity. The chapter provides revolutionary insight for many youth workers who are depending on programs to prepare their students for long-term spiritual growth.

The Purpose of Ministry

Ministry can be defined as "meeting needs with love." God has blessed every believer with special gifts to be used for ministry. In youth ministry we need to clearly communicate that these God-given gifts don't come with an age limitation. Students shouldn't have to wait until they are adults to minister. A healthy youth ministry will constantly encourage students to discover their gifts and put them into practice through ministry and mission opportunities. When the purpose of ministry is applied, you will graduate student ministers rather than program attendees, who are spectators with few roots to keep them planted in God's ways. Student ministers won't graduate from their faith when they graduate from the youth ministry.

> **A healthy youth ministry will constantly encourage students to discover their gifts and put them into practice through ministry and mission opportunities.**

Chapter 10 shows how to challenge students to put feet to their faith and do the work of the ministry. It also shows how to challenge your student ministers to become student leaders.

Balancing the Five Purposes

Most youth ministries would get the following letter grades for their efforts toward the five purposes:

Fellowship	A
Discipleship	B
Worship	C+
Ministry	C-
Evangelism	D+

These grades are a sweeping generality of what I see when training youth workers across the country, and it may or may not be an accurate reflection of your ministry. How would you grade the purposes in your youth ministry? Do you find yourself having a strong evangelistic emphasis without many mature students because discipleship is weak? How about the other way around? Do you have strong discipleship yet haven't seen any new Christians in years because you have no evangelism effort? Or does your youth ministry have strong worship, discipleship, and fellowship, and you wonder why it is not growing (no evangelism) and why the students are apathetic (no ministry)? Most youth ministries excel in at least one of these purposes but usually at the expense of the others.

Keep thinking about your youth ministry. Have you found a balance between evangelism, fellowship, discipleship, worship, and ministry? When you do, you will uncover an exciting image of biblical health and a purpose-driven youth ministry.

The Five Purposes at Saddleback Church

As we attempt to build healthy members at Saddleback Church, we want everyone to know the five biblical reasons we exist. Our pastor devised a slogan and put the purposes into five *m* words for easy retention. The slogan is "A Great Commitment to the Great Commandment and the Great Commission will grow a Great Church." The five *m* words are *mission, membership, maturity, ministry,* and *magnification.* The adults in our church learn them like this:

Mission: We communicate God's Word through evangelism.
Membership: We incorporate God's people into our fellowship.
Maturity: We educate God's family through discipleship.
Ministry: We demonstrate God's love through ministry.
Magnification: We celebrate God's presence in worship.

As we were working on this purpose component within our youth ministry at Saddleback Church, we felt like some of the *m* words weren't student-friendly. Most students, especially the unchurched, don't identify with words like *mission, membership,* and *magnification.* Because we want students to understand and participate in the purposes of our ministry, we chose to communicate the purposes with words that students could more easily embrace.

My pastor well understands the big picture of the purposes and believes that there are several ways to say the same thing. The five purposes of the church don't have to be communicated to our students with the same words our church uses. This freedom allows us to change and personalize the words without compromising the purposes. Words are important, but actions are more important. Our students learn the five purposes through these words:

Reach is our word for evangelism
Connect is our word for fellowship
Grow is our word for discipleship
Discover is our word for ministry
Honor is our word for worship

This chapter has explained to you the five purposes; the next chapter demonstrates how to write a purpose statement that your youth ministry and church can see, understand, and act on. Use the exercise in "Making It Personal" to brainstorm for words that will work as the skeleton for your purpose statement. Focusing on the five words will help communicate and reinforce the five purposes so that others can help you pursue God's purposes for your youth ministry. But if you already have a purpose statement that you believe is effective and you like the wording even though it doesn't clearly reveal the five purposes, that is okay. The priority of a purpose-driven youth ministry isn't to identify five magic words that will make stationery look nice; it is to build a youth ministry that clearly reflects evangelism, fellowship, discipleship, ministry, and worship.

MAKING IT PERSONAL

1. Below are three ways the same purposes can be communicated. Write down any words that immediately come to mind to convey the common term.

KEY WORDS	COMMON	SADDLEBACK CHURCH	SADDLEBACK YOUTH MINISTRY	YOUR WORDS
1. "Love ... God"	worship	magnify	honor	_____
2. "Love ... neighbor"	ministry	ministry	discover	_____
3. "... make disciples"	evangelism	missions	reach	_____
4. "baptizing them ..."	fellowship	membership	connect	_____
5. "teaching ... to obey"	discipleship	maturity	grow	_____

2. Of the five purposes, with which do you most resonate?

3. On which purpose do you spend most of your ministry time? Is this consistent with your answer to the above question? Why or why not?

4. Take an inventory of your youth ministry programs and note which purposes they fulfill.

5. What letter grade would you give the five purposes as seen in your youth ministry?

    Evangelism   _____
    Fellowship   _____
    Discipleship   _____
    Ministry   _____
    Worship   _____

6. Perhaps your youth ministry emphasizes a few purposes more strongly than others. Create an action plan that brings balance to your ministry. What steps can you take to strengthen your ministry?

7. What will it take to ensure that your ministry expresses all five purposes?

NOTES

1. (Grand Rapids: Zondervan, 1995.) I encourage you to get Rick's book to share with your senior pastor. Not only will it be a great gift, but it will eventually benefit your youth ministry. A healthy church is a supportive force behind a healthy youth ministry.

2. Warren, *The Purpose-Driven Church*, 81, 83.

3. See chap. 3, n. 1, for a list of passages to study within your youth ministry context.

4. Of the five purposes, the connection between baptism and fellowship has been the toughest for youth workers to grasp. In an explanation, Rick Warren writes, "In the Greek text of the Great Commission there are three present participle verbs: *going, baptizing,* and *teaching.* Each of these is a part of the command to 'make disciples.' Going, baptizing, and teaching are the essential elements of the disciple-making process. At first glance you might wonder why the Great Commission gives the same prominence to the simple act of baptism as it does to the great tasks of evangelism and edification. Obviously, Jesus did not mention it by accident. Why is baptism so important to warrant inclusion in Christ's Great Commission? I believe it is because it symbolizes one of the purposes of the church: fellowship—identification with the body of Christ. . . . Baptism is not only a symbol of salvation, it is a symbol of fellowship" (*The Purpose-Driven Church*, 105).

THREE

Why a Purpose Statement Is Important and How to Create One

During a recent PDYM seminar, I had lunch with David, a passionate but frustrated youth worker from Nashville. He had a list of struggles he wanted to talk through. He had a hard time getting volunteers, and the volunteers he had didn't seem to understand why the youth ministry existed. They were nice people who were basically clueless about the big picture of the ministry. Some of his volunteers were a source of conflict because they tried to promote their own agendas. He was also tired of being interrogated and second-guessed regarding his program choices. He told me that he questioned his leadership and his call.

David was inadvertently keeping a secret from his youth ministry team and from his church. He knew the five purposes of his ministry, but he kept them hidden. He wasn't doing it intentionally; he just didn't recognize the importance of making them known. David's eyes lit up when I spoke about the importance of communicating the purposes through a purpose statement. He nodded his head and said, "Yeah, that's it! I've been assuming everyone knows what we are trying to accomplish. Obviously, this is too big of an assumption."

David considered students, parents, and his volunteers as valuable people who had no idea why their youth ministry existed. Most of them liked David, and the ministry had some quality things happening, but the sense of clarity and direction was missing.

I told David that putting the five purposes into a written purpose statement and learning to lead from them (chapter 4) would help solve some of his problems and make a positive impact on his ministry. I make that same promise to you.

What a Purpose Statement Will Do for Your Youth Ministry

A Purpose Statement Will Clarify Your Ministry's Existence

When you reveal a purpose statement, you will take away the mystery of your ministry. A clear purpose statement will help you

- make sense of your programs,
- utilize your volunteers more effectively, and
- provide direction for your students' spiritual maturity

Once you communicate God's purpose for your ministry, you won't have to ask the *why* question again. The new question will be *how*: How do we accomplish what God has called us to do? The why must be answered before the how can make sense to others.

Saddleback Church's youth ministry purpose statement answers the *why* question.

> The why must be answered before the how can make sense to others.

Our youth ministry exists to REACH nonbelieving students, to CONNECT them with other Christians, to help them GROW in their faith, and to challenge the growing to DISCOVER their ministry and HONOR God with their life.

Our purpose statement leaves no question about why we exist. It doesn't give specific answers to how we will accomplish the why, because the how is not an important element for a purpose statement. The how will change as your programs change, but the why should never change.

A Purpose Statement Will Attract Followers

Proverbs 29:18 (KJV) says, "Where there is no vision, the people perish." This verse became a reality in my early years of youth ministry when I wasn't sure why it even existed. Prior to discovering our purpose and learning the importance of communicating it, I watched students and volunteers wander aimlessly. They became emotionally detached and left our ministry because there was no clear communication about why we were doing what we were doing. The ministry was directionless, and people felt like their presence didn't matter.

I have since learned that many people in the church are followers and have a great need to be led and encouraged in the right direction. They want to be part of a ministry that has a purpose, and they will follow if they know where they are going and agree with the destination. People are attracted to ministries that honor their time and provide meaning for their lives. People are selective with their time and won't expend much effort if they sense a lack of direction.

A Purpose Statement Will Minimize Conflict

A clear direction will help you manage conflict in your ministry. When God's purposes are not communicated, people will create their own purposes and lobby for them. When I first came to Saddleback, I got to know the few youth ministry volunteers by asking them their understanding of the purpose of our youth ministry. Each person named a different purpose, yet each answer was sharp, passionate, and convincing. One said, "We exist to get students excited about worship." Another said, "We're about building fellowship and providing small-group opportunities." Yet another said, "We want to reach lost students through evangelistic events." As I got to know these volunteers, it became clear that their definitions of purpose were directly related to what they thought should be happening. All of them had good intentions, but they could not agree on the purpose of our ministry, and this led to conflict.

Prior to my purpose-statement years, I personalized all of the negative comments directed at our ministry. Since I hadn't communicated our purpose, people were confused and asked a lot of questions. Their questions—even the innocent ones—felt like attacks, and I interpreted them as a lack of loyalty. With hindsight, I've come to learn that these people weren't disloyal; they were just mystified by lack of direction.

Now that we have a purpose statement, conflict about direction is almost nonexistent. When there is conflict over purpose, I don't take it personally, because I'm confident of God's purpose for our ministry. When someone attacks our purpose, he or she is pointed back to the five New Testament purposes and reminded of why we exist. At Saddleback we never argue about our purposes. We have disagreed over the *how* of our ministry or over *style* but never over the *why*.

If you were to join our volunteer staff at Saddleback Church, I would ask you to agree with the purposes of the church. Without buy-in there is too much potential for personal agendas and conflict. I decided long ago that I don't have time to fight the saints in the church. Neither do you. Your battle time should be reserved for the Enemy. A clearly communicated purpose statement will help you maximize this battle time.

> I don't have time to fight the saints in the church. Neither do you.

A Purpose Statement Will Create Personal Excitement

If you can't get fired up about your ministry's purpose, you are in the wrong ministry. When people understand your purpose and agree with it, it will create excitement among leaders, parents, and students. I'll never forget the look of "Aha!" on the face of one of our volunteers after he heard me teach on our purpose. He came to me smiling and said, "Now I get it! That was great! Thanks!"

Recently, I was preparing my weekend message while eating and studying at Taco Bell (my favorite office). I was sitting behind some students who were ditching class from a nearby high school. I looked at the students, assumed that they were unchurched, and filtered them through our purpose statement: "We exist to REACH nonbelieving students." They are one of the five reasons (evangelism) we exist as a ministry. My mind was whirling, thinking of ways our youth ministry might reach these students, and I asked God for wisdom greater than my own. On my way to refill my drink, I stopped by their table and invited them to our New Year's party. We had a few seconds of small talk and I left. I write this not so that you will think I'm courageous for talking to non-Christian students, but as an example of what a leader does when he or she is passionate about purpose.

A Purpose Statement Will Professionalize Your Ministry

I am passionate about youth ministry. I desire to see our profession continue its growth as a significant career choice for those called to ministry rather than as a stepping stone to a *higher* ministry or pastoral position. As an advocate for youth ministry, I want youth workers to be highly regarded and appreciated for what they do; a purpose statement will communicate health, quality, and professionalism.

> **The fastest way to show a church that things are happening is to carefully launch a purpose statement.**

During my PDYM seminar, youth workers ask, "Why are you spending time on developing a purpose statement when we need program ideas? Our church is looking for something to happen quickly so that they can see we have something going on." Actually, the fastest way to show a church that things are happening is to carefully launch a purpose statement. Doing so is like hanging a banner over the church door that shouts, "We're serious about what we're doing. Our youth ministry has purpose. We're more than adolescent day care."

How to Create a Purpose Statement
Check Out the Direction of Your Church

Before you write a purpose statement, you need to clarify the direction your church is heading so that your youth ministry purpose statement will work in harmony with the direction of your church. Youth ministry is not intended to be a separate entity within the church, but one supportive element of the overall mission of the church. Be very careful to protect this. As youth ministry becomes more professional, we risk the danger of developing tunnel vision and believing that youth ministry is the only ministry in the church. This is a wrong and divisive attitude.

You should discuss with your pastor or governing leadership the purposes of your church. If there is nothing written that explains why your church exists (not what it believes, but why it exists), you may need to help the leadership move toward discovering the purposes of worship, evangelism, fellowship, discipleship, and ministry as described in chapter 2.

You can approach the pastor of a purposeless church in one of two ways. You can say, "Pastor, I can't believe it; our church is so lame; it's unbelievable that we don't have a purpose statement." Or you can keep your position and ask, "Can you help me understand why our church exists? I'm reading this book that talks about the importance of discovering and defining our purpose. I like what I'm reading, but I don't want to take our youth ministry in the wrong direction."

If you find that your church has nothing in writing regarding the five purposes, begin a dialogue about them with your pastor. Be sure to use your meeting time to ask if he or she objects to your writing a specific purpose statement for your youth ministry. If there is no objection, you should begin by getting others involved. (If your church has an existing purpose statement that your pastor wants you to use, move on to chapter 4. But as you move on make sure that your leadership team understands the five purposes discussed in chapter 2.)

Teach the Youth Ministry Leadership the Five Purposes

Once you know your church's direction, teach others in your ministry about why your church exists. You will have better success in writing a purpose statement if you allow your people to be a part of the discovery process by studying the Scriptures with them and teaching about the five purposes.[1]

You will need to decide who to involve in this process; not everyone in your ministry needs to take part. It is okay to be selective and involve the leaders (both student and adult) who have invested their time and energy in the ministry and really care about its direction. At the writing stage, a smaller team will be more efficient. But when you're ready to launch your purpose statement, you should teach it to everyone in your ministry. (If you're the only leader of your ministry, don't wait for a team before you write a purpose statement. Craft one with your senior pastor and use it to invite others to be a part of your ministry.)

You may even ask your leadership team to read this book so that your shared vision will create momentum. Thus no one will be surprised by the new emphasis, thereby creating more support for the ministry's direction. At every PDYM seminar I teach, I watch youth ministry teams drag into the seminar, questioning if the day is going to be worth their time. At the end of the day, the team leaves with a united mission about becoming purpose driven.

Encourage the Youth Ministry Leadership to Put Their Thoughts in Writing

Don't feel that you must carry the entire burden for wording the purpose statement. Once you have spent some time teaching a group of people the five purposes of the church, have them help you craft the purpose statement. Ask them to think of five key words to express the five purposes (see chapter 2), show them some sample purpose statements, and then encourage them to spend some time praying and writing out a purpose statement.

Although the five purposes of the church are inspired by God and unchangeable, the language of your purpose statement is negotiable. Use words that will best communicate the meaning of the five purposes. In addition to Saddleback Church's youth ministry purpose statement on page 57, here are three other samples. I would caution you not to immediately copy any of these and thereby short-circuit your own discovery process. Doing your own work will help you better understand the five purposes and to write a *personal* purpose statement for your youth ministry.

Purpose Statement of Saddleback Church

Saddleback Church exists to bring people to Jesus and MEMBERSHIP in his family, develop them to Christlike MATURITY and equip them for their MINISTRY in the church and life MISSION in the world, in order to MAGNIFY God's name.

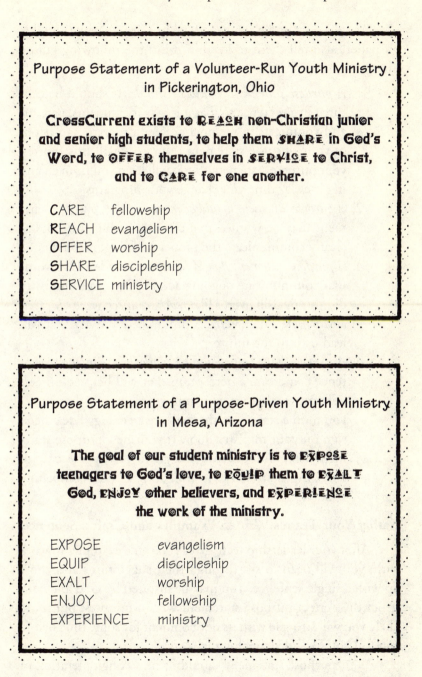

Purpose Statement of a Volunteer-Run Youth Ministry in Pickerington, Ohio

CrossCurrent exists to REACH non-Christian junior and senior high students, to help them SHARE in God's Word, to OFFER themselves in SERVICE to Christ, and to CARE for one another.

CARE   fellowship
REACH   evangelism
OFFER   worship
SHARE   discipleship
SERVICE ministry

Purpose Statement of a Purpose-Driven Youth Ministry in Mesa, Arizona

The goal of our student ministry is to EXPOSE teenagers to God's love, to EQUIP them to EXALT God, ENJOY other believers, and EXPERIENCE the work of the ministry.

EXPOSE   evangelism
EQUIP   discipleship
EXALT   worship
ENJOY   fellowship
EXPERIENCE ministry

As you encourage your leadership to put their thoughts on paper, also tell them to keep in mind the following guidelines:

1. *A purpose statement should be simple.* It should be captured in a sentence so that it is easy for students, parents, and volunteers to memorize. Keep program names out of your purpose statement. Not only will this shorten your purpose statement, but it will keep you from changing it every time you change your programs.

2. *A purpose statement should be meaningful.* A purpose statement may be worded in a clever way, but if it doesn't clearly communicate the proper meaning, it is useless.

3. *A purpose statement should be action oriented.* Use words that communicate ongoing action. Our youth ministry did this by using verbs like *reach, connect, grow, discover,* and *honor.* These verbs communicate activity that will lead us into the future.

4. *A purpose statement should be compelling.* Since one sentence can create a perception that will help volunteers determine whether your ministry is worth their time, you need a statement that will create energy like a neon sign on your ministry door. If your new purpose statement isn't noteworthy enough to justify the cost of changing stationery, it probably is not compelling enough.

Gather Your Team's Written Examples and Craft a Sentence

After your leadership team gives you some examples to work with, you will need to sift through their suggestions and come up with a single sentence. You may be inspired by God and construct the perfect purpose statement within minutes, but more likely you will struggle with its development for some time before you feel comfortable launching it.

Your purpose statement shouldn't be a conglomeration of individual members' pet words or phrases. Don't get caught up in trying to make people happy by combining all of their contributions. Group consensus on the wording isn't important. What is important is arriving at a clear statement that will allow you to lead with confidence. Consensus becomes important later when others are asked to make a commitment to support your ministry's purpose. You don't have to be the sole creator of the purpose statement, but you will need to coordinate its birth, own it, sell it, explain it, and illustrate it.

What to Do Once the Purpose Statement Is Written
Seek the Wisdom of Others

Once you have a well-crafted purpose statement, you would be wise to show it to others—pastors, friends, parents, other youth pastors—who weren't involved in the composition process and ask for their advice. Proverbs 15:22 says, "Plans fail for lack of counsel, but with many advisers they succeed." A good leader seeks out advisers. If you're afraid of other people's opinions, you're not a leader. Proverbs 19:20 says, "Listen to advice and accept instruction, and in the end you will be wise." After listening to the advice of many, interpret the information, pray about it, and share it with your pastor.

> **If you're afraid of other people's opinions, you're not a leader.**

Get Support from Your Pastor

Any time you make a significant change in your ministry, it is wise to consult your pastor. You owe it to the senior leadership to communicate major changes that are being discussed within your ministry. Don't ask your pastor to do any of the work related to the purpose statement, but ask for support regarding the wording—as well as the direction of your ministry—before you make the statement public.

Why do you need an advocate? Because you may find that, after you launch your purpose statement and make some changes in your ministry, people will question you. Some may say, "We've never had a purpose statement before. Why do we need one now?" They may not even like the direction the five purposes take you. You may find they love fellowship and don't want to pursue evangelism since it will attract new students and upset the status quo. Angered people may attempt to sabotage your efforts by bypassing you and complaining directly to your pastor. You don't want your boss to be caught off guard. When your pastor is informed, there can be no surprise by the opposition. Your pastor can verbally support your direction and thus diffuse negative momentum.

Launch It with Wisdom

Once you get your pastor's support, make your purpose statement public. It is best to launch your new purpose statement at a time that lends itself to natural change: the beginning of January when everyone expects change; in June during graduation season or movement to the next grade level; or in late August or early September at the beginning of the new school year.

Think through how you will communicate these purposes so that your team will sense your confidence with the direction God has laid out for your ministry. When you announce the purpose statement, use it as an opportunity to teach those who weren't involved in its creation where the five purposes for the church are found in the Bible. Make sure they know these are God's eternal purposes for a healthy ministry and not your own brainchild.

Give People an Opportunity to Process Their Future Participation

Before we went public with our purpose statement at Saddleback, I anticipated a little difficulty. Some of the volunteers had worked in the youth ministry before I arrived, some didn't like change, and some were older than I was and thought they knew what was best for the ministry. Even though they were members of a purpose-driven church, they felt that the youth ministry needed to fulfill only the fellowship purpose. The holy huddle youth group brought them comfort.

I clearly explained the five purposes of the church and showed everyone the statement we would use to communicate the purposes. Even though my pastor wasn't there, I relayed his excitement so that the volunteers would know this was a team direction. If I had to do it over again, I would ask my pastor to attend this volunteer meeting so he could more appropriately show his verbal and nonverbal support.

After explaining the purposes, I gave everyone two weeks to prayerfully consider whether or not they could fully support the statement. I told them they could "get off the ship" and there would be no hard feelings. I didn't want them to feel like they needed to hide from me at church if they no longer wanted to work with students in an attempt to fulfill the purposes. I related to them that ministry changes sometimes create opportunities for people to move in new directions. Our youth ministry ship had been resting comfortably at the dock (stuck at the dock was more realistic) for a while, and it was now time to set sail. In a positive way, I said, "It's time to jump ship if you're not able to go in our new direction." They needed to be either 100 percent supportive or, for the benefit of the ministry, find another place to serve within our church. This was not a mean-spirited act; it was an act of leadership.

Fortunately, most people were thrilled with a clear sense of direction. They became hopeful and energized. Thus, I had an easy transition. But it is not always this smooth for everyone. Some of my youth worker friends could have had Jesus himself explain the five purposes and still had people complain. Some church cultures breed criticism and oppose all new ideas. Some of your people who don't like change or don't like you may see the introduction of a purpose statement as an opportunity to change ministries. Don't view the reshuffling as negative. It can be a positive move, since the people you attract in the future will join a united, purpose-driven team.

Put Leadership Behind Your Purpose

If you are the point person for your ministry and what you've read so far sounds too terrifying, you may be rethinking your role as *the* leader. Not everyone who thinks he or she is a leader is one. Leaders have to make some tough decisions and find the courage to do what's right. They are not always liked by everyone. Someone once told me that if I was liked by everyone, I probably wasn't an effective leader.

Building a purpose-driven youth ministry will take a tremendous amount of commitment, perseverance, and leadership. After you read the next chapter, you will know if you have what it takes to be the type of leader who can inspire your youth ministry toward the five purposes of the church. Just about anyone can create a purpose statement, but it takes leadership to use it to make a purpose-driven youth ministry.

> Building a purpose-driven youth ministry will take a tremendous amount of commitment, perseverance, and leadership.

MAKING IT PERSONAL

1. Does your church have a purpose statement? If so, do you know it?

2. Does your youth ministry have a purpose statement? If not, do you think your youth ministry needs one? What do you think a purpose statement would do for your youth ministry?

3. If your youth ministry does have a purpose statement, can you write it from memory? Why or why not?

4. Do your youth ministry leaders—both students and adults—have a clear understanding of the direction of your youth ministry?

5. Using the five words you wrote under question 1 at the end of the last chapter (page 53), try writing a purpose statement.

6. Study the verses listed in note 1 below and discuss their implications for the purpose of your ministry.

NOTES

1. In Rick Warren's *The Purpose-Driven Church* (Grand Rapids: Zondervan, 1995), 96–97, the following Scriptures are given as potential study verses: Matthew 5:13–16; 9:35; 11:28–30; 16:15–19; 18:19–20; 22:36–40; 24:14; 25:34–40; 28:18–20; Mark 10:43–45; Luke 4:18–19, 43–44; John 4:23; 10:14–18; 13:34–35; 20:21; Acts 1:8; 2:41–47; 4:32–35; 5:42; 6:1–7; Romans 12:1–8; 15:1–7; 1 Corinthians 12:12–31; 2 Corinthians 5:17–6:1; Galatians 5:13–15; 6:1–2; Ephesians 1:22–23; 2:19–22; 3:6, 14–21; 4:11–16; 5:23–24; Colossians 1:24–28; 3:15–16; 1 Thessalonians 1:3; 5:11; Hebrews 10:24–25; 13:7, 17; 1 Peter 2:9–10; 1 John 1:5–7; 4:7–21. You can see another example of all five of these purposes lived out through the eyes of the early church in Acts 2.

FOUR

Conveying Your Purpose and Leading by Example

Youth workers love discovering God's five purposes for the church (see chapter 2), and they actually have fun crafting a purpose statement (see chapter 3). Unfortunately, their enthusiasm often diminishes when they encounter the material you'll find in this chapter. What you're about to read requires leadership. It will challenge you to move beyond the discovery of God's five purposes and the creation of a purpose statement, asking you to jump into the application phase.

In this leap, you will most likely find the leadership requirement difficult. Leadership separates a purpose-driven youth ministry from an event-and-activity-driven youth ministry. In many ways the application of this book depends on your ability to be a leader. Conveying the purposes is a huge task for any leader, but pursuing this challenge will strengthen your youth ministry.

> **Leadership separates a purpose-driven youth ministry from an event-and-activity-driven youth ministry.**

How a Leader Conveys the Purposes

Knowing why your youth ministry exists and having an articulate purpose statement will be of little value if you aren't communicating, driving, and supporting your purpose. The more people understand and rally behind your purpose, the healthier your ministry will become. This is where the true test of leadership will be played out. Are you ready to take the next step and help your ministry get beyond good intentions and into God's purposes?

You must take on three responsibilities to make God's purposes known within your youth ministry: communicate the purposes, repeat the purposes, and make sure that key people memorize the purpose statement.

A Leader Communicates the Purposes

Your purpose cannot become a common purpose until people know it. Until then you will be trying to build a ministry with misinformed, confused, and uncommitted players. It would be like suiting up nine unwilling baseball players in new uniforms then asking the whole team to play in left field without a coach. People may be involved, but they won't be effective until they are completely informed and in position.

To aid students, volunteers, parents, and church leaders in retaining your purpose statement, you will need to continually communicate it. Some ideas to help you communicate to each of these groups follow.

Students
- Use your five key words over and over again.
- Put your purpose statement on all of your literature. Your students should see your purpose statement every week.
- Teach on each of the five purposes throughout the year.
- Challenge your committed students to memorize the purpose statement.
- Make your purpose statement visible with a banner or poster in your meeting room.

Volunteers

- Have them memorize the purpose statement as part of their commitment to youth ministry.
- Record yourself explaining the purposes and give them each an audiotape to review.
- Ask them to teach on the purposes to their small groups at least twice a year.
- Regularly ask them if they know and understand the purposes.
- Begin the purpose statement challenge (explained on pages 74–75).

Parents

- Explain your purpose statement at every parent meeting.
- Print your purpose statement on ministry stationery so it is seen on all letters sent home.
- Ask and assign parents to pray specifically for one of the five purposes.
- Write a parents' letter every other month explaining one of the purposes.
- Show them how every program is designed to fulfill a specific purpose (you will see this more clearly in chapter 5).

Church Leaders

- Send each person in leadership a copy of your purpose statement and a brief description of each purpose.
- Ask each elder or church leader to pray specifically for one of the five purposes as it relates to your youth ministry.
- When explaining your programs to church leaders, always say, "This program fulfills our _____ purpose."

A Leader Repeats the Purposes

After you've done a good job of conveying your purposes to all of the above groups, do it again. A good leader will constantly communicate the purposes and remind people of the importance of knowing them. No one will know the purposes or value them as much as the point person of the ministry. I'm always amazed that the people who I think should know our purposes don't. Consistent repetition will help your followers catch the vision of the ministry.

> No one will know the purposes or value them as much as the point person of the ministry.

Prior to coming to Saddleback Church I worked at another church for eleven years. I communicated our purpose statement with an image of a funnel (at Saddleback we use the image of a baseball diamond, as you will see in chapter 12). I taught it all the time. I talked about the funnel, showed diagrams of the funnel, and even gave funnels out as gifts. I went wild with the funnel concept because I wanted people to understand why we did what we did.

Prior to one of our volunteer staff meetings, everyone secretly arrived an hour before me to create an antifunnel campaign. They made funnel hats, drew funnels on their shirts, painted funnels on banners, and decorated the room with funnels. They drew circles around funnels with a slash through the circle communicating "No more funnels." They had protest signs that said, "Get rid of the funnel" and "Stop the funnel abuse."

When they saw me walking toward the room for the meeting, they scurried behind couches and hid to see my reaction. When I walked into the room, they all shouted, "Surprise!" and they got on their knees and begged me to release them from the bondage of the funnel. My immediate external reaction was to smile and laugh at the escapade, but internally I was devastated.

Here was my volunteer staff whom I had been leading, nurturing, and sharing ministry with for years saying, "Enough is enough; we get the point." I felt like my leadership had been attacked.

Later that night I called a mentor and shared this stinging experience. This man, who was very successful in business, said, "Doug, what they did is one of the greatest compliments I've ever heard. Most followers don't hear about purpose enough to know it, let alone get tired of it. I would be thrilled if my employees realized why our company exists. Most don't have any idea of our business outside their main responsibility. Besides, your volunteers weren't making fun of your purposes, they were having fun with your visual process. So back off on the funnels for a while, but never back off on your purposes." I did just that. I kept the funnel rhetoric to a minimum. Interestingly though, I noticed that the volunteers continued to use the funnel language when they described our purpose.

In Nehemiah 4:6–15, the people who were rebuilding the wall of Jerusalem were tiring under the stress of having to deal with their enemies. Halfway through the fifty-two-day project, Nehemiah had to remind them of their purpose. Nehemiah gives us a good leadership example. It is wise to remind people of God's purposes for your ministry every twenty-six days (or once a month) so that they don't lose sight of them.

A Leader Makes Sure Key People Memorize the Purpose Statement

Even after you convey your purpose statement and repeat it, you will find that some of your key people need to be nudged to memorize it. It is important for key leaders to memorize the purpose statement so that they will be more likely to repeat it and teach it to others. This will also help them lead with confidence because they will know where they are going.

I created a little game called "The Purpose Statement Challenge" to help my volunteers memorize our purpose statement. It goes like this: If one of our students memorizes our purpose statement and says it in front of our group, he or she can then pick any volunteer to repeat our purpose statement. If the volunteer can't repeat it, he or she either owes the student five dollars or a lunch.

When we first started this game, I pulled a ninth grader aside and asked him to memorize the purpose statement during the week and come Sunday morning prepared to make some money. When Sunday rolled around, the student (Andy) came forward and spit out our purpose statement with ease. While the volunteers began ducking under their chairs, Andy pointed to Cynthia, one of our oldest volunteers. Cynthia walked up, didn't even attempt the purpose statement, and handed Andy five bucks. We did this for several weeks until our volunteers either knew it or went broke. Our leaders were taking drastic measures (everything short of tattoos) to memorize it. One woman learned the purpose statement to the tune of "Jesus Loves Me" and sang it in front of the students. Whatever it takes!

To make the memorization easier, I had the students and volunteers begin by focusing on the five key words. When they understood the progression of those five words, the surrounding words came easier, (to give them a little more hope) I also told them that our purpose statement is only a few words longer than John 3:16, which many of them had easily memorized as a child.

What to Do After Your Purpose Statement Is Known

As you live with the task of communication and repetition, you will find that there are at least four other responsibilities you must take to lead a purpose-driven youth ministry: monitoring the purpose statement, managing your time by the purposes, modeling the purposes in your life, and creating programs to fulfill the purposes.

Monitor the Purpose Statement

Monitor your purpose statement by occasionally evaluating the wording. If God didn't give you the specific words to use, then you shouldn't be surprised when the wording shows itself fallible. You may need to reword your purpose statement for better clarity. Our first purpose statement had four key words to communicate the five purposes. It made sense to me, but I noticed that others weren't making the connection, so we changed the wording to make the meaning clearer.

Here is another example of how we had to monitor an existing purpose statement after we had already launched it. An earlier purpose statement reads:

> Our youth ministry exists to REACH nonbelieving students, to CONNECT them, to GROW them in their faith, and to challenge them to DISCOVER their ministry and HONOR God with their life.

At first glance you may not even notice the differences from the one you read on page 57. Shortly after communicating our purpose statement to our church, a student's mother came to me and said, "Several parents are really happy that you have some direction for the youth ministry, but I'm a little disappointed because I don't think you're doing what your statement says you'll do. I don't see any growth in my son's faith."

We were reaching her son. He was attending a few programs, but he wasn't a Christian (he told me himself). Based on the above wording, the mom's complaint was valid. Our purpose statement had told her that if we reached her son, we would *connect* and *grow* him in his faith. We had reached her son, but he wasn't growing in his faith. Why? Because he didn't have a faith. We needed to change the wording because it is impossible to help someone grow in a faith he or she doesn't have. We had to be more specific. The underlined words are the additions we used to make our purpose statement more specific.

> Our youth ministry exists to REACH nonbelieving students, to CONNECT them with other Christians, to help them GROW in their faith, and to challenge the growing to DISCOVER their ministry and HONOR God with their life.

Manage Your Time by the Purposes

When you understand why your ministry exists, you will want to more carefully focus your time. Chapter 17 suggests more specific time management techniques, but here I want to encourage you to begin evaluating your time based on your purposes.

When junk mail comes across your desk and you find an invitation to a student event, stop and evaluate the opportunity. You will always have dozens of opportunities, but you need to decide if your time is going to be managed by your opportunities or your priorities. Your priorities should be your five purposes. Examine your opportunities and ask yourself: "Will this help us better accomplish one of our purposes?" "Is this opportunity relevant to our purposes?" "What type of purpose will it help fulfill, and do we need that help right now?" If it won't help you accomplish your purpose, it will drain some of your time. A leader learns to determine what is important, since not everything is worthwhile. If you allow yourself and your ministry to get too busy, your effectiveness will decrease. Keep from being managed by your opportunities and try to be managed by your purposes. The old adage "If you aim at nothing, you'll hit it every time" is true. What is also true is that if you aim at everything, you'll seldom hit your target. Your purposes, however, will keep you aiming straight at the target.

As you look at the time you allot to different elements of your ministry, you may want to begin thinking, *How much time do I give to each of the five purposes during a given week or month?* This evaluation will begin to show you not only where your time is going but also which purposes get your best attention.

You need to decide if your time is going to be managed by your opportunities or your priorities.

Model the Purposes in Your Life

If you are a leader who lives out the purposes, you will *pull* people instead of *push* them. Pushing them to do what you want is tough, tiresome, and unrewarding. The leader who tries to push people in the right direction finds resistance. You will be much more successful at pulling others in the right direction if they observe you in action. Your example will cause them to want to emulate your actions.

I live out the Saddleback youth ministry purposes by, among other things, trying to *reach* unbelieving students. I was recently at a church event where there were many rough-looking unchurched students. Many of our churched students were scared of them and didn't want anything to do with them. To be honest, I was a little frightened myself. I didn't have much in common with them, and I didn't know enough about drugs to talk their language. But I understood that we exist to reach those students, and if I didn't greet them, the chances were good that our adult and student leaders wouldn't do it either. Because of this, I took another leader into the pack with me (the biggest one I could find), and we started meeting these students. I soon saw other adult and student leaders being *pulled* to make their way over to greet these students.

> I can't talk about the importance of servanthood if I'm not stacking chairs or picking up papers at the end of a program.

Everyone watches leaders! I can't talk about the value of being in a small group, for example, if I'm not in one myself. I can't talk about the importance of servanthood if I'm not stacking chairs or picking up papers at the end of a program. Leaders model important values and provide a breathing example of the purpose statement.

Create Programs to Fulfill the Purposes

Since programs are intended to influence students (not just stir up activity), a leader will change and design programs to best reflect the ministry's purposes. He or she understands that the purposes are more important than programs and will make sure that the purposes are enhanced regardless of the program's destiny. This leader recognizes that programs are a means to an end and not an end in themselves.

> **Programs are a means to an end and not an end in themselves.**

As you better understand the five purposes and work through some of the ideas in the next chapter, you will probably begin to think about making strategic changes in your ministry. Keep in mind that most people don't like change. Change creates conflict and will put your leadership to the test. If you believe in God's purposes, you should be willing to handle the complaints that come as a result of program adjustments. The only consolation through the journey of conflict is knowing that you are doing the right thing to build a healthy youth ministry on God's eternal purposes. (I will take you through some important steps for implementing change in chapter 19.)

One more component that is vital to discuss before you begin creating programs to fulfill the purposes is the different commitment levels of students both in- and outside your ministry. The next chapter (component #3: potential audience) shows a way to identify different commitment levels. When you are able to focus the purposes toward different commitments, you will find yourself creating a strategy with programs that have a purpose. This is where the purpose-driven youth ministry really begins to take shape!

MAKING IT PERSONAL

1. Do you think you are the type of leader who can help make God's purposes for the church known? Why or why not?

2. How would you teach the five purposes to the students in your group?

3. How well are the purposes known among your students, volunteers, and parents?

4. What are some specific ways leaders could help students understand the five purposes?

5. If you have a purpose statement that was written a long time ago, is it still relevant and understandable for your youth ministry?

6. What do you think of the purpose statement challenge described on pages 74–75?

7. Which of the five purposes do you find most difficult to model in your life? Why?

COMPONENT THREE

POTeNTial AUDieNCe

FIVE

Identifying Students' Commitments

By now you may be eager to jump in and begin creating programs to fulfill God's five purposes. I want to spare you the trouble that Patrick Denton, a youth worker of eight years, experienced when he made the mistake of rushing into programming too soon. At one of my PDYM seminars, Patrick was excited to discover the five purposes. He determined that his ministry was out of balance because most of his programs were designed to fulfill the purpose of discipleship and the other four purposes were basically neglected. He was so thrilled about his new understanding that he left the seminar right after the purpose segment to figure out how to add the other purposes to his programs.

Several months later Patrick called me and explained how his premature enthusiasm and changes had created big problems in his ministry. Patrick made some significant alterations in his Wednesday night program, Full House. He added new components to Full House so that it would maintain a balance of the five New Testament purposes. Prior to the changes, Full House had been a successful Bible study that fulfilled the purpose of discipleship. Patrick's students were bringing their Bibles and enjoying the study of God's Word. He didn't have large numbers of students attending, but the ones who were attending were consistent, committed, and growing in their faith.

Patrick redesigned Full House to include some wild games that would be attractive to unchurched students and fulfill the evangelism purpose. After the games, he provided snacks and encouraged students to eat together in small groups—fellowship purpose. When everyone was done sweating from the games and had finished eating, he pulled them together to sing songs to fulfill the worship purpose. He then taught his usual Bible study to cover the discipleship purpose, and he concluded the programs in the church kitchen so that students could make peanut butter and jelly sandwiches for the community's homeless—ministry purpose. Patrick believed he had designed the ultimate youth ministry program fulfilling the five purposes of the church.

Patrick left the seminar too early. And you can guess what happened to Full House after six months. The crazy games attracted some new students, but they usually left after grabbing the food. They didn't want to sing or listen to a Bible study. The few students who did stay didn't know anything about God, so Patrick had to simplify his teaching. At first the program changes seemed like a good idea to the original Full House students who wanted a place to invite some of their non-Christian friends, but after the newness wore off, they didn't feel like they were getting any depth from Patrick's teaching. They also missed the intimacy and accountability they had had with committed Christians. Even though they really liked Patrick, many of them stopped attending and went with their Christian friends from school to another church that had a deeper midweek Bible study and no games.

At the end of six months, Patrick had about the same number of students attending as before the changes, but now his students were either new or non-Christians, and the group was void of spiritual depth. In addition, parents were complaining to Patrick about their kids going to other churches.

Patrick had focused on the purposes, but he hadn't thought through the various commitment levels and the receptivity each commitment allows. His programming mistakes give us an opportunity to learn a few principles.

Putting Programs Before People Brings Problems

Patrick's First Problem: One Program Can't Effectively Fulfill All Five Purposes

When you aim at all five purposes in one program, you can't hit any with power. Instead of hitting the bull's-eye, Patrick was spraying shrapnel everywhere. He tried to create an evangelistic appeal with games and discovered that he needed more evangelistic energy, depth, and quality to keep the unchurched. But he didn't have time to do all this at Full House because he felt the need to get to the other purposes. With this programming, he found he couldn't give any of the purposes enough focus, and this resulted in poor quality. Patrick's biggest mistake was that he introduced all of the purposes without thinking through how his unique potential audience could be better reached by one of the purposes.

> **When you aim at all five purposes in one program, you can't hit any with power.**

Patrick's Second Problem: One Program Can't Effectively Target All Students

It is a fairly safe assumption that the students in your youth ministry have different levels of spiritual commitment (we have some who want to know the Hebrew word for atonement and others who want their parents to pay them to attend any program). Since students are so different, Patrick shouldn't have expected one program to meet everyone's needs. Some students need the basics, and others need to put their long-term faith into action. Some non-Christian students need to hear a clear presentation of the gospel, while others need to learn and develop spiritual disciplines. Patrick tried to meet everyone's need with one program and found himself frustrated because his audience was so diverse and his program too general.

Solutions

As you begin to evaluate your existing programs in relation to the five purposes, you need to ask two important questions about each of your programs:

1. What primary purpose (evangelism, worship, fellowship, discipleship, or ministry) does this program (for example, Full House) fulfill?
2. Who are we trying to target with this program?

If your answer to the first question is "all of them," your program isn't much different from Patrick's and you can expect his problems. If your answer to the second question is "Students," you are being far too general. What kind of students? I can think of at least five types in our youth ministry:

- the non-Christian student
- the new Christian
- the student who knows a great deal about the Bible but is apathetic about most things we do
- the growing student
- the spiritual leader

These potential audiences exist whether we want to recognize them or not. Recognition will lead to effectiveness. Your programs will become more successful, while fulfilling God's purposes, if you spend some preliminary time identifying the different audiences in your ministry. If you don't do this, you may find yourself in Patrick's situation, creating programs for students who don't exist within your ministry.

> Your programs will become more successful, while fulfilling God's purposes, if you spend some preliminary time identifying the different audiences in your ministry.

In the rest of this chapter, I will show how you can identify the potential audience of students both within and outside your church and design programs specially meant to reach them.

How to Identify Your Potential Audience

At Saddleback Church we identify our potential audience by a series of five concentric circles we call the "Circles of Commitment" (see fig. 5.1).

Fig. 5.1

These circles accomplish two significant tasks. First, they help illustrate our potential audiences. When we know who we are trying to reach, we can design our programs to focus on one of God's five purposes *and* target our potential audience. Second, the circles help communicate the goal of our youth ministry: to reach students from our community and move them to core commitments. As you read through our descriptions, you may find that your youth ministry doesn't have a certain type of student listed. Focus on the word *potential*. You may not have committed students now, but the students you do have possess the potential to become committed students. The following descriptions represent our five potential audiences.

> When we know who we are trying to reach, we can design our programs to focus on one of God's five purposes AND target our potential audience.

Community Students

We recognize *community students* as teenagers living within a realistic driving distance of our church. More specifically, we look at the schools within a ten- to fifteen-mile radius of our church as our potential community audience. We don't view Southern California students as our potential community audience. We don't even consider all of the students in the county as our community audience. Instead, to keep our ministry manageable we focus on the schools and neighborhoods represented in a fraction of our county. There are approximately twenty-six thousand junior high and high school students at schools within twenty miles of our church property. The only common commitment these students share is their *noncommitment* to attend church.

This number of students indicates that there are too many unreached teenagers in our community. It is a number that shouts for something to be done to reach these students with the good news of Jesus Christ. This massive number also tells us that there should never be any competition between other church youth ministries in our area. Why? Because less than ten percent of teenagers in our community are involved in churches. This means that more than twenty-three thousand unchurched teenagers need to hear about God's love; our community, then, has a significant target audience for the purpose of evangelism. Chapter 6 concentrates on how to reach community students by expressing the primary purpose of evangelism.

Crowd Students

The next circle represents what we call *crowd students.* Crowd students are those who come to a weekend youth service[1] and fill out an information card. Our weekend program is designed for our regular students and their unchurched friends. We view this as our entry-level program.

Some of our crowd students are invited by regulars, others are forced by their parents to attend, and still others attend regardless of their parents' church involvement. These are our regular attendees; some are Christians and some are non-Christians. Their commitment is that they attend Saddleback Church and refer to it as their home church.

If we can get students excited about regularly attending one of our weekend services, we have a great opportunity to draw them into the rest of our ministry. Chapter 7 goes into further detail about how we program for the crowd student with a youth service that fulfills the purpose of worship.

Congregation Students

Once students give their lives to Christ, our goal is to place them in a small group where they can connect with other Christians and grow in their faith. Students who move beyond the crowd level and commit to attending our midweek small groups are considered *congregation students.* We constantly encourage our weekend students (crowd) to take the next step and get involved in our midweek small groups where they will be known, cared for, held accountable, and connected with other believers. We view this intimacy as fulfilling the purpose of fellowship. Chapter 8 tells more about congregation students and their commitment to small groups.

Committed Students

We define *committed students* as those who are committed to developing spiritual habits, such as personal Bible study, prayer, accountability with another believer, Scripture memorization, giving, and commitment to the church body. Chapter 9 gives a unique way to prepare committed students through the purpose of discipleship.

Core Students

When committed students discover their giftedness and want to express it through ministering to others, they become *core students.* This is my favorite aspect of youth ministry. I love watching students fulfill God's purpose for their lives by discovering their gifts and expressing them in ministry. Remember, *discover* is the key word that represents the purpose of ministry in our purpose statement. These ministering students don't graduate from their faith when they graduate from the youth ministry.

What may have started with an evangelistic effort to reach community students comes full circle when core students become student ministers. Core students also have the opportunity to become student leaders—leaders who become key players in a growing youth ministry through understanding the big picture of why their youth ministry exists. Chapter 10 provides more information on core students doing ministry and on student leadership.

In no way do I want to suggest that Jesus used the five circles of commitment in his strategy to reach the world, but it is apparent that he ministered to people at all different levels of faith. He had a spiritual influence in the towns he traveled through (community), and he often taught large groups (crowd). In Luke 10 he sent out the seventy-two (congregation). He led a band of twelve disciples (committed), and he had an inner group of Peter, James, and John (core).

> **Jesus ministered to people at all different levels of faith.**

The circles are not *the* model for visualizing students' commitments. If you can use this model to help you better identify a student's commitment, then do so. The circles will help you make better sense of your programs. If you like the model but don't want to use the words or definitions I use, don't feel limited to them. I have a friend who has termed his potential audience as "unknown, unconvinced, convinced, connected, and committed." Use what works for you. Just remember that it is not as important to be original as it is to be effective.

What to Do After You Identify Your Potential Audience

Define Your Potential Audience by Commitments

After you identify your potential audience, ask, "To what is each audience committed?"

Community students are committed to *not attending church*—they are living apart from Christ;

Crowd students are committed to *attending our church*— they are hearing about Christ;

Congregation students are committed to *a small group*— they have a relationship with Christ and with other Christians;

Committed students are committed to *spiritual habits*—they are growing in Christ;

Core students are committed to *doing ministry*—they are serving because of Christ.

The clearer the picture you have of what each commitment level looks like, the easier it will be for you to relate to students at their respective levels.

Realize That Each Group Size Will Decrease as Commitment Increases

The circles of commitment constantly remind us of our potential audiences. They also reveal a realistic view of what a purpose-driven youth ministry looks like. Since each circle represents a deeper commitment, you will begin to experience some attrition at each level beyond community. That is a normal element of the maturity process.

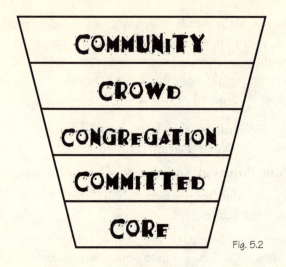

Fig. 5.2

Focus on the Word "Potential" and Start with Who You Have

A key word in this potential audience component is *potential*. You may transfer our circle concept into your setting and realize that you have a few crowd students, a few congregation students, and none in the committed or core. That's okay. If you have *any* students in your youth ministry, you have the *potential* to move them toward the core. Start building your youth ministry with the ones you have and begin praying and designing your programs to move students toward the next level of commitment.

When I first came to Saddleback, there were thirty-five students in the youth ministry. I identified the majority of these students at the crowd level, and that is where we started. They were our potential audience. We designed a program to meet the needs of crowd students and also began a small-group program for those students who were ready for the next step in their faith. This small-group focus became our congregation program. It wasn't until my third year at Saddleback that we had an established committed program. And it wasn't until my fifth year that our core really exploded. While we had core students during our second year, we didn't have a strong program. I write this to encourage you. You don't need to start by developing all five potential audiences today. A healthy, purpose-driven youth ministry doesn't happen quickly. Building health takes time. Be patient about the progress of your programs.

Express Your Heart Louder Than Your Hoops

Some youth workers don't like the type of commitment structure we have at Saddleback Church. I have been asked, "Don't students resist your categories and feel like they are jumping through spiritual hoops?" Actually, I have never experienced any student opposition to the circles of commitment. The circles simply define where students are and where we want to take them. Students in our ministry are familiar with the circles because we teach on them a few times a year and regularly refer to moving the community to the core. In all of our communication we express our hearts; we want to see students grow spiritually. We understand that the circles are a human-made model used to identify our potential audience. They are not spiritual circles and should never be confused as such.

The circles provide us with an identification, not an identity. We are careful to not assign a "value" to a student based on commitment level. We don't have acknowledgment ceremonies at which we say, "Hey, everyone, Phillip has just moved from the crowd circle to the congregation circle. Let's give him a hand." The purpose of the circles is not to isolate students, but to recognize commitment levels so we can enhance growth by being more strategic in our program designs.

> **The circles provide us with an identification, not an identity.**

How to Design a Purpose-Driven Strategy

Now that you know the five purposes of the church and have identified your potential audience, you are ready to ask, "What types of programs will fulfill the five purposes *and* reach our potential audience?" A formula I like to use for programming is

potential audience + purpose = program

For example,

community students + purpose of evangelism = New Year's Eve program

Thus the New Year's Eve program becomes a strategy for reaching community students by fulfilling the purpose of evangelism. Figures 5.3, 5.4, 5.5 show three different strategies for implementing this formula in different youth ministries. No one example is *the* right way. There are many diverse ways to target various audiences. In addition to potential audience and purposes, every ministry must take into consideration

- the direction of the church
- the available time of the leaders
- the amount of adult help
- the accessible resources

These are just a few of the variables that will impact your strategy, the programs you design, and how often you do them. If you have limited time, no help, and no resources, you won't be able do everything you would like to do. Keep in mind that your programs don't all have to be weekly programs. You may choose to fulfill the purpose of worship for your committed students through a night of praise singing once a month (or quarterly, depending on your time).

In the following examples you should notice the term *primary* before both purpose and program. I use that to indicate the *main* biblical purpose and program for each specific commitment level. For example, at the New Year's Eve program, fellowship will occur. A few students will be there for ministry, but the primary purpose

Example 1		
Part-time Youth Minister, First Presbyterian Church		
WHO are we trying to target? **Potential Audience**	**WHAT** is our purpose? **Primary Purpose**	**HOW** will we attempt to do this? **Primary Program**
Community	Evangelism	Yearly outreach event
Crowd	Fellowship	Quarterly special events/socials
Congregation	Discipleship	Sunday school
Committed	Worship	Midweek praise & worship
Core	Ministry	Monthly service project

Fig. 5.3

Example 2		
Volunteer-Run Youth Ministry, Our Savior Lutheran Church		
WHO are we trying to target? **Potential Audience**	**WHAT** is our purpose? **Primary Purpose**	**HOW** will we attempt to do this? **Primary Program**
Community	Evangelism	Occasional campus visitation
Crowd	Discipleship	Sunday school
Congregation	Ministry	Student-led ministry teams meet midweek
Committed	Fellowship	Monthly social gathering
Core	Worship	Quarterly night of praise

Fig. 5.4

Example 3		
Full-time Youth Minister, Saddleback Church		
WHO are we trying to target? **Potential Audience**	**WHAT** is our purpose? **Primary Purpose**	**HOW** will we attempt to do this? **Primary Program**
Community—Chapter 6	Evangelism	Friendship evangelism challenge
Crowd—Chapter 7	Worship	Weekend worship services
Congregation—Chapter 8	Fellowship	Midweek area Bible study small groups
Committed—Chapter 9	Discipleship	Self-initiated discipleship tools
Core—Chapter 10	Ministry	Student leadership (monthly)

Fig. 5.5

is evangelism. Another example involves our small groups (see chapter 8): The primary purpose is fellowship because in small groups we spend most of our time connecting with other believers. The purpose of discipleship emerges in these small groups, because, we begin with a Bible study.

If you can get a handle on the formula primary purpose + potential audience = program, you will save time and headaches trying to make your programs effective. As God leads you, realize that your programs will be expressed in a unique way. The eternal purposes of God never change, and a potential audience exists in most churches, but programs can and should change as often as necessary to reach your potential audience and best fulfill God's purpose for your ministry.

Figure 5.6 shows how we at Saddleback Church purposefully pursue our potential audience.

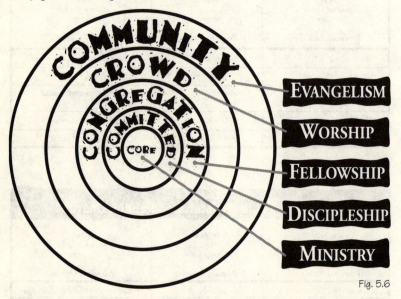

Fig. 5.6

The next five chapters further explain how to design programs to reach the five potential audiences and express the five purposes. I discuss important transferable principles as well as present some specific ways the youth ministry of Saddleback Church creates programs for these audiences.

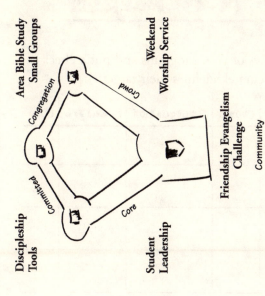

**Area Bible Study
Small Groups**

**Weekend
Worship Service**

**Friendship Evangelism
Challenge**

Community

**Discipleship
Tools**

**Student
Leadership**

Congregation

Crowd

Committed

Core

Fig. 5.7b

The five primary programs listed in Fig. 5.5 are laid out in a progressive order around this baseball diamond. This diamond is the process we use to communicate movement. You will read a detailed description of each of these programs in chapters 6–10. We use some additional programs, which we term our secondary programs, that will be described in chapter 12. You will see how these secondary programs assist movement from the community to the core. You will also understand why we use the symbol of the baseball diamond to communicate movement.

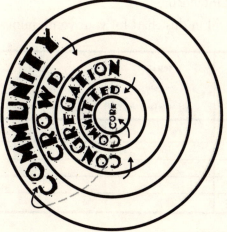

Fig. 5.7a

The above circles are an example of our intended movement. We want to move the community student to the core and the core student back out to reach the community student.

Making It Personal

1. Write down the names of your programs and put a check in the box that most accurately defines their target(s).

PROGRAM	COMMUNITY	CROWD	CONGREGATION	COMMITTED	CORE

2. Do any of your programs need to be more focused? If one of your programs is targeting more than one audience, what might you do to make it more focused?

3. Do the students who attend your programs know for whom the programs are intended?

4. How would you fill in this chart for your youth ministry?

WHO are we trying to target? Potential Audience	WHAT is our purpose? Primary Purpose	HOW will we attempt to do this? Primary Program
Community		
Crowd		
Congregation		
Committed		
Core		

5. What is the approximate numerical breakdown of students involved with your ministry?

  Community ____
  Crowd ____
  Congregation ____
  Committed ____
  Core ____

6. Write your own definition for each potential audience (see pages 88–90).

  Community

  Crowd

  Congregation

  Committed

  Core

7. What are the defined steps that students take to move to the next level of commitment in your ministry?

NOTES

  1. Our weekend worship services are held at the same time as our adult worship services. At the time of this writing, we have three meetings each weekend—Saturday night at 5:00 and Sunday morning at 8:45 and 11:00. These programs all have the same format. Chapter 7 discusses these services further.

COMPONENT FOUR

PROGRAMS

SIX

Reaching Community Students
Fulfilling God's Purpose of Evangelism

Aaron Gutridge was the star football player at Tustin High School. Every week the local newspaper reported on his outstanding playing. Everyone at his school knew who he was, and he had tremendous influence on campus. He did not grow up in a church, he wasn't a Christian, he came from a broken home, and the only time he referred to God was on the football field when he cussed.

Aaron was invited to our church's Friday night "Overtime" program by his friend Matt, one of our committed students. Overtime is a pizza party after the football game. In order to eat pizza, Aaron had to fill out an address card. Once he did this he moved from an unknown community student to a potential crowd student. He was no longer a complete stranger.

The following Tuesday I wrote Aaron a letter. I thanked him for visiting our church and invited him to join Matt for our Sunday morning program, which is designed for crowd students. I was pleasantly surprised the next Sunday when Matt brought Aaron, and Aaron brought five unchurched friends from the football team. This particular Sunday was the first time Aaron had ever heard a message about God's love. After church we invited the guys to a Sunday afternoon basketball game with some of our adult leaders. They accepted, we played, the leaders won, and Aaron and his competitive buddies returned the next several Sundays for rematches. Within a couple of months, Aaron's motivation to attend church changed when he surrendered his life to Jesus Christ. He became active in our midweek area Bible study and small groups, which are aimed at congregation students. Within a year he showed an eagerness to grow in his faith and develop the habits of a committed student. Soon Aaron was in our student leadership group, which is geared for core students. After high school, Aaron played football in college where he continued to grow in his faith. Today he is a full-time youth pastor.

When you look closely at Aaron's story, you will see that, in cooperation with God's sovereignty, a number of factors worked together to reach him and help him move from the community to the core: a nonthreatening community program for him to attend (Overtime), a committed student who invited him (Matt), a follow-up plan (a letter), an entry-level program at which he could hear the gospel (crowd program weekend service), some relational contact through the basketball games (adult leaders), and other programs to supplement his growth (that is, congregation, committed, and core programs). I would love to tell this type of story about all the students who shows up at a community event, but I can't. Spiritual growth like Aaron's is our goal, but it doesn't happen with every student.

Evangelism Isn't a Program; It's a Process

If you want your youth ministry to reach unchurched community students, you must make a strong commitment to breathe evangelism into your ministry. Youth ministries that are successful in reaching unchurched students view evangelism as essential and not as just a good idea. If you plan to prioritize evangelism, you need a strategy to make sure the purpose of evangelism isn't reduced to a program. Evangelism isn't a program; it's a process—a process of a person modeling his or her transformed life to someone in need of God's transformational grace.

> **We dont' have the resources to create programs attractive enough to compete with the world.**

I don't believe that we should be training students to rely on fancy programs to fulfill the purpose of evangelism. A consistent evangelistic program isn't easy to pull off. Our church is minutes from Disneyland and a hundred other entertainment activities, and we don't have the resources to create programs attractive enough to compete with the world. Neither do you. We do have life-changing content (the truth of God's Word) and caring relationships with which the world can't compete. This *truth* is what I want our students to understand. I want them to take some personal responsibility for evangelism and live their lives with eyes that are searching and hearts that are beating with compassion for their lost friends.

Throughout my years in youth ministry, I have been blessed to see hundreds of ordinary students reach out to their friends and introduce them to Jesus Christ. It has been a glorious mix of our youth ministry and students doing the possible and watching God do the impossible. I can't define the impossible work of God, but I can tell you what we've done to be faithful to the purpose of evangelism in our youth ministry.

Evangelism in our youth ministry encompasses an understanding and a practical expression of three elements:

1. The development of an evangelistic attitude
2. The continual challenge to become evangelistic
3. A worship service to which students are proud to bring their friends (see chapter 7)

The rest of this chapter explores the first two elements as a route toward developing the purpose of evangelism in your youth ministry. Chapter 7 demonstrates how Saddleback Church's worship service acts as an open door from the community into the crowd.

An Evangelistic Youth Ministry Expresses an Evangelistic Attitude

Jesus said in Matthew 9:12–13: "It is not the healthy who need a doctor, but the sick.... For I have not come to call the righteous, but sinners." *The Message* translation reads, "I'm here to invite outsiders, not coddle insiders." Many youth ministries do an excellent job of coddling insiders and a lousy job of reaching the lost.

Youth ministries that are fulfilling the purpose of evangelism are usually the ones in which the youth ministry leadership, the church staff, and the students understand evangelism and share a passion to see it expressed. If the purpose of evangelism isn't shared and supported by your overall church leadership, you will fight a constant battle. Tension builds when youth leaders want to reach the lost and the church leadership wants to coddle insiders. I have watched this conflict destroy many youth workers.

> **Tension builds when youth leaders want to reach the lost and the church leadership wants to coddle insiders.**

Expressing the purpose of evangelism in your youth ministry requires a unified evangelistic attitude in which those involved understand the difficulty of evangelism yet push ahead, compelled by the biblical conviction to reach the lost. This contagious attitude invades the church and invites leaders who love students and sense an evangelistic purpose within their own lives. There are at least four ways to express an evangelistic attitude.

"We Know It's Tough, But We're Going to Do It Anyway"

Evangelism is tough work. It is much easier to take care of the righteous than to go after the unrighteous, since unbelievers aren't as receptive to our methods and our message as are Christians. The apostle Paul said that "the message of the cross is foolishness to those who are perishing" (1 Cor. 1:18).

Student evangelism is difficult for me as a youth worker. If I start talking to a community student on campus who doesn't know anything about me or Christ, I'm seen as a threat. I have been questioned several times by parents who have seen me with their kids and don't know anything about me. I don't blame them for asking who I am and what I am doing on campus when I don't have teenagers. They are suspicious that I may be some sort of pervert or cult leader.

Evangelism is also tough for students. They live in constant fear of rejection. They are afraid that they won't be understood, that they won't have all the right answers, or that they will be labeled as Jesus freaks. These natural fears paralyze them and keep them quiet about their involvement with church and their relationship with Jesus. This is also an issue for many youth workers who fear rejection.

Evangelism also becomes difficult when some church families believe that youth ministry should take care of their kids and not be concerned with those outside the church. I have had parents tell me, referring to community students, "The church shouldn't be bringing in these types of students. These are the students my son sees all day at school, and he shouldn't have to deal with them at church." After I finish being sick, I try to politely explain the biblical purpose of evangelism. Youth ministries that try to fulfill the purpose of evangelism should have their share of non-Christian students. If your youth ministry isn't making the coddlers unhappy, you probably aren't expressing an evangelistic attitude.

For some youth ministries the hindrance to evangelism is the actual church leadership and/or elder board. These churches value evangelism as long as it isn't messy. Unfortunately, student evangelism can be messy, and the churches that place the purpose of *cleanliness* above the purpose of *evangelism* give more power to the janitor than to the Holy Spirit. Non-Christian students don't understand the sanctity of the church property. They don't realize that the fellowship hall was carpeted by the late Mrs. Jennings and that food on the memorial carpet is synonymous with blasphemy. Community students don't think about changing their language when they come to church—they talk like they always talk—and they smoke, litter, and loiter. They can cause problems by not respecting things that churched teenagers are taught to respect. (If you're thinking that I just described your regular students, this puts you in good company with Jesus! The religious leaders weren't too happy with the group of people he was attracting either.)

Finally, evangelism is tough because of the enemy. Eternal salvation is the subject of a very real spiritual battle because Satan doesn't want anyone to be effective in leading others to Christ. An evangelistic attitude faces all opposition with a dependency on God's power and a vision for the lost.

"We View Evangelism as Nonnegotiable"

Bible students understand their part in evangelism. Jesus didn't make it optional when he commanded in Acts 1:8: "You will be my witnesses." Developing an evangelistic attitude means viewing evangelism as a biblical command. Evangelism must become a clear conviction, or you will be tempted to give up when your students don't respond to your challenge to reach their friends. They will listen to your messages and agree with the conclusion, but they will distance themselves from the action because evangelism is tough. When you view evangelism as a nonnegotiable command, you won't give up even when you meet resistance.

"We Want Leaders Who Like Adolescents"

Evangelistic youth ministry must have leaders who love teenagers. If you're going to reach students, you have to like being with them. A good missionary doesn't go into a village and hate the people because they don't understand his language. In the same way, evangelistic youth leaders don't despise community students just because they don't understand God's way. Evangelistic leaders love all teenagers, not just the Christian students who are easy to love.

Youth ministries that successfully reach unchurched students are almost always led by a leader with a burden for the lost. This person understands the words of Jesus: "There will be more rejoicing in heaven over one sinner who repents than over ninety-nine righteous persons who do not need to repent" (Luke 15:7). It is impossible to get close to the heart of God without getting close to those for whom his Son and our Savior gave his life.

"We Must Have Leaders Who Model Evangelism"

If the point person of a ministry isn't eager to evangelize, the volunteers and students won't be, either. Anything difficult—like evangelism—usually has to be pushed by leadership. The majority of teenagers I've worked with did not jump for joy when they learned about their responsibility to evangelize. Most would rather not do it. They are comfortable with the friends they have at church and don't feel an inherent need to reach the lost. But when they see evangelism modeled by their leaders and diligently taught from Scripture, they gradually understand its purpose and make it a priority. An evangelistic youth ministry challenges the leaders to set the pace and be evangelistic with their coworkers, neighbors, and families.

An Evangelistic Youth Ministry Challenges Students to Become Evangelistic

In chapter 4 it is stated that one of the jobs of leadership is to continually repeat the purpose of why your ministry exists. If you want to reach community students, you need to emphasize evangelism as you repeat the purposes. At Saddleback Church we are constantly teaching and reminding our students of the command for evangelism, even at the earliest stages of their faith. We want students to understand that those outside the faith are attracted to Christians before they are attracted to Christ. Jesus told us in Matthew 5:14 that we are to be lights and to shine so that others will be prompted to give their lives to God. This verse introduces lifestyle as an important factor of evangelism. Students need to be reminded of this all of the time.

We don't expect all of our students to be *evangelists*, but we do expect them to be *evangelistic*. We don't expect our students to have the courage to stand on a lunch table in the middle of campus and preach (evangelist), but we do expect them to shine bright and develop a heart for their lost friends, pray for them, and bring them to appropriate church programs (evangelistic).

Challenge Students with Strong Evangelistic Themes

During my last year (of eleven) at the church where I served before coming to Saddleback Church, my zeal for evangelism became drained. The students sensed it and followed my lead; this resulted in evangelistic apathy. When I came to Saddleback Church I had a restored passion, and I wanted my students to know it. I started with a small youth group, but we soon grew as students heard and understood the following three themes continuously.

"We Are Going to Grow"

I wanted students to know right away that we have a command to reach out and make followers of all people. "All" is quite a few people! I explained that our intention wasn't to be the largest youth ministry in town, but to fulfill what Jesus asked us to do in the Great Commission. I told the students that if we didn't grow, we were sending a message to our non-Christian friends to go to hell. We were saying to them that they are not worth our effort. If we take seriously the command of evangelism, we will grow. I am not ashamed of this in any way. I am not encouraging an outdated youth ministry message that bigger is better. Rather, I am suggesting that evangelism is better and it always results in growth.

> If our group doesn't grow, we are sending a message to our non-Christian friends to go to hell.

"We Will Not Become a Holy Huddle"

Coming into a small youth group, I found myself constantly talking about the holy huddle syndrome or S.M.O.T.S. meetings (Secret Meeting of the Saints). I didn't want our youth ministry to be a club, and I made sure everyone understood that. I rarely refer to our ministry as a youth group because a group mentality doesn't grow; it's comfortable being a group. A ministry grows. A ministry views itself as evangelistic.

This is a difficult roadblock for some youth workers. They often ask, "Shouldn't I encourage my students to be separated from the world? Don't I want them listening to Christian music and hanging around with Christian friends? Shouldn't their entire *world* be Christianity?" My response is yes to the first two questions and no to the last. Their entire world shouldn't be Christianity, but it should be Christ. And Christ came to save the lost, not to form a club.

> Students' entire world shouldn't be Christianity, but it should be Christ.

"This Program Is Not for You"

There are times when I tell my regular students not to attend a specific program if they don't bring a friend. I'm tired of creating evangelistic programs to aid students with their personal witness and having only churched students attend. If you go to the effort of designing an evangelistic program, you must tell your regular students whom the program is intended to reach.

Be careful about which programs you say, "Bring your friends." I remember asking a student, "Why didn't you bring a friend tonight?"

He said, "I didn't know this was intended for my friend."

I said, "Every time I announced the program I said, 'Bring a friend.'"

His next words really made me think. "Yeah, but you're always telling us to bring our friends to everything." That night I learned a valuable lesson. I needed to be specific about what programs were intended for evangelism.

Even now, as our ministry has experienced amazing growth, we continue to repeat these three themes about evangelistic growth; people forget what isn't emphasized. We don't want to get comfortable with the students who are saved and lose sight of those who don't know Christ.

Challenge Students with Evangelistic Baby Steps

When you are helping students capture a vision for the lost, give them baby steps that they can handle. Nothing is more defeating than evangelism training that has students memorize the four happy hops to heaven and then sends them out to talk to strangers about what they memorized. Most students don't connect with "stranger" evangelism. God uses this form of evangelism, but it drastically limits evangelism to a fearless few. If you provide your students with techniques they can master, they will become confident and eventually more courageous in sharing their faith with their friends. You are more likely to give them hope by breaking the process down into workable steps than by overwhelming them with a responsibility that even most adults fear.

Here is an example of the baby steps we challenge our students to take.

Step 1: Tell your friend that you're a Christian.
Step 2: Invite your friend to an appropriate program.
Step 3: Tell your friend why you're a Christian.
Step 4: Tell your friend how you became a Christian.
Step 5: Ask your friend if he or she would like to become a Christian.

This process is what we call our *friendship evangelism challenge*. While it is more of a verbal challenge than an actual program, we still refer to it as the primary program we use to reach community students.

Programming for Community Students: Saddleback Church Model

Saddleback Church has primary and secondary youth ministry programs designed for each potential audience. The primary programs are explained here and at the end of the next four chapters. (Chapter 12 lists and describes our secondary programs.) My prayer is that our program examples will trigger some ideas for you. I hope that when you read about what we are doing at Saddleback Church, you will be *underwhelmed* because of the simplicity of our youth ministry programs. Because we are purpose driven, we don't put a lot of value in maintaining programs. If a program isn't reaching its potential audience or expressing one of the five biblical purposes (evangelism, fellowship, discipleship, ministry, worship) we modify or discontinue it.

Primary Community Program:
Friendship Evangelism Challenge

At the beginning of the school year, we teach a series called *friendship evangelism challenge*. We provide each student with a wallet-size card and ask him or her to write the names of five non-Christian friends on it (see fig. 6.1).[1] We then challenge our students to pray for these friends every day and ask God to provide the opportunity and courage to take the steps to share their faith. One youth ministry has taken this idea and started a H.I.T. list of the friends for whom they are praying. H.I.T. is an acronym for "hearts in transition."

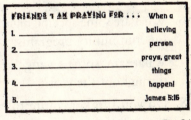

FRIENDSHIP EVANGELISM

1. Tell your friend you're a Christian.
2. Invite your friend to an appropriate program.
3. Tell your friend why you're a Christian.
4. Tell your friend how you became a Christian.
5. Ask your friend if he or she would like to become a Christian.

FRIENDS I AM PRAYING FOR . . .

1. _____
2. _____
3. _____
4. _____
5. _____

When a believing person prays, great things happen! James 5:16

Fig. 6.1

On the back of the friendship evangelism card is the five-step process for sharing one's faith, the baby-steps referred to on page 112. Some students will take all five steps with a friend during the first week of school. Others may take all semester to get through the first two steps. We encourage our students to complete step two by the end of the first semester with at least three of their five non-Christian friends.

Some of our adult leaders are formally assigned to follow up on students who have committed to accept the friendship evangelism challenge, but all of our leaders are encouraged to ask students about their efforts on an informal basis. The more we talk about friendship evangelism, the more eager our students become to share their stories about how they are working on the five steps.

MAKING IT PERSONAL

1. How would you define your personal passion for evangelism?

2. When was the last time you discussed your faith with an unbeliever? How well do you model evangelism to your students?

3. Name some students in your youth ministry who need to be challenged to develop an evangelistic attitude.

4. Name some students in your ministry who express a concern for the lost. Has anyone encouraged those students lately?

5. Rate on a scale of 1 to 10 your youth ministry's evangelistic attitude (1 = holy huddle; 10 = passion for lost).

    1   2   3   4   5   6   7   8   9   10

6. What are some specific nights you would define as "hot nights" for community programs?

7. What are some evangelistic themes you need to repeat throughout the year?

8. Do you think a commitment to friendship evangelism will work with some of your students? Why or why not?

9. Name someone on your team who could oversee the implementation and follow-through of friendship evangelism. How can the rest of the staff support this person?

NOTES

1. Community students are the only students for whom we don't have a primary program. Our primary program (friendship evangelism challenge) is directed *to* them and not *for* them. As I said earlier, we don't want students to rely on a specific evangelistic program. Evangelism is a process for students to get excited about, not a program for them to attend. We have continual programs *for* our other audiences—crowd, congregation, committed, and core.

SEVEN

Keeping Crowd Students
Fulfilling God's Purpose of Worship

Let's assume that Stacy is one of your regular students who has accepted the friendship evangelism challenge. She has been praying for five of her friends and finally has found the courage to invite her friend Kayla to one of your programs. Stacy should bring Kayla to your crowd program, the open door to your youth ministry. Do you have a program to which your regular students can feel comfortable inviting their community friends? If so, this program will involve both Christians and non-Christians.

At Saddleback Church a student like Stacy would bring her friend to one of our three weekend worship services (one on Saturday night, two on Sunday), where our junior high and high school crowd programs meet separately from one another and from the adult worship services. These services target crowd students while fulfilling the primary purpose of worship. The weekend may not seem like the stereotypical time for unchurched students to enter a youth ministry, but Saddleback isn't a stereotypical church. The strategy of our church is to draw community seekers of all ages to our weekend worship services.[1]

Some youth workers get confused at this point because they try to imagine their regular students bringing non-Christian friends to a traditional Sunday school class or worship service. Our weekend worship services are anything but traditional, and students who attempt the friendship evangelism challenge have no problem bringing their friends to church. Many students tell their non-Christian friends, "It's not what you think it is; trust me and give it a try."

As I mentioned in chapter 2, many youth workers have limited the purpose of worship to singing. Worship is bigger than that! We define it as expressing our love to God. We attempt to fulfill the purpose of worship by communicating our love to God through praying, singing, giving, testifying, thanking, and listening to God's Word in our weekend worship service.

The style of our weekend worship service seeks to break the stereotype that church is boring. Worship doesn't have to be sleep-inducing. Since our worship service targets the crowd student, we try to create a unique blend of fun, student involvement, and a clear message. Although the word "fun" doesn't seem to fit a traditional definition of worship, we want students to have a great time when they come to church. We want them to say what David said, "I was glad to go to the house of the LORD. . . . Worship the LORD with gladness" (Psalm 122:1; 100:2 NLT).

I believe God values variety in worship, since he appreciates variety in humanity. A preference of worship style seems to me to be more sociological than theological. The Bible doesn't command a particular style of worship, although Jesus gives us two important requirements in John 4:24 to worship in spirit (love) and in truth. During our weekend worship service, we teach the truth and do everything with an attitude of love so that both believers and nonbelievers will have an opportunity to see how wonderful God is.

The response of the crowd at Pentecost (Acts 2) was mixed. Some mocked the apostles, while others were amazed at what they heard. God wasn't put off by the scoffing, though, He added 3,000 people to his kingdom that day. The connection between worship and evangelism seemed to work back then, and we see it working in our setting today.[2]

As you read this chapter, please note that my intention isn't to convince you to move your crowd program to Sunday morning. Your crowd program may be your midweek program; it may be held once a month; or it may be scheduled only quarterly. Perhaps you even design it to fulfill the primary purpose of fellowship. Again, there is no one strategy that works for all youth ministries; your programming will be dependent on your available time, help, and resources.

> **A preference of worship style seems to be more sociological than theological.**

Your Crowd Program: An Open Door to Community Students

As you think about your crowd program as an open door to community students, you should consider four transferable principles helpful for reaching and keeping crowd students:

1. a positive environment
2. an element of fun
3. student involvement
4. an understandable message

A Crowd Program Needs a Positive Environment

Students spend several hours a day in a school environment that isn't usually positive. It can be negative, competitive, hostile, and cliquish. A crowd program should radiate an noticeably positive environment in comparison with the world. Early in my youth ministry career I heard someone say, "Until students are environmentally comfortable, they won't be theologically aware." I've translated this to mean, "Until students feel that they are loved, they won't be able to understand the spoken Word of love." If students walk into your crowd meeting and don't feel cared for, appreciated, and valued, they will have a tough time making a connection between what they are feeling (environmentally comfortable) and what they are hearing about God's love (theologically aware).

Jesus modeled this environmental approach with the woman at the well in John 4. He created a positive environment by

> **Until students are environmentally comfortable, they won't be theologically aware.**

breaking Jewish tradition and speaking to a Samaritan. She was amazed that Jesus would talk to her. He then gave her an understandable message on love—he would give her living water so that she would never thirst again. The environment was created before the theology was spoken.

You can establish a positive environment for your crowd program in several ways. The list below shows a few simple differences between a positive and negative environment.

Positive Environment

- contemporary music is playing
- adults and student leaders greet those entering the meeting
- photographs of students enjoying the youth ministry cover the walls
- seating is arranged to make the room feel inviting

Negative Environment

- the senior citizens' choir is singing to the accompaniment of organ music
- adult and student leaders have formed a "heckle tunnel" and are ridiculing students for their appearance as they enter the meeting
- the Ten Commandments are posted on the walls and students' names are listed next to the commandments they have broken
- seating is arranged by height, weight, and popularity

Although the negative list is quite exaggerated, each point indicates a glaring and common mistake for you to avoid. There are at least two more ways to create a positive environment.

Develop the Ten-Minute Rule

The environment of your meeting room should be established at least ten minutes before the first student arrives. We make a fatal mistake in believing that a meeting begins when all the students arrive. Many of us are rushing around trying to get things ready for the meeting, and students are walking into a hectic room where no one has the time to greet them appropriately. In this setting, if a student is greeted at all, it is done hurriedly. The student is then left alone so that we can finish our tasks.

Even though visitors are usually brought by their friends, they still feel awkward and alone when they walk into a new environment for the first time. You won't get a second chance to make a good first impression; many visitors will evaluate your entire ministry based on how they were greeted when they arrived. Crowd students should walk into a friendly room: music playing, a few people greeting, and photographs on the wall to give visiting students something to look at and occupy their time so that they won't stand out as new.

> **Many visitors will evaluate your entire ministry based on how they were greeted when they arrived.**

Your greeters should be caring students who stand at the entrance and welcome everyone with a smile and a touch. Student leaders should meet visitors, carry on conversations with them, and integrate them into the program. If a student shows up alone, a student leader should try to connect the visitor with another student. Visitors are slightly impressed when adults greet them—that is supposed to happen. But new students are deeply impressed when a peer makes a verbal connection and then takes an interest by helping them feel comfortable and introducing them to others.

When was the last time you were with a crowd of people and didn't know anyone? How did you feel? Because we feel so comfortable in our meeting rooms, we often forget the pain of being alone. The ten-minute rule will help you prepare for the crowd's arrival so that new students can receive a personal greeting.

Promote Safe Touch

We all know that touching students can be a sensitive topic, but I stand firm in my belief that human touch adds to a positive environment. We teach our leaders that any type of safe contact—handshakes, hugs, high fives—is good and should be expressed as often as possible. The students in our ministry don't naturally shake hands with one another; it isn't their usual form of greeting. Instead, they stand there and communicate with a monosyllabic grunt, "Heh." But when I meet students, I always extend my hand. They may think I'm a little corny, but at the same time, my handshake may be the only positive, safe adult touch they have had all day (or all week for that matter).

Every weekend before our crowd program begins, I move around the room and try to touch and greet as many students as I can. I do this so that when I get up to teach God's Word later in the program, students will know that I have acknowledged their presence.

A Crowd Program Needs an Element of Fun

Most non-Christians or uninvolved students maintain the unfortunate stereotype that church—and by association, God—is boring. Having a good time at church is one of the most powerful ways to shatter the *boring* stereotype. God wired us with the capacity to laugh, and we shouldn't view fun as ungodly. When you create a program at which students experience fun, they are more likely to connect with you and your message.

I have received my share of criticism from church members for promoting "too much fun" in our youth ministry. Nevertheless, I am unapologetic for planning fun for crowd students. We continually hear from these students, "I never imagined that church could be fun." When I see a crowd student laughing and having a good time, I see a student who is receptive to discovering that the source of his or her laughter is the creator of fun—God himself.

> God wired us with the capacity to laugh,
> and we shouldn't view fun as ungodly.

As you process this principle, separate *fun* from *funny*. Fun and humor are not the same thing. Don't feel the pressure to be something you're not (if you're not the comedian type), but do work at creating a fun environment.

A Crowd Program Needs Student Involvement

Students need to be involved in both the crowd program and in the overall ministry. If crowd students can find an opportunity to connect with someone or something they like, they will have an easier time making a transition into other opportunities for growth.

When programming for crowd students, we always ask, "Is this something a student could be doing?" For example, if we want a drama, a video, a humor bit, or a crowd-breaker, we try to find students to make it happen.

One way a crowd student can get involved in Saddleback Church's youth ministry is to join one of our many ministry teams. They include such teams as the drama team, video team, greeting team, band team, and others (see page 217 for a complete list). We try to make these teams an easy access to involvement. For example, let's say Josh Moine shows up at our crowd program and expresses interest in playing in the band. We say, "You're in! You're the newest member in the band." We don't use a spiritual litmus test to see where he is spiritually before he joins. If Josh isn't a Christian, we have confidence that he will meet Christ while he is rehearsing and playing in the band. For example, the band ministry leader (a core student) starts every rehearsal with a short devotion and prayer. Josh will hear more about Christ by playing in the band and hanging out with other band students than he will if he simply attends, and leaves a crowd program.

Getting students involved can happen throughout the entire crowd program and doesn't have to be limited to ministry teams. For example, students can be involved through

- creative teaching methods
- spontaneous melodramas[3]
- interactive games
- role plays
- panel discussions
- testimonies

One way to gain the interest of crowd students is to show them that the program isn't solely dependent on adults. We want crowd students to see other students participating throughout the program—and not just the *perfect* students. Any student should be able to get involved easily if he or she chooses.

A Crowd Program Needs an Understandable Message

Our world of increasing moral decay is forcing teenagers to look harder for answers and truth. Crowd students are much more eager to explore and discover spiritual truth than when I first began youth ministry. I once believed that an entertaining message was needed to reach crowd students. I now see an entertaining attitude as an aid to communication, but more impressive is a message that makes sense.

Because a crowd audience is a mix of both Christians and non-Christians, it is important to teach a message that challenges both. Because God's Word is true, it is relevant for everyone. So when I teach our crowd audience, I speak to the needs of teenagers and use the Bible as my source. When it comes time for the application of the truth, I usually present different action steps for seekers and Christians. I may say, "For those of you who are checking God out, I encourage you to ...," and I give specific action steps for the seekers. I say, "For those of you who are Christians, I challenge you to...," and I give specific action steps geared for believers. Most visiting crowd students tell me that the few messages they have heard at other churches weren't specifically for teenagers. This is one of the main reasons I feel a tremendous responsibility to present God's Word in an understandable manner. There are several ways to make messages more palatable.

Try to Answer Their Questions About the Messenger

New crowd students, recently making their way in from the community, are sizing up the teacher before, during, and after the message. They are unconsciously asking three questions:

1. Can I trust you?
2. Do you care about me?
3. Do you know what you're talking about?

Forms of these questions have been around since ancient Greek culture when Aristotle identified three qualities of successful communication. He taught that a great communicator must have *ethos, pathos*, and *logos*. *Ethos* is related to the word *ethical*. A speaker is ineffective if he or she can't be trusted. *Pathos* refers to a communicator's empathy or understanding. A strong communicator may be eloquent, but without showing love, he or she is nothing. And *logos,* the root of our word *logic,* refers to one's knowledge about a subject.

The *ethos* and *pathos* of communication are visible in your character. New crowd students will sense this about you and make a judgment about your trustworthiness and concern. Again, this is why it is important for you to mingle around the room touching students and having conversations with visitors. These conversations will impact their perception of your *ethos* and *pathos* before you begin your message.

Give Your Message a Creative Title

Once you answer the questions of trust (ethos), concern (pathos), and knowledge (logos), you still have to answer the question, "Why should I listen to you?" A creative title won't keep students focused through an entire message, but it will ignite their interest and grab their immediate attention.

I like to use "how to" titles to interest students who view God's Word as a history book that is irrelevant to their lives. An automatic sense of relevance is built into a "how to" title because it communicates action. I want to set the stage for students to think, for example, "Today he's going to teach me from the Bible how to improve my friendships." Some creative examples of "how to" titles are

- "How to Shout Without Screaming" (evangelism)
- "How to be Attractive Without Looking Good" (Galatians 5—fruit of the Spirit)
- "How to Find Love When you Feel Like Puke" (Jonah)
- "How to Perform Your Own Heart Surgery" (hardness of heart)
- "How to Find Intimacy in a Crowded World" (Matthew 9—Jesus heals the bleeding woman)

Spend time making your titles creative, interesting, and enticing. Most students are used to seeing a message title like "Hosea: An Example of God's Love." A catchier title would be "Would God Want You to Marry a Prostitute?" Ask your students which message they would be more interested in hearing. (You might also survey their parents to see which title would get you in trouble!)

Let's say you are preparing a message on what the Bible teaches about explosive language and James 2 is your text. You could title it "What the Bible Says About Your Tongue" or give it a creative title like "How to Tame a Belching Dragon." The latter title is a little gross, yet intriguing. It will help you grab crowd students' attention.

Develop an Introduction to Capture Their Interest

After the creativity of the title wears off, draw your students into the message with an introduction that makes them want to listen. I may tell a story of my first love: "It was second grade. Her name was Margaret Montgomery. I was pushing her on the swings when she accidentally knocked me down into the sand. I started crying. She laughed at me and broke up with me the next day." I would reminisce about the joys and sorrows of an eight-year-old's first love. This humorous illustration would help me introduce a message on "How to Find a Love That Won't Leave You."

When teaching the crowd audience, I regularly teach topics. For example, I ask myself, "What does the Bible say regarding friendships?" I do the same thing with topics such as temptation, family, sex, peer pressure, language, and so on. At other programs, for students with more spiritual depth, I teach through books of the Bible or on contextual passages.

Topical teaching offers great opportunities to use real-life illustrations. Tell stories about your failures or personal struggles. Students can relate to failure. Such authenticity will make you more approachable since students are more likely to relate to and trust people who have failed rather than people who appear to be perfect.

Simplify Your Message

No one will deny that Jesus was a master communicator. He spoke in simple language, told stories, and used word pictures. Study the simplicity of Jesus' teaching style and try to emulate it. When you are teaching crowd students, don't try to impress them with everything you know. You should be trying to impress them with how great God is and how his ways can be understood and applied today.

Don't fall into the temptation of including everything you know about doctrine, Christian living, and theology in each message. You will have several opportunities throughout the year to teach more. In the past I have put information into my message that would impress my deceased seminary homiletics professor instead of prepare a message that a living fourteen-year-old crowd student could understand.

It's depressing, but, even when they understand the message, most students will forget it within twenty-four hours. Because your messages won't be retained for long, try to simplify them to one key statement. I like to call that statement my "big idea," which is the one truth, principle, or thought I want students to remember. For example, if I am teaching on Jonah, my big idea may be,

"You can run from God, but you can't hide." Once I establish the big idea, I repeat it several times throughout the message.

> **I have put information into my message that would impress my deceased seminary homiletics professor instead of prepare a message that a living fourteen-year-old crowd student could understand.**

Use Understandable Bible Passages

When you read a Bible passage to students, make sure you use a translation they can understand. This point isn't intended to create a translation debate, but if students don't understand what is being read, they probably aren't going to be motivated to read the Bible on their own. When I go to the movies and see an attractive preview, I want to see the movie. If I don't like the preview, I'm not drawn to the movie. This principle applies to students and God's Word. If students don't understand what they hear, they won't be drawn to read it on their own.[4]

Provide Notes So Students Can Follow Along

Give crowd students a fill-in-the-blank outline so they can be involved in the message (see fig. 7.1). Even non-Christians will take notes when given the opportunity. Many of our students play a silent game of "Figure out the fill-in before Doug gives the answer." This game was first brought to my attention by a volunteer who views her ministry as being concerned about everything. She felt that students weren't paying close enough attention to the message and that they shouldn't be making a game out of it. I told her that I love for students to play this game. She was shocked (which I enjoyed). It's not distracting; I don't acknowledge that they do it; and it creates better learning, since they are using more brain power in an attempt to guess the right answer. Students even come up afterward and tell me that their guess was better than my answer.

HOW TO KEEP FROM SHRINKING

ESSENTIALS FOR A NEW YEAR

"There are three things that will endure—faith, hope, and love—and the greatest of these is love."
(1 Cor. 13:13 NLT)

- Faith is our
- Hope is our
- Love is our

"Patient endurance is what you need now, so you will continue to do God's will. Then you will receive all that he has promised." (Heb. 10:36 NLT)

A CONTINUAL GROWTH PLAN

"We have around us many people whose lives tell us what faith means. So let us run the race that is before us and never give up. We should remove from our lives anything that would get in the way and the sin that so easily holds us back. We do this by keeping our eyes on Jesus, on whom our faith depends from start to finish." (Heb. 12:1–2a EB)

1. Find _____

"We have around us many people whose lives tell us what faith means"

- Faith:
- Hope:
- Love:

2. Remove _____

"We should remove from our lives anything that would get in the way and the sin that so easily holds us back"

- Obstacle #1:
- Obstacle #2:

3. Focus _____

"We do this by keeping our eyes on Jesus"

- Bible (time in God's Word)
- Prayer (time with God)
- Accountability (time with another believer)

4. Don't _____

"So let us run the race that is before us and never give up"

- Spiritual growth comes from a lot of little

  _____

- Spiritual growth is

  _____

Our ministry exists to REACH non-believing students, to Connect them with other Christians, to help them GROW in their faith, and to challenge the growing to DIS COV ER their ministry and  HONOR God with their life.

Figure 7.1 is an example of a message outline. We have preprinted stationery that has a "Moving Toward Maturity" slogan at the top of the page and the keywords of our purpose statement along the right-hand side. In addition to filling in the blanks, I want our students to see our purpose statement every week.

Give Them Specific Action Steps

Growing up in the church, I heard a thousand sermons that I didn't know how to apply. I believe it is poor communication to finish a message without any reference to application. The first message that ever provided me with practical application not only changed my life, it also influenced my communication style. I want students to hear action steps so they'll think about how the Bible's truth can influence their lives. I want them to be hearers and doers of the Word (see James 2:14–26).

Providing action steps is often the most difficult part of constructing a message. Putting yourself in your students' world and trying to imagine what they can do with the material you are teaching them will help you make your lesson more relevant to students.

PRAY	This should be the foundation for everything you do.
POINT	Based on your passage or your topic, what do you want students to remember? This is the "big idea." Start with the end in mind.
PLOT	This refers to organizing your thoughts. Plot your key points out on paper and think through the logic track.
PERSONALIZE	Make it personal. Include your life illustrations. Remember to share failure stories.
PRACTICAL	This is the action area. Give students some direction about what you just taught them.

Fig. 7.2

Take Time to Prepare

If you plan to implement the above ideas, you need to take time to prepare, because preparation will impact your presentation. Shooting from the hip doesn't work over the long haul. You may be able to get away with it occasionally, but you'll lack depth and clarity if you don't spend time preparing. The chart on the previous page may help you prepare your next message.

Programming for Crowd Students: Saddleback Church Model

I want to reiterate that this isn't the only type of crowd program that works. There are several ways to reach the crowd student. You may not be able to design this type of program if you don't have the time, help, and resources. Your crowd program may be totally different—but just as successful—if you have a positive environment, an element of fun, student involvement, and an understandable message.

Our Primary Crowd Program: Weekend Worship Services

At the time of this writing, Saddleback Church's weekend crowd program meets in a portable building. For the majority of my many years in youth ministry, I have not had the luxury of having my own youth room. I have often had to share rooms with other ministries. The shared portable building we are in now isn't an inviting room. It has no windows, a low ceiling, and narrow walkways that are usually lined with students. We have to work hard to create a positive environment when the facility works against us.

When students walk into our weekend crowd program, they are greeted and welcomed by another student and handed a bulletin. The bulletin is nothing fancy, but it serves many purposes. It gives the greeters a little more reason to be standing by the door and it gives crowd students something to hold and hide behind. Also, the bulletin contains our announcements, promotion for our small groups (the next commitment level), words to the songs our band plays, and a fill-in-the-blank message outline with Scriptures.

The room reverberates with either taped music or our live band's tunes.[5] On our large-screen TV we have a video playing—either a sports highlight or a humorous blooper segment. The room is filled with round tables and chairs for the students and volunteers. I prefer this setup to rows of chairs because tables allow more natural conversation, and they make the room feel less formal. It also gives our adult leaders a specific ministry opportunity (within a program that is mostly student-run) because they can host a table. In addition, student leaders can take primary responsibility to make sure that people at the table feel welcomed, comfortable, and connected with the other students nearby. Our goal is for everyone to be greeted *at least* four times: once at the door, once by me, once by the table leader, and hopefully, once by another student at the table.

Each of our weekend services is about an hour and ten minutes long (we repeat the same service three times: Saturday at 5:00 P.M. and Sunday at 8:45 A.M. and 11:00 A.M.). Our time schedule looks something like this:

11:00	Begin with student band and two upbeat songs
11:08	Welcome with humor/fun element
11:15	Student ministry team highlight
11:20	Student drama
11:25	Band and choir
11:35	Student testimony
11:40	Message
12:10	End

Band Begins

Our band is good! Although it didn't start that way, it has become as good as any student band I have ever heard. One reason for this excellence is that our church makes music a priority, and the students are taught at an early age that they can use their musical skills to build up our church. We have learned the importance of having a "farm system" of backup talent so that we don't have strong years followed by weak ones.

The two opening numbers are usually songs from the hottest new Christian artists. These are intended to be performance songs rather than sing-alongs. When the band begins playing, it's the cue for everyone to find a seat.

Welcome with Humor/Fun Element

This welcome probably should be done by a student, but I have a special affection for it. I like to do the welcome since it is the only time during the morning that I'm up front before I speak. I feel a sense of comfort when I can get up and welcome visitors. (We don't highlight or point out visitors, but we encourage students at the table to greet one another.) Then I introduce the humor element.

The humor element may be a fun game we do with a few students on stage or it may be a table game that gets students to interact, laugh, and compete against other tables. We usually give the winning table a box of donuts. Occasionally we show a short movie clip from a comedy movie or TV show if we can tie it in with the topic I'll be teaching later.

Student Ministry Team

As I mentioned earlier, we have several different types of ministry teams (see page 217 for a complete list). During this section of our weekend program we "show off" one of these teams. We usually have our video team create a short (three-minute) documentary on one of the ministry teams. Not only does this highlight and affirm those on a ministry team, it is also an advertisement to get new students involved in one of our teams.

Student Drama

We use our student drama team every week. Most often the students write an original (usually humorous) sketch that fits with the topic I'll be teaching. Some weeks the dramas would get an A grade and other weeks a C–. Regardless of quality, I see drama as a powerful tool to communicate a truth that I will be reinforcing with the message.

Band and Choir

Our second set of songs is usually praise songs. Some feel that this is a departure from crowd programming. It is, if you consider that most non-Christian crowd students don't know what they're singing about if they sing at all. However, we have found that good music and authentic worship by Christians is a witness to unchurched students. Non-Christians usually don't sing, but they do watch others and listen to the words. If the band is good and the words make sense, they are not turned off to singing. They have already been impressed with the musical ability of the student band, and now they are hearing the gospel sung, and spiritual seeds from music are being planted.

I don't encourage youth workers to use singing at their crowd programs if they don't have quality music. Prior to Saddleback Church I never used singing during our crowd program. We didn't have good student musicians, and only a few "front row" students did all of the singing. It was embarrassing for an unchurched student. Praise singing is definitely not needed to start a crowd program.

Student Testimony

Almost every week a student shares about his or her faith. About half the time we use core students, and the other half we use students at various faith commitment levels. We want our crowd students to hear real-life stories of faith in Jesus Christ. Paul wrote in Romans 1:12 that it is beneficial for us to "be mutually encouraged by each other's faith." This is my favorite part of our crowd program, since I love to hear how God is working in students' lives.

When we ask students to think through their testimony and write it out, they are more articulate and their testimony is more powerful. In the past I have had students say, "Uh . . . well . . . Doug just asked me to share a little about my faith . . . and . . . uh . . . I really don't know where to start. . . . I guess I've been a Christian all my life. . . ." This isn't good for a crowd program, so we use a testimony tool to help students think through and focus their message (see fig. 7.3). Then a member of our ministry staff calls the student, listens to what he or she has written, gives input, helps with clarity, and encourages the student with prayer.

WRITING YOUR PERSONAL TESTIMONY
The Example of the Apostle Paul

One of the privileges and responsibilities of Christians is to share with others our faith in Christ. Although many methods and plans can be used to communicate our faith, none is more effective than sharing how the love, grace, and mercy of Christ have changed our lives.

People to whom we witness may evade issues, attempt to discredit biblical and historical facts, or blame their condition on others. But it is hard to discount the authentic testimony of a believer whose life has been transformed.

Completing this worksheet will better equip you to give a logical and organized presentation of who Jesus Christ is and what he has done in your life.

Let's use the story of Paul's conversion as a pattern for your testimony. Read the Bible text: Acts 26: 1–23

Paul's attitudes and actions before his conversion—vv. 1–11

Lived as a Pharisee—v. 5 (see Gal. 1:13–14)

Imprisoned many saints—v. 10

Condoned the deaths of many saints—v. 10

Persecuted Christians—v. 11

Circumstances surrounding Paul's conversion—vv. 12–18

1. Where was he going?
2. What time was it?
3. What did he see?
4. Who was with him?
5. What did he hear?

Read 2 Cor. 5:17; Gal. 6:15

Changes in Paul's attitudes and actions after his conversion—vv. 19–23

What evidence of Paul's repentance and conversion can be found in the following verses?

6. Verse 19 _____
7. Verse 20 _____
8. Verse 21 _____
9. Verses 22–23 _____

Read 1 John 1:5–9; 2:3–6

Now go to the next page...

Fig. 7.3

Writing Your Personal Testimony
YOUR TURN!

Introduction

➡ Name _____

➡ Year in school (or age) _____

➡ School _____

➡ City _____

Attitudes and actions before I became a Christian—If appropriate, include family or church background. Avoid naming religious denominations, since this may alienate some of your listeners.

1. _____
2. _____
3. _____
4. _____
5. _____

Circumstances surrounding my conversion—Consider time, date, place, people, motivation, etc. This is a natural place to summarize the gospel: the death, burial, and resurrection of Jesus Christ.

1. _____
2. _____
3. _____
4. _____
5. _____

Changes in my attitudes and actions since my conversion—Be enthusiastic!

1. _____
2. _____
3. _____
4. _____
5. _____

Miscellaneous comments[6]

Fig. 7.3 con't.

Message

The elements of an understandable message have already been described in this chapter (see pages 122–28). They include

- creative titles and introductions
- simple stories and word pictures
- an understandable Bible translation
- fill-in-the-blank notes
- specific action steps

If your teaching time is dictated by a designated curriculum, you may want to buy a book on creative teaching methods to enrich your presentation of the assigned teaching.

MAKING IT PERSONAL

1. What program do you see as your "open door" to community students?
2. Evaluate your crowd programs in regard to the following (1 = poor, 2 = needs help, 3 = okay, 4 = good, 5 = great):
   ____A positive environment
   ____An element of fun
   ____Student involvement
   ____Understandable message

   How can you improve on any areas with low scores?
3. Do you arrive early to programs to help create a positive environment? Why or why not?
4. Can a visiting student get involved in your ministry easily? Is there a path clearly defined for his/her involvement?
5. If you are a teacher, which area needs the most attention from you: *ethos, pathos,* or *logos*?

6. Are you gathering any input from visitors regarding their first impression of your crowd program? How could you facilitate this process?

7. Do students view your crowd program as one to which they feel comfortable bringing their unchurched friends? How do you know this?

NOTES

1. If students want to attend a church service with their family and attend the junior high or high school service, they need to be at church for two services. At Saddleback we have four adult services in addition to three youth services. Both programs are offered simultaneously. Some families worship together at one service, and then during the next service, the student attends a student service while the parents are involved with a ministry in our church (for example, teaching children's Sunday school). Some students attend the youth services instead of attending with their parents, and some students attend our weekend services even though their parents don't go to our church.

2. Just like in Acts 2, we see both responses. Some students mock, others are amazed. Though our goal is, of course, for all students to be amazed and respond to the gospel, we don't fear those who mock, because we are confident of the relevance of our style and the clarity of our message.

3. With the help of Laurie Polich and Duffy Robins, two other youth workers, I have written a book called *Spontaneous Melodramas* (Grand Rapids: Zondervan, 1996), which contains twenty-four ready-to-use melodramas (twelve from the Old Testament and twelve from the New Testament). They are easy to use, fun, and a great way to get students involved.

4. See appendix C regarding *The One-Minute Bible for Students*. It is a great tool for getting students to develop an appetite for regular Bible reading.

5. If the word "reverberates" makes you extremely nervous, you have two viable options: (1) get used to it or (2) turn down the music. I don't think it would be a good idea to consider option 3, which is to get rid of the music. Teenagers and music just seem to go together.

6. The testimony tool can be found in *Ideas Library: Camps and Retreats, Missions, & Service Ideas* (Grand Rapids: Zondervan, 1997).

EIGHT

Nurturing Congregation Students
Fulfilling God's Purpose of Fellowship

Crowd programming focuses on attracting and keeping a broad number of students, but congregation programming focuses on nurturing your students in small groups. I am regularly asked, "How do I grow my youth ministry?" My most common response is, "Take care of the students God has entrusted to you. Nurture them!" Jesus used a story to illustrate this stewardship principle in Matthew 25:21: "Well done, good and faithful servant! You have been faithful with a few things; I will put you in charge of many things. Come and share your master's happiness!"

Nurturing students means faithfully helping them grow in their relationship with God. The most substantial and measurable spiritual growth happens among students who have trustworthy, accountable, and healthy relationships with either an adult leader or a peer. These relationships are attainable for congregation students through fellowship. As we learned in chapter 2, fellowship happens in youth ministry when students are known, cared for, held accountable, and encouraged in their spiritual journey.

In youth ministry circles we have grossly overused and generalized the word *fellowship* to include just about everything we do with students. We have a fellowship hour that meets in the fellowship hall, and the three students who don't come into the youth room are out-side fellowshiping. We fellowship during our annual trip to the amusement park, and we promise fellowship during every announcement—"Hope you can make it; it will be a great night of fellowship." Yet our all-inclusive word seems to fall short of the New Testament image of fellowship.

> **In the early church, fellowship was more relational than recreational.**

In the early church, fellowship was more relational than recre-ational. It included sharing (1 John 1:7) and breaking bread (Acts 2:42) with other believers, as well as developing intimacy with Christ (1 Cor. 1:9) and with other believers (Gal. 2:9). This is a much dif-ferent image than hanging out with students and playing volleyball.

The most effective way to produce biblical fellowship in stu-dents' lives is through their participation in small groups. Because they provide more personal attention than do larger programs, small groups are a long-term solution to the bigness of our cul-ture. They provide the sense of belonging, for which teenagers are desperately searching, that makes cliques, gangs, and cults so attractive. In the church, small groups are essential, especially to adolescent spiritual maturity. All of the healthy youth ministries I have observed maintain a small-group structure.

> **Small groups are a long-term solution to the bigness of our culture.**

A quality small group will connect students to other students and build a sense of community within a youth ministry. Some youth workers say, "We don't need small groups. Our youth group is already a small group; we only have fifteen students." No, that's a crowd. Students can hide in a group that size, but they can't hide in a small group of four or five. When small groups are utilized, the *small* youth ministry is able to handle growth. Students receive care they wouldn't receive from a crowd program. Once I finally realized and admitted that I wasn't capable of caring for everyone in our youth ministry, I learned to rely on small groups. That's when the ministry really began to explode. Other adults changed roles from chaperones to shepherds, and their commitment to youth ministry increased as students began to express hurts and expect care. A focus on small groups helped close our back door; we no longer had students leaving as fast as they were coming.

1 Thessalonians 2:8

We loved you so much	Youth ministry is an expression of God's love for students. You can express this personally through your small group.
that we were delighted	It is so rewarding to watch a student spiritually mature. Observing growth should produce delight for you.
to share with you	Sharing is what we do in our small groups. We share our lives—the good and the bad.
not only the gospel of God	Our shared gift to students is nothing less than the very gospel of God. This is the source of truth we have to offer.
but our lives as well,	We are much more than teachers who offer only truth and facts. We also share our lives and invest in relationships without worrying about the interest and return.
because you had become so dear	One of the goals of our small group is for your students to become "dear" to you. This road to endearment is paved with patience and effort.
to us.	There are no lone rangers in our youth ministry. You are part of a team: rely on others and be reliable.

Fig. 8.1

Small groups are not new to youth ministry, and dozens of excellent books are available on the mechanics of small-group ministry. While I don't intend to reiterate what has already been written, I do want to reinforce the benefits of developing a small-group ministry and share a few practical ideas on what your leadership might do to ensure healthy small groups.

The Big Deal About Small Groups

These words of the apostle Paul could be a theme verse for small groups: "We loved you so much that we were delighted to share with you not only the gospel of God but our lives as well, because you had become so dear to us" (1 Thess. 2:8). In programming for crowd students, we introduce and share the *gospel*, but in small groups we share our *lives* with one another. Breaking down this verse as shown on page 139 helped our small-group leaders at Saddleback Church see the power available through small-group ministry (see Fig. 8.1).

There is, of course, more to youth ministry than supervising games, preparing messages, organizing camps, and playing the guitar. Those are important tasks, but a leader who can nurture a group of students and provide an environment of love will experience a depth of ministry never reached in just being up front and running the show. Not only will the small-group leader benefit from a more intensified ministry, but the students will benefit in at least four ways.

> A leader who can nurture a group of students will experience a depth of ministry never reached in just being up front and running the show.

Small Groups Allow Students to Be Known

Most students enjoy being part of a crowd, but if they had to choose between being an unknown face in a crowd and being known by a small group, they would choose the latter every time. Even though I am the youth pastor at my church and am expected to know everyone, I don't. I *recognize* many of the students who show up at our weekend crowd program, but I don't *know* them. I do, however, know the students in my small group. I not only know their names, I know their families, struggles, fears, strengths, and sins. And they know mine. This intimacy is why we want to grow larger and smaller at the same time—larger because of friendship evangelism and smaller through small groups. Even in the midst of a growing youth ministry, a student can be known through a small group and nurtured by a small-group leader who loves God and loves students.

> **We want to grow larger and smaller at the same time.**

Small Groups Make Students Verbal

During a larger crowd program, most students will listen to a message but have little opportunity to speak and share their opinions. Even if opportunities are given, many students will keep to themselves for fear of asking "dumb" questions. In a small group an emotional platform is created where students can express their opinions and not feel left out. Recently, at the conclusion of our small group, a student timidly asked, "What do you guys think about masturbation?" It was obvious that he needed some answers and wanted to share his struggles with the guys he'd spent months with building community. This student never would have been able to verbalize this question in a larger group.

Small Groups Allow Students to Personalize Their Faith

Small groups allow for personal application of Christianity. Our students hear many sermons, but those messages are often difficult to apply until they are discussed. Small groups allow for discussion about how the truth can be implemented specifically in students' lives. For example, if we are talking about being witnesses for Christ, a student in my small group can talk about particular ways *he* can talk about Christ at *his* school. All of a sudden, the teaching moves from an impersonal, up-front platform presentation to the small group and into *his* life.

My PDYM seminar is good for youth workers to hear. It can be inspiring and challenging, but it is hard to apply until it is talked about and put into a personal setting. Some youth workers attend the seminar and return to their church and put their PDYM notebook on a shelf to rest forever. Many of our students are doing the same thing with the Bible. If it is not discussed and applied to their life setting, they view it as interesting but irrelevant.

Small Groups Encourage Accountable Relationships

When a student in my small group says that he plans to put into action a truth that he has heard, he knows that this group of guys will *ask* him about the application the next week. Sharing opens the door to accountability to other members in the group. Christians without accountable relationships open themselves to potential trouble. The Christian life is too difficult to live in isolation. The Bible sheds some light on our need for one another. James 5:16 says, "Confess your sins to each other and pray for each other so that you may be healed." Quality small groups allow students to share struggles and prayer requests, and they teach students that they can rely on church family during difficult times. A feeling of community is developed in a small group as members grow in a scriptural understanding of loving one another. We are told to

- serve one another (Gal. 5:13)
- accept one another (Rom. 15:7)
- forgive one another (Col. 3:13)
- greet one another (Rom. 16:16)
- bear one another's burdens (Gal. 6:2)
- be devoted to one another (Rom. 12:10)
- honor one another (Rom. 12:10)
- teach one another (Rom. 15:14)
- submit to one another (Eph. 5:21)
- encourage one another (1 Thess. 5:11)

Consistency and Benefits of Small Groups

The more consistent a small group is, the stronger the benefits. Figure 8.2 illustrates this truth by graphing the results of meeting in small groups. Every youth ministry can implement these three different types of groups to help students connect with one another.

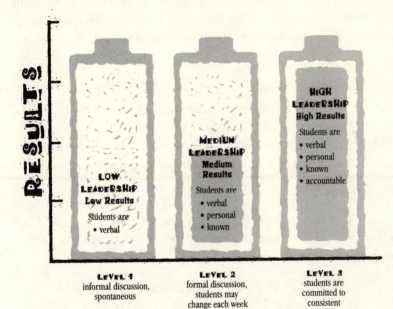

RESULTS

High Leadership High Results
Students are
• verbal
• personal
• known
• accountable

Medium Leadership Medium Results
Students are
• verbal
• personal
• known

Low Leadership Low Results
Students are
• verbal

Level 1
informal discussion, spontaneous

Level 2
formal discussion, students may change each week

Level 3
students are committed to consistent attendance

LEADERSHIP

Fig. 8.2

Level 1 Small Group

This is the informal, spontaneous small group. Students are randomly placed into groups at the beginning or end of a youth-group meeting. There is little to no consistency from meeting to meeting. The purpose is usually to get to know one another and/or to get students to discuss various questions. A level 1 small group is viewed as *a* component of a program, but it is not essential to its overall strength. Leadership is not necessary for the spontaneous small group. It can be effectively run from the front of the room by providing all small groups the questions and then giving each group a limited time to answer them.

Level 2 Small Group

This type of group expresses medium consistency in that it usually has the same students in it each week, but they have no formal commitment to consistent attendance. A level 2 group focuses more on the discussion than on interpersonal relationships; its goal is to get through the questions and interact with the teaching. Often, the leader has more of a teaching and facilitator role. This small-group format is an essential part of a program.

Level 3 Small Group

This type of small group focuses more on the students than on the teaching. The content may be a starting place to get the group headed toward discussion, but the focus is on intimacy, lifestyle, and accountability. This small group is the program rather than a part of a program. The small group members are the same each week, and their attendance is consistent and expected. The aim isn't to grow the group and bring in new members; rather it is to develop trust and friendship with those who are committed. The leader of this small group plays the role of pastor, shepherd, and counselor.

What Your Leadership Needs to Provide for Healthy Small Groups

Consistent, intimate small groups don't just appear. Like life, they are a process and not a one-time program. A healthy small-group strategy requires hard work from leadership. Applying the following principles will help to ensure healthy small groups.

> Consistent, intimate small groups don't just appear.

Determine Small-Group Values

It is important to establish what relational and attitudinal values you want to appear in all your small groups. While small-group leaders have different personalities and styles, they should treat small-group members alike. It is your responsibility to determine and define the values you expect to see. Though you may do this in concert with all of your small-group leaders, you must ultimately believe in the nonnegotiables and be the bottom line for them. Some examples of small-group values follow.

Authenticity: All leaders must model a genuine, transparent walk with Christ. They must be sincere leaders, not show-offs.

Confidentiality: Small groups must be a safe place to be honest. What is shared in the group must stay in the group.

Nurture trust: Students should feel like they have safety to share their feelings and power to ask questions. No question is silly or stupid.

Love for others: This is a learned value that begins with respecting one another. Students must be allowed to finish sharing their thoughts without being interrupted.

It is your responsibility to make everyone aware of the values you and your leadership decide upon. You can't take for granted that all your leaders will know the values and understand how they are to be applied in small groups. When I made this mistake, I found small-group leaders who were wanna-be teachers and turned their groups into classrooms, while still others created an environment where no disagreement was allowed. I learned never to assume that we all had the same values. Your values should be clear, concise, and consistently communicated to all involved.

Establish the Administrative Boundaries

Too many small groups fail because their leaders didn't establish boundaries at the outset. It is important to think through the issues and establish ground rules so that everyone knows what to expect. Here are some questions you may want to consider prior to starting your small groups:

- What is the intended outcome of the small groups?

- How will we divide students into groups (for example, grade, school, interests)?
- How will students know who is in what small group?
- For how long will the groups stay together (for example, eight weeks, one semester)?
- Will they be open groups into which anyone may enter at any time?
- Will they be closed groups into which new students may not join until the end of a time commitment?
- May students form their own groups with friends?
- Will the groups be coed or single-gender groups?
- Will the groups be student-led or adult-led or a combination?
- What will we do when a boys' small group ends in five minutes and the girls meet for an hour?

There is no one right answer for any of these questions. Your answers will depend on your goal for small groups, as well as your students, leaders, meeting times, and available meeting space. For example, regarding the first administrative question from the list, here are ten ways small groups can be divided.

1. age
2. sex
3. school
4. neighborhood
5. available meeting times
6. interests (for example, sports, drama, music)
7. natural friendships
8. personality types
9. spiritual maturity level
10. drawing names

What works for our ministry may not work for yours. We like to allow students to form small groups based on natural relationships so there is some built-in accountability. If the natural relationships are a problem for the small group, we may intervene and redirect some students to another small group where the personalities mesh better. We usually have our students write down the name of one friend they would like to be with in a small group, and we work to accommodate their requests. We always want to stay attuned to relationships and, if students aren't compatible, rework small groups. In all of these small-group decisions, we ask God to provide us with his wisdom.

Lighten the Load for Small-Group Leaders

If our small group leaders have time to invest in youth ministry above and beyond their commitment to a small group, I want that time to be relational with students and not spent in preparation. (Remember, the primary purpose of our small groups is fellowship. If it was discipleship I might have a different view of where they should invest their limited time.) I try to lighten their load in another way. I like to help them with their small group preparation time by providing them with a list of discussion questions for each study.

They are not necessarily expected to read the questions word for word, but they are to use them as a starting point to build their discussion strategy. Most find it helpful to have a list from which to choose. (We also provide answers for the questions pertaining to Scripture.)

Start with some basic open-ended questions, and then create questions that move to more specifics about the Scripture being studied. Finally, conclude with questions that push for personal application. Try to provide more questions than your small-group leaders will need so they can choose the best from the list. An example of our curriculum follows in Figure 8.3.

Provide Basic Skill Training

I have gone to seminars on small-group dynamics and have even taken a similar class in seminary, but I have learned more through experience than through lecture. Give small-group leaders some fundamental skills, but don't overwhelm them with theory and rhetoric. Provide them with some basics and allow them

BODY POWER: TOY OR TOOL?

1 CORINTHIANS 6:12–20

[12]"Everything is permissible for me"—but not everything is beneficial. "Everything is permissible for me"—but I will not be mastered by anything. [13]"Food for the stomach and the stomach for food"—but God will destroy them both. The body is not meant for sexual immorality, but for the Lord, and the Lord for the body. [14]By his power God raised the Lord from the dead, and he will raise us also. [15]Do you not know that your bodies are members of Christ himself? Shall I then take the members of Christ and unite them with a prostitute? Never! [16]Do you not know that he who unites himself with a prostitute is one with her in body? For it is said, "The two will become one flesh." [17]But he who unites himself with the Lord is one with him in spirit. [18]Flee from sexual immorality. All other sins a man commits are outside his body, but he who sins sexually sins against his own body. [19]Do you not know that your body is a temple of the Holy Spirit, who is in you, whom you have received from God? You are not your own; [20]you were bought at a price. Therefore honor God with your body.

OPENING QUESTIONS

(Answers will vary.)

1. What is the most expensive and valuable thing you own?

2. Are you picky about its use or do you treat it like junk? Are you protective of it or do you let others mess around with it?

3. If people don't treat their best stuff with respect, what does it tell you about them?

4. What about your own body? Would you consider it an expensive thing?

5. What parallels do you see between the use of an expensive piece of property and the use of your own body?

6. Some people see the body as a toy; others as a tool. How would you describe the difference between these two perspectives?

Fig. 8.3

SCRIPTURE SPECIFIC

1. Trace the word "body" through this passage. If this was everything you knew about your body, what would you know about it?

2. In verses 12 and 13 Paul quotes two of the Corinthians' favorite sayings. What are they?

3. What do you think these sayings meant? What view of the body—toy or tool—do they communicate?

4. How did Paul contradict and counteract these sayings? (Look for his words in verses 12 and 13 after the dash.)

5. Paul says that our bodies are members of Christ himself (v. 15). Then he asks, "Shall I then take the members of Christ and unite them with a prostitute?" What point is he driving at here?

6. In verse 18 Paul seems to say that sexual sin fits into a special category all its own. Does this mean that sexual sin is worse than other sins?

7. What is the one command we are given for dealing with sexual temptation (v. 18)? What are some examples of when we need to flee immorality?

8. The bottom line is "Honor God with your body" (vv. 19–20). How can we do that?

PERSONAL APPLICATION QUESTIONS

1. Do you think the sexual guidelines that most Christians set up for today's teenagers are too loose or too tight? Why?

2. What do you think are the top three sources of sexual temptation for students today?

3. What is one fresh insight you can take from today's Bible passage that can help you battle sexual temptation?

4. Who is one person you can talk to about sexual questions and temptations?

to learn through their personal experience. Below are some of the do's and don'ts we used at a recent small-group training:

- Don't be afraid of silence.
- Do show that everyone's input is valued.
- Don't feel like you have to have all the right answers.
- Do keep the group focused.
- Don't move to a new question too quickly. Ask, "Would anyone like to add to that?" The priority is dialogue, not getting through all the questions.
- Don't dominate the conversation.
- Do ask God to give you his eyes and ears.

Whatever you determine to be your basic do's and don'ts, keep the list in front of your leaders. You may want to spend five minutes reviewing one item from your list at each volunteer staff meeting.

Express a Vision for Starting New Groups

If a youth ministry is reaching community students through friendship evangelism, the crowd will grow. As the crowd program grows, more students will be moving to the congregation and entering small groups. If healthy small groups are to stay small, you will constantly need to identify potential small-group leaders.

In our high school ministry, most of our small groups are adult-run, but they have a student leader who can fill in for the adult if necessary. We also challenge our junior-year students to pray about leading a small group of freshmen students during their senior year. Not only does this help us keep seniors more actively involved in ministry, but it makes their junior year an exciting learning year. We encourage them to glean everything they can from their current small-group leaders and envision themselves as small-group leaders the next year. (Our junior high small groups are led by adults or older high school students.)

Pour into Your Leaders

If you are the point person of your ministry, you should be spending most of your time with your leaders. You might prefer to spend more relational time with students, but remember, the time spent with your small-group leaders is essentially time spent with the students in their groups. If small-group leaders are growing, they will challenge their small-group members.

Programming for Congregation Students: Saddleback Church Model

Our Primary Congregation Program: Area Bible Study Small Groups

Our small groups meet at homes in our community. These weekly meetings are called area Bible studies (ABS). We use the words *Bible study* instead of *small group* for marketing purposes, since most Christians place a higher value on Bible study than on small groups. The ABS does have a time of Bible study, but most of the time is spent building small-group community. We meet in homes for several reasons.

Homes Are More Comfortable

Most of the meeting rooms on our church property are portables. Each portable is shared with other ministries, so we don't have a youth room that we can make comfortable. Besides, few buildings can compare with the warmth of a host home. We try to limit each ABS home to thirty students and six small-group leaders for a five-to-one student-to-leader ratio.

Homes Get Families Involved

We like to use our students' homes, because this involves their parents. Some host-home parents become involved with greeting, while others lead small groups. We have even had a few couples thank us for making their marriages stronger. They opened their home up for an area Bible study and then left for a date! A once-a-week date night impacted their marriage. In turn, their dating was a great example for our students.

Home Groups Allow More Pastoral Responsibility for Our Volunteers

Volunteers won't stay involved with a youth ministry for an extended amount of time if they don't have significant responsibilities. By using homes, we provide volunteers the freedom to express their pastoral hearts because they don't have to sit and watch me be the youth pastor. When volunteers meet in a home, they become a youth pastor to the students in their small group.

Home Groups Lessen the Driving Distance, Are More Accessible to Students, and Allow for Different Meeting Nights

The strategic positioning of our meeting places throughout the community allows us to reach more students who can't get a ride to the church property. Meeting in homes also gives us the freedom to have alternate meeting nights and times. In the past, we had students say, "I work on Wednesday nights and can't attend," or "I have band practice that night." Now we have our ABS small groups Monday through Thursday, which provides more meeting options.

A Typical Area Bible Study Schedule

> 6:50 Leaders arrive
> 7:00 Students begin arriving
> 7:15 General greeting and announcements
> 7:20 All-group teaching time
> 7:40 Small-group time
> 8:30 Finish

Leaders Arrive: 6:50 P.M.

ABS home groups are led by adult volunteers. We have three primary roles for our adult leaders: teacher, pastor, and small-group leader.

The teacher's main responsibility is to come to an ABS prepared to teach a fifteen- to twenty-minute Bible study. We write the curriculum and provide it for all our teachers so that every ABS has the same material. The teacher also acts as a small-group leader.

The role of the pastor (a layperson, volunteer) in each home is to oversee the entire ABS and specifically care for the small-group leaders. The ABS pastor's tasks are to make sure students get connected with other students, remind leaders to contact students who have been absent, monitor the size of groups to keep them small, assist leaders with students' spiritual growth, and serve as a small-group leader. (If you can't use the term *pastor* in your church, find another word that communicates care, for example, *shepherd, lay minister, mentor,* and so forth.)

The other adults who attend an ABS act as small-group leaders. They encourage the ABS teacher and provide pastoral care to their specific small group.

Students Begin Arriving: 7:00 P.M.

We use the first fifteen minutes as time to unwind, mingle, greet one another, eat snacks (if the host home chooses to provide them), and wait for a few late arrivals. We have learned that the later we wait to start, the later students arrive. I have heard many youth workers complain that their students are always late, but in reality they are the ones who have *trained* their students to be late by continually compromising the starting time.

General Greeting and Announcements: 7:15 P.M.

Because at Saddleback Church our small-group ministry is held in twenty-plus homes, all our ABS pastors need updating on information to be disseminated to our congregation students. Our ABS pastors call an information line to hear a recorded message of the announcements that need to be communicated during the week.

All-Group Teaching Time: 7:20 P.M.

Because the emphasis on ABS is fellowship through small groups, we are not overly concerned about the skill level of our teachers. However, we have been blessed to find teachers who do a good job of working through the curriculum and making it understandable for our students.

While outstanding curriculums are available through denominational publishing houses and Christian bookstores, we have chosen to write our own at this time. All curriculums need to be adapted in some degree or another. No curriculum writer knows your students, your setting, and your goals like you do. Our most successful ABS consisted of our students reading through the *One-Minute Bible for Students.* We used one of the weekly readings and wrote a Bible lesson that could be studied by and applied to small groups. (See appendix C for more on *The One-Minute Bible for Students.*)

We put most of our lessons in a spiral-bound notebook that students can use for taking notes during the teaching time and for recording prayer requests in their small groups. Students can take the notebooks home for further study or to give their parents an opportunity to see what they are learning.

Small Group Time: 7:40 P.M.

After the teaching time we break up into small groups that meet in different areas of each ABS home. Each small-group leader is given a handout of questions from the teaching curriculum (see fig. 8.3 for an example).

Our ministry team has chosen to have same-sex small groups. We believe it is easier for students to develop long-term accountability when they are in a small group with members of the same sex. We provide other opportunities throughout our ministry programs and at camps for coed small groups to discuss topics and situations.

Finish: 8:30 P.M.

Some small groups end earlier than others (usually the guys' groups), but students tend to hang around the house until 9:00 P.M.

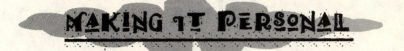

MAKING IT PERSONAL

1. Who are the students you as an individual are caring for?

   • _____

   • _____

   • _____

   Have they become "dear" to you (see 1 Thess. 2:8)?

2. What are the pros and cons of your small group ministry as it exists right now?

3. Using the labels explained on pages 143–44, what type of small group do you have?

4. What are three important small-group values?

5. What do your small-group leaders need in order to become more effective at helping students grow spiritually?

6. How can you help your students see the importance of small groups?

7. What is the most difficult aspect of running your small group?

NINE

Preparing Committed Students
Fulfilling God's Purpose of Discipleship

The saddest times in my youth ministry career are when I am reunited with a former youth ministry student who no longer gives his or her faith any priority. I wish I could say that all the positive stories about former students who are now in full-time ministry or raising godly families balance out my sadness for the others. Unfortunately, they don't! I'm always left to wonder what went wrong in their lives, and I often allow guilt to raise its ugly head and question my role in their spiritual development—"If only I had done more, they might still have a vibrant faith."

Several years ago I ran into Jake Brazelton, a former youth ministry student, at the mall. He was in his late twenties and living in complete opposition to God's ways. He had graduated not only from our youth ministry, but he also had graduated from his faith. None of our leaders would ever have guessed that Jake would wander from his faith; he had been a consistent participant for four years. We could count on his attendance at all our programs. I hate to admit it, but he was even in my discipleship group.

Jake and I talked for nearly an hour. After our conversation I realized that he knew *about* the Bible, Christian doctrine, and theology, but he had never quite learned how to maintain his faith and grow on his own. As a teenager his spiritual growth came as a result of attending youth ministry programs. As long as there was a program, he was growing. Our programs became his drug, and he was an attendance addict. I asked myself, "Where did I go wrong?"

God used my conversation with Jake to prompt me to seriously evaluate our youth ministry. I eventually realized that we had designed a youth ministry that encouraged committed students to become faithful to our programs or to their discipler more than they were committed to Christ and following his way. Too many conversations with former students like Jake caused me to rethink and radically change our discipleship strategy.

The Mystery of Discipleship

I have read dozens of books on discipleship, and the only consistent element I have found is the inconsistent definition of the task. In each of these books, I tried to find a specific definition of discipleship that would lead to a distinct discipleship program for students. I never found one. Thus, I learned that the *business* of making disciples is difficult.

Added to the multifaceted methods of discipleship are the unique growth patterns of adolescents. Because students respond to spiritual input in different ways, we can't franchise a discipleship program that will work with every student. The bottom line is that there is no one way to disciple students.

My definition of discipleship is simply "helping students become more like Christ." For some students it takes less than six months before we see measurable growth; for others it takes six years! Because of this, our discipleship attempts must have a personal and relational element to them. In the beginning my style of discipling students had been fifty percent educational and fifty percent relational. Most youth ministry discipleship programs have basically this same structure reflected in different methods. They have a component of teaching combined with an element of adult attention. For example, in the case of Jake Brazelton, we would meet together (relational) and go through a series of discipleship booklets (educational). I thought that Jake was being discipled and that I was fulfilling the discipleship cycle laid out in 2 Timothy 2:2: "The things you have heard me say in the presence of many witnesses entrust to reliable men who will also be qualified to teach others."

I envisioned this fifty-fifty style when I read the Gospels. Jesus taught his disciples (educational) as well as walked and lived with them (relational). But Jesus did something else I never fully realized prior to my conversation with Jake. Jesus informed his disciples that he would be leaving them. He verbally prepared the disciples for his absence.

This preparation element was missing in my previous years of discipling students. I had encouraged our leaders to disciple students by spending time with them and teaching them about the Christian faith. What I neglected is what students like Jake needed the most: I didn't focus on a strategy that would help our committed students develop the habits, or spiritual disciplines, necessary to grow on their own when they were no longer in the youth ministry. For many students at my church, our discipleship plan reinforced their commitment to—or dependency on—programs and people. We had created an educated dependence when we should have prepared students with the habits necessary for spiritual independence.

Now I have come to understand that students need more than information and relationships. Youth ministries are filled with Bible-literate students who bear no fruit. These students have all of the right answers (knowledge), but they make wrong daily choices. At some point, students must be weaned from depending on the flesh and begin walking in the Spirit. This isn't going to happen when we establish a program-based discipleship plan. It happens best when the formula looks something like this:

33.3 percent educational

33.3 percent independent spiritual habits (or disciplines)

33.3 percent relational

Because the word *discipline* carries negative connotations, we focus on the more neutral word *habits* and encourage our students to develop habits that will prepare them for their long-term journey in the Christian faith.

A New Method of Youth Ministry Discipleship

I'm a little leery any time I read the word *new* when it relates to ministry. I'm sure there are youth ministries doing what I'm about to explain with the following action steps, but I know of no other written source that reflects this type of discipleship strategy.

Put Your Enthusiasm Behind Habits Instead of Programs

If students are going to maintain their faith over the long haul, they must develop consistent spiritual-growth habits, in addition to attending a small group program where they learn to study, discuss, and apply God's Word. The encouragement to establish habits may be the greatest gift we can give to students as they face life's challenges, choices, and crises. The question is simple: "Long after the youth ministry days of programs and role models are gone for a graduating senior, what will sustain that young person's faith under trial?" The answer: the grace of God and learned habits.

That is why our youth ministry enthusiastically and consistently focuses on the development of spiritual disciplines as a key part of our educational and relational time. Using the warm incubator of a student's small group, leaders are able to give encouragement and resources rather than expecting a student to attend an additional discipleship program another night of the week.

Define the Habits of a Committed Christian

Before you can find appropriate resources to help your students develop spiritual habits, you must first identify the habits you want your graduates to carry with them. While there are several truths we want our students to understand about Christianity (educational), there are only a few spiritual habits we want them to develop during their time in our youth ministry. At Saddleback Church we have defined six habits we want committed students to take with them. These six habits may be different from the ones you would choose, but don't disregard this idea (end result) simply because our lists (means) may differ. The principle of helping students develop habits is transferable to your youth ministry regardless of the ones you define.

We defined our six habits by asking, "What habits are important for lifelong independent spiritual growth?" Another way of looking at it is, "What are the habits *you* rely on to maintain an authentic relationship with Jesus Christ?" The ones we listed are the ones I have been developing and relying on since I began my own spiritual pilgrimage as a teenager. We want our committed students to

- have consistent time with God through prayer and Bible reading
- have an accountable relationship with another Christian
- commit to the body of Christ and our church body (not just the youth ministry)
- understand and participate in giving/tithing
- memorize Scripture
- study the Bible on their own (beyond reading)

Because we focus on the word *habits,* we have made our list into an acronym using the word *habits.* It is a little forced but is nevertheless a helpful aid to memorization.

H ANG time with God

A CCOUNTABILITY with another believer

B IBLE memorization

I NVOLVEMENT with the church body

T ITHING commitment

S TUDY Scripture

Remember, these are simply the habits we want students to develop. This list does not include all the *information* we want them to know before they graduate from our youth ministry. We try to cover the educational element of discipleship through our various teaching times during our weekend services, area Bible study small groups, and secondary discipleship programs geared for committed students (see "Bible Institute" in chapter 12).

Find or Create the Tools to Help Build the Habits

Once you define the habits, it is important to ask, "What tools (or resources) will help my students develop these habits?" Granted, the provision of tools doesn't ensure that a student will be discipled and walk with Christ for his or her entire life. (Even the Pharisees were faithful in using "tools"!) It will, however, add to your confidence that you haven't handicapped students by creating a dependence on yourself or on a particular program.

It is not enough, however, to say, "I want students to study the Bible before they graduate." They need a resource to help them study the Bible and grow in their faith. This means depending on a Christian bookstore to provide it or creating something.

I've done it both ways. At this point in my ministry, I prefer to create tools because it keeps them affordable and because students seem more receptive to what I create than to what I buy. It is easy to buy a growth booklet or a journal, but when you create one, students know that it is especially important to you.

Most youth workers don't have the time, help, and resources to create their own materials. Even those who can create their own can't compete with the fancy layouts and colorful printing jobs of published resources. But you have something a publisher can't express—your heart. When I give something that I have created to my committed students, they accept it as a gift from me. (I have never had a student say, "Oh, I wish you had bought me something instead.") The time it takes to create something helpful communicates that I care about their spiritual journey. Don't feel guilty, though, if you don't have time to create the resources you want. Purchase them or have students purchase them.[1]

Focus on Encouragement

In addition to the role you play as creator or finder of resources, you also play the role of encourager. You should constantly urge students to develop the habits you have defined. Better yet, encourage the small-group leaders, who in turn shepherd their students in the development of these habits.

One of the ways I motivate committed students is through a monthly letter (like the one below) to those using our H.A.B.I.T.S. tools. Because students have to sign up for each resource they take (see fig. 9.1), I have accurate records of our committed students. I send these students pastoral letters and give them an occasional phone call to find out how things are going.

My dear friend,

I hope this letter finds you doing well! I'm writing to encourage you in your study of God's Word through ROOTWORKS. I've been getting all kinds of feedback from those who have taken it.

- "It's the best Bible study I've ever done!"
- "Uh, well ... I have it ... I read the first page, but to be honest, it's under my rat cage."
- "Fields, I can't believe it! I found three typos."
- "I'm going to start soon; I promise."

I'm so thrilled that you have expressed a desire to study the Bible that I wanted to write to you and say, "Way to go!"

Here are some suggestions to help you with this discipline:

1. Don't give up! Let me or your small-group leader know how you are doing.

2. Do a little at a time. Habits are formed by doing something every day for at least twenty-one days straight. Studying the Bible can become a habit.

3. Pray for a new insight from God each time you study the Bible.

4. Mark the mistakes you find and let me know so I can correct them.

5. Share any new insights with your S.A.G. Five partner.

6. If you don't understand a question or an answer, forget about it and move on. Don't let that keep you from finishing a lesson.

Know that I love you and thank God for you.

Doug

PS: If you want more information on some of the other discipleship tools we are trying to put into your hands, let me know (e.g., Quiet-Time Journal, Bank of Blessings, Hidden Treasures).

YES! I want to develop
Spiritual H.A.B.I.T.S.

I am signing up for:

☐ Bank of Blessings   or   ☐ Rootworks (don't get both at once)
☐ S.A.G. Five (☐ help me find a partner)
☐ Hidden Treasures   ☐ Quiet -Time Journal

Name: _____

Phone: _____   Grade: _____

School: _____

Address: _____

Turn this in at the information table to pick up your tools.

Fig. 9.1

In addition to receiving my encouragement, every committed student has the support of a small group. The small-group leader is the one who does most of the encouraging and plays the role of discipler with hands-on oversight and mentoring. Because we focus on students developing the H.A.B.I.T.S. on their own, neither the committed student nor the discipler has to be out

> The small-group leader is the one who does most of the encouraging and plays the role of discipler with hands-on oversight and mentoring.

another night of the week attending a discipleship program. The tools are our discipleship program.

Programming for Committed Students: Saddleback Church Model

Our Primary Committed Programs: Discipleship Tools

Before we look at the specifics of each tool, note two things. First, no student requests all the tools at once. We encourage students to take only the tools they are ready to use. Second, there is a cost to producing and/or buying tools. If your church can't afford to add the cost of the tools into your budget, you will need to find another way to pay for them. You may want to encourage parents to pay for the tools, or you may want to find financial sponsors in your church who will purchase the resources and pray for the students who use them.

Habit 1: Quiet-Time Journal. Have a Consistent Time with God Through Prayer and Bible Reading

When you look at a page from one of our quiet-time journals (fig. 9.2), you will see that it is really nothing more than a few key questions and a blank space to write in, enhanced by a little graphic design. We have found that half-sheet-size (5-1/2" x 8-1/2") journals work best. The small writing area and large graphic treatment let students know that they don't have to do much writing. We put only thirty-one pages in each journal so that students can replace their journals several times throughout the year and feel a sense of accomplishment. We make it clear that they are not obligated to finish the journal in a month. Thus, they don't have to feel guilty if they don't complete it in that time frame (see fig. 9.3). When students ask for

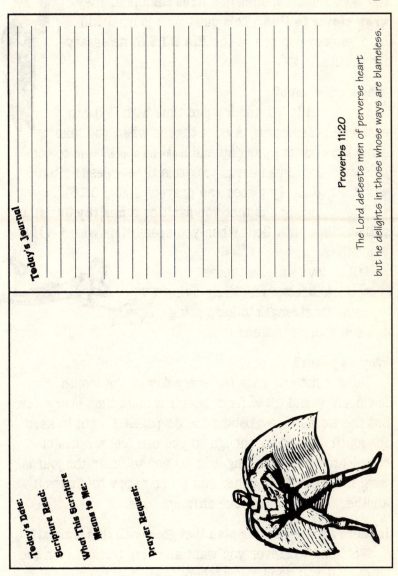

Today's Date:

Scripture Read:

What This Scripture Means to Me:

Prayer Request:

Today's Journal

Proverbs 11:20

The Lord detests men of perverse heart
but he delights in those whose ways are blameless.

Fig. 9.2

My gift to you

This journal is my gift to you to **help you grow** as a Christian. I can think of nothing more **EXCITING** than watching students' **lives change** as they **grow closer to God.** This quiet-time journal will help you develop one of the **H.A.B.I.T.S.** necessary for growth.

Why a quiet time?

Our world is **noisy** and **busy,** and time with God can easily be passed over. A quiet time is when you take some time out of your day and make an appointment to connect with God. Even Jesus took this time—"Jesus often withdrew to lonely places and prayed" (Luke 5:16).

The bottom line is that you can't be a **healthy Christian** without time with God. When you spend time with **GOD** you will:

fall in **love** with him more
receive **direction** for daily living
have his **strength** to keep going
grow more like **him**

Why 31 pages?

No, it's not one page for every day of the month. You obviously would *benefit* from having a quiet time every day, but there's no secret behind the 31 pages. I want to keep the journal **SHORT** enough so you can feel a sense of completion. However long it takes you to finish the journal, we'll **CELEBRATE** together and I'll be happy to give you another one (we have four different types).

Is there a Bible-reading plan that goes with this journal?

No! Read whatever you want and *keep track* of it in the journal. If you don't know where to read in your Bible, you might start with the gospel of **John** or the book of **Philippians**. Or, if you need a reading plan, you can read through **The One-Minute Bible** or pick up a Bible-reading plan from our information table.

What's the deal with a Proverb on every page?

I love the book of Proverbs because it is filled with wisdom for everyday living. There happen to be 31 chapters in Proverbs, so it was a convenient way to expose you to more of God's Word. It's for your *reading pleasure.*

What do I need to write on the journal page?

Whatever you want! You can write out your **prayers,** list what God is teaching you, write a letter to God, write about your *spiritual journey,* describe what you want to learn, write what you think God would say to you if he was writing to you—there are no rules. It's your spiritual journal. It's not intended to be a diary in which you record everything you did yesterday—they are your pages—write what's in your heart.

What do I do when I finish?

Ask for another one. *Look back* over your journal pages and reflect on what God is doing in your life and what you're learning. Transfer your ongoing prayer requests to your next journal and **celebrate** God's growth in your life!

I'm excited about your growth,

Doug

"Delight yourself in the Lord, and he will give you the desires of your heart."
Psalm 37:4

Fig. 9.3

new journals, we have an opportunity to affirm them, to celebrate their growth, and to ask them about their times with God.

Habit 2: S.A.G. Five. Have an Accountable Relationship with Another Believer

S.A.G. stands for Student Accountability Group, and five is the number of minutes we ask students to pray together during the week. We coach all of our committed students to find one Christian friend on their campus with whom they can pray and develop an accountable relationship. We don't ask them to pray in the middle of the campus or to stand on lunch tables to draw attention to their spirituality; we do ask them to meet somewhere at school and pray together.

We regularly remind students to seek out a S.A.G. Five partner, and we always end our camps with a challenge to students to find a partner before they go home. The camp experience can quickly fade if a student doesn't have some encouragement from a friend. Students usually keep their same S.A.G. Five partner for the entire school year.

Once students have partners, we make a big deal about their partnership. We ask them to sign the S.A.G. Five covenant (see fig. 9.4). We give them a wallet-size card on which to record their partner's phone number, which serves as a gentle reminder of the commitment (see fig. 9.5).

Habit 3: Hidden Treasures. Memorize Key Scriptures

The title of this resource comes from a combination of the New International Ver-

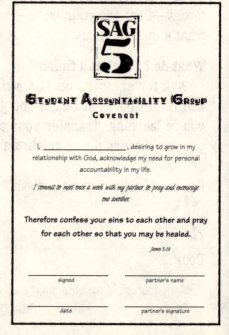

SAG 5

STUDENT ACCOUNTABILITY GROUP
Covenant

I, _____, desiring to grow in my relationship with God, acknowledge my need for personal accountability in my life.

I commit to meet once a week with my partner to pray and encourage one another.

Therefore confess your sins to each other and pray for each other so that you may be healed.

James 5:16

_____   _____
signed   partner's name

_____   _____
date   partner's signature

Fig. 9.4

> I desire to grow in my relationship with God, and I **Student** acknowledge my need for personal accountability in my life. I commit to meet once a **Accountability** week with my partner to pray and encourage one another. **Group**
>
> partner _____   partner's phone _____

> Therefore **confess** your sins to each other and **pray** for each other so that you may be healed. *James 5:16*

Fig. 9.5

sion and the New American Standard Bible translations of Psalm 119:11: "I have *hidden* your word in my heart that I might not sin against you" (NIV, emphasis added) and "Thy word I have *treasured* in my heart …" (NASB, emphasis added).

Hidden Treasures is a simple flash-card Bible memorization tool. When committed students sign up for Hidden Treasures, we give them a set of three to five verses. Each verse is printed on a 3" x 5" card, laminated and single-hole-punched. We hang the cards on a large silver ring. After students have memorized a set of verses, we give them the next set. We include a short note explaining why we chose those verses or encouraging them to not give up.

Habit 4: Attend Church. Commit to the Church Body, Not Just to the Youth Ministry

This is the only habit of the six for which we don't have a specific resource to give students. We are always talking to our students about attending church and being involved in our church body. We speak highly of Saddleback Church events, and we model involvement by supporting church-wide programs. The periodic letters we send to our committed students remind them of the importance of being involved with the church beyond their youth ministry experience.

Habit 5: Bank of Blessings. Practice the Discipline of Financial Giving

Of the other resources listed, this is the most difficult to get students excited about. To generate a better understanding of giving, I created a giving kit called the Bank of Blessings. The kit

includes a tape-recorded message wherein I talk about the importance of giving, as well as a four-lesson Bible study on tithing, a stack of offering envelopes, and a decorated container in which to collect one's offering (see fig. 9.6).

Of the five resources, this is the one for which we don't do much follow-up. We do want to know if students understand everything they studied on tithing and we want to answer their questions, but we don't want to pressure them into giving to please their leaders rather than giving out of their love for God.

Fig. 9.6

Habit 6: Rootworks. Know How to Study Scripture

This Bible study tool gets its name from Colossians 2:6–7: "As you received Christ Jesus the Lord, so continue to live in him. Keep your *roots* deep in him and have your lives built on him. Be strong in the faith" (NCV, emphasis added). I have selected specific books from the Bible and written questions for students to answer after they have read the Scripture. The questions motivate them to think about what they are reading and to take time to process God's Word. While the quiet-time journal encourages devotional reading, Rootworks encourages a deeper study of the Bible. See figure 9.7 for a sample study from the book of Philippians.

Rootworks

Questions for Philippians 1:12–14

1. What has happened as a result of Paul's imprisonment?

2. What does Paul's experience say about how God can work through difficult circumstances?

3. How does Paul's experience relate to the following verse? "And we know that in all things God works for the good of those who love him, who have been called according to his purpose" (Romans 8:28).

4. Do you ever feel imprisoned at school or chained to someone?

5. How might your "imprisonment" serve to help you talk about God?

Questions for Philippians 1:15–18

1. Paul is talking about two types of preaching being conducted while he is in jail. One group has sincere motives while the other group has greedy motives. Paul recognizes the mixed motives, but he is thrilled that the message of Christ is getting out regardless of motives. What is an example of a church having greedy motives?

2. What can one do when he/she recognizes impure motives?

Fig. 9.7

MAKING IT PERSONAL

1. What is your definition of discipleship?

2. How have you been measuring spiritual growth?

3. When did you develop your spiritual disciplines? Describe your pattern of spiritual growth.

4. Create a composite of a committed Christian. What do you see as the habits of a committed Christian?

5. What resources will help students develop habits for growth?

6. What specific steps can you take to get students excited about spiritual habits?

NOTES

1. I have created tools to help students develop the H.A.B.I.T.S. mentioned in this chapter. They are self-published and available for purchase through Making Young Lives Count (see page 397). They are also available on computer disk so that you can edit my material and personalize it for your individual ministry without any copyright problems. You can get a sample pack of all of the tools or a production pack, which comes with original art, computer disks, and ready-to-use masters.

TeN

Challenging Core Students
Fulfilling God's Purpose of Ministry

One of the greatest joys youth ministry leaders can experience is watching core students embrace ministry. Dedicated core students are usually the ones who develop a heart for ministry and find an opportunity to serve, no matter where life leads, after graduating from your ministry.

The word *core* becomes confusing when it is removed from the context of the circles of commitment (see fig. 5.1, p. 87). Many youth workers I've met say, "I have core students, but they're not the minister type; many of them are apathetic." In the PDYM nomenclature, those types of students wouldn't be considered core students. At Saddleback Church we refer to them as *regulars*. They attend everything, but they don't desire to grow spiritually or to minister to others.

The more our staff focuses on teaching students about service, the more I am surprised at how open students are to the concept of ministry. They enjoy discovering that they are gifted and that God wants to use them. In some churches, getting students to do ministry isn't as big a challenge as convincing the church congregation and leadership that teenagers can play a vital role in the body of Christ.

173

In some churches, getting students to do ministry isn't as big a challenge as convincing the church congregation and leadership that teenagers can play a vital role in the body of Christ.

Challenging Students at All Levels to Do Ministry

Students at all commitment levels can fulfill the purpose of ministry. Some highly motivated students may even want to start their own ministries.

Even though not all of your students will want to minister, they shouldn't have to move through all the circles of commitment before they hear about ministry and are allowed to serve. It would be crazy to say, "Although you express a desire to care for others, you can't until you jump through our 'congregation' and 'committed' hoops first."

Chapter 7 stresses the importance of getting crowd students involved in a ministry team without giving them a spiritual litmus test. Even non-Christians can serve others. Their motive isn't obedience to God, but obedience to God may follow service. Every year I watch students give their lives to God *after* they have done missions work in a Mexican village.

The following steps will help you inform your students about and get them interested in doing ministry.

Stop Treating Students as the Future Church

I detest hearing church members say, "We must have a strong youth ministry because youth are the future of our church." Students aren't the future of the church; they're the present church, just like all other believers. While this future-church message may seem innocent and empowering, it is actually defeating. We should be challenging youth to be ministers and to participate in the faith today instead of sitting back and waiting until they are adults. The apostle Paul encouraged young Timothy's ministry by saying,

"Don't let anyone look down on you because you are young" (1 Tim. 4:12). We need to communicate that same message.

> **Students aren't the future of the church; they're the present church.**

Jesus never said, "Take up your cross and follow me when you're an adult." The Bible is clearly void of any age requirement for serving. God shattered age limits with biblical heroes like David, Jeremiah, and Mary. A sign of a healthy church is one that helps all Christians, regardless of age, to discover their gifts and express them through serving in ministry.

Continually Communicate Ministry Messages

All students should hear about the joy of participating. Even during crowd programs, we stress that our youth ministry is about active participation and not passive observation. We repeat that message often because it is important. Peter tells Christians that he will keep reminding them of the truth: "I will always remind you of these things, even though you know them and are firmly established in the truth you now have" (2 Peter 1:12). We need to remind students that a life of *observation* is a wasted life, but a life of *participation* in the work of the kingdom is the reason we were born.

Teach Students That They Were Created for Ministry

For many students, the truth that all Christians are called to ministry is revolutionary. Not everyone is called to be a pastor, but all believers are called to do the work of the ministry. In Ephesians 4:11–12 we are told, "It was he who gave some to be apostles . . . and some to be pastors and teachers, to prepare God's people for works of service, so that the body of Christ may be built up." My role as a pastor, then, is to prepare God's people (students) for works of service (ministry). What an honor, yet what a humbling and sobering responsibility!

At Saddleback Church we teach that every Christian is

- *created* for ministry (Eph. 2:10)
- *saved* for ministry (2 Tim. 1:9)
- *called* into ministry (1 Peter 2:9–10)
- *gifted* for ministry (1 Peter 4:10)
- *authorized* for ministry (Matt. 28:18–20)
- *commanded* to minister (Matt. 20:26–28)
- to be *prepared* for ministry (Eph. 4:11–12)
- *needed* for ministry (1 Cor. 12:27)
- to be *rewarded* according to his or her ministry (Col. 3:23–24)

We can't assume that students will discover these truths on their own. Even most of the adults I know don't understand that they were created to do ministry. We must, therefore, teach and repeat these truths.

Help Students Discover Their Spiritual Gifts

Christian students have not only been invited to play in the game of ministry, they have been given the equipment to play well. One of the thrilling roles I have as a youth worker is helping students understand that they have been gifted by God (Rom. 8; 1 Cor. 12; Eph. 4). I love to say, "Congratulations, you're gifted!" It is wonderful to see their eyes get big when they find out that God has gifted every believer. I enjoy giving them a simple spiritual-gifts test to further spark their interest. This short test gets them thinking about their *gift tendency*, which aids in their gift discovery.[1] By taking part in different ministry opportunities, students will discover their spiritual gifts.

Challenge Students to Discover Their S.H.A.P.E.

At Saddleback Church we teach our entire church body that God has uniquely "shaped" every individual to do something in ministry. We teach them the five elements that can help them discover their personal ministry by using the acronym S.H.A.P.E.

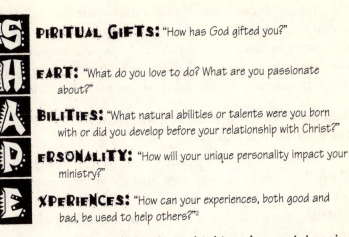

SPIRITUAL **GIFTS:** "How has God gifted you?"

HEART: "What do you love to do? What are you passionate about?"

ABILITIES: "What natural abilities or talents were you born with or did you develop before your relationship with Christ?"

PERSONALITY: "How will your unique personality impact your ministry?"

EXPERIENCES: "How can your experiences, both good and bad, be used to help others?"[2]

One way to get your students thinking about ministry is to teach a S.H.A.P.E. series. Spend at least one teaching session in the series on each of the five elements to discovering one's gifts. I call my S.H.A.P.E. series "How to Get into Shape."[3] I teach it about every twelve to eighteen months, since getting students involved in the ministry is one of our key values. (In addition to teaching the S.H.A.P.E. principles in this series, we also teach them in Class 301.)

After I teach the series, we help students interested in ministry find a place in one of our twenty-nine student-led ministry teams. Although anyone can join a ministry team, only core students (those in small groups who are participating in the H.A.B.I.T.S.) can lead a team or start their own ministries. This way we insure that we have growing Christians at the helm of ministry teams.

How to Help Core Students Start Ministries

Have Students Complete a S.H.A.P.E. Profile

At the conclusion of the S.H.A.P.E. series or after Class 301 (see chapter 12), we encourage committed students to complete a S.H.A.P.E. profile. The profile is filled with questions prompting students to think about their spiritual gifts, heart, abilities, personality, and experience. I encourage you to adapt it for your youth ministry. When students fill out the profile, we tell them to prepare their minds and hearts for ministry.

If students don't show interest during the S.H.A.P.E. series or don't return the S.H.A.P.E. profile after Class 301, we don't force them to complete the profile. Being wise stewards of our time, we want to first focus on those who express some degree of self-motivation. We meet one-to-one with those students.

Help Students Get Started in a Ministry Based on Their S.H.A.P.E.

When a leader and student meet to discuss the student's S.H.A.P.E. profile, they explore how the student might use his or her unique S.H.A.P.E. to serve God. The leader either assists in placing the student in a ministry or helps the student to create a new one. Let's use Josh as an example. Josh is a sophomore in high school, and his S.H.A.P.E. profile answers were as follows:

Spiritual Gift: His highest score was for the gift of hospitality.[4]
Heart: He has expressed a passion to make others feel comfortable, to plan, and to organize.
Abilities: He is good at sign language, cooking, and fixing things.
Personality: He is outgoing.
Experience: He became a Christian because he liked the leaders at his hometown church, who went out of their way to make him feel comfortable during his first visit.

When Josh and I sat down to go over his S.H.A.P.E. profile, he didn't have an answer to the last question on the profile: "If I could design a specific way to serve God around my personal S.H.A.P.E., and I knew I couldn't fail, it might be . . ." Since Josh didn't have any specific ideas, I knew it was my job to encourage him to serve in an existing ministry or help him create one. We created one. We dreamed up the idea of Josh becoming the host, chef, and leader for our monthly Dinner for Ten ministry (see p. 216). Prior to the days of Chef Josh, our dinner was pizza. Now Josh arrives early to prepare a special meal and stays throughout the dinner to welcome guests and help them feel comfortable. Josh has discovered a great ministry within our church, one of which I am particularly fond!

Not every student's S.H.A.P.E. profile points directly to a particular ministry or a logical ministry. Many times I have scratched my head and pleaded with God to give me some ideas so that I wouldn't have to say, "Uh, … I don't know where you can serve," thus squelching a student's excitement. And at other times, interestingly enough, a student's answers haven't pointed to the ministry he or she had in mind. Why does this happen? Because God's path isn't always the logical path. All the giftedness testing in the world can't and shouldn't attempt to "box" God in. When this happens we have two options: (1) Keep praying and dialoguing over the next several weeks until there is more clarity on placement. Or (2) encourage the student to jump into a "ministry of choice" until God leads elsewhere.

Nori, for example, chose option 2. She really wanted to start a baby-sitting ministry. I never would have thought of that ministry based on her S.H.A.P.E. profile, but she decided to get a group of teenagers together to baby-sit for the children of our adult volunteers during monthly staff meetings. She also made baby-sitting available so that our volunteers can go on dates during the week. She was mature enough to see that if our adult leaders have quality marriages, they will make better role models and ministers. When other students saw that baby-sitting could be a ministry, they said, "I can do that! I can be a part of that ministry!"

Keep in Touch with Their Discovery Process as Well as Their Faith

We can't assume that once we get students involved in ministry, we can leave them alone. Many students won't discover their ministry until they have tried several different opportunities. We may need to help them search for new opportunities through which to express themselves.

In addition to their ministry, we also want to keep in touch with how they're doing in their walk with God. If our core students aren't in our student leadership program (see page 180), they can get lost in the busyness of doing ministry. We want to continually show our student ministers that they are valued.

For students doing ministry in the core (meaning they participate in or lead a small group and they practice discipleship H.A.B.I.T.S.), we maintain monthly accountability through a few simple questions we call our Core Accountability Report (fig. 10.1). Although we see these students every week, this sheet gives them an opportunity to update us on what is happening in their relationship with God and in their ministry. It is not mandatory that they fill out the report, but most core students like to fill it out because they know we are concerned with their lives and they want to update us on their ministry.

How to Turn Student Ministers (Core) into a Student Leadership Team

Participation in student leadership should require a deeper level of commitment and accountability than is expected from students in ministry programs.

Based on what you have already read, you can see that it is possible for students to have a ministry but not be in student leadership. We have several core students who either don't have time for student leadership or aren't ready for the additional commitments we require.

For example, Candice and Amy are two of our core students. Both are in a ministry (the drama team) and both are in a small group (congregation). Candice is at the beginning stages of forming the H.A.B.I.T.S. of a disciple (committed), while Amy has been committed to them for several years. Neither of these girls is in our student leadership. Amy is too busy with work and school commitments, while Candice's lifestyle doesn't reflect the type of behavior we expect from our student leadership. She continues to be tempted by the party scene and occasionally drinks. Even though she is following our process for growth, she is not *being* the type of Christian who appropriately reflects our student leadership.

You may raise your eyebrows and come to Candice's defense with, "No one's perfect." True, but God has a higher standard for leaders. The theme verse for our student leadership is Ephesians 4:1: "I urge you to live a life worthy of the calling you have received."

Core Accountability Report

1. How have your times with God been this month?

2. What is one thing you've learned about your relationship with God this month?

3. How is your current ministry going?

4. How can I pray for you this month?

5. Is there anything else you'd like me to know?

Fig. 10.1

Recognize Jesus' Definition of Leadership

Jesus gave his disciples an image of leadership that should be our standard for student leadership. Matthew 20:25–28 says that Jesus called his disciples together and said to them, "You know that the rulers of the Gentiles lord it over them, and their high officials exercise authority over them. Not so with you. Instead, whoever wants to become great among you must be your servant, and whoever wants to be first must be your slave—just as the Son of Man did not come to be served, but to serve, and to give his life as a ransom for many." Not only did Jesus shatter another pharisaical paradigm, he also gave a prescription for greatness: Be a leader who serves.

Servant leadership is not attractive to most students; it opposes the impulse to race for the front seat of the car or to be first in line to eat. If your present student leadership is unhealthy, you may need to "close shop" for a few months. Explain to your students that you are trying to make some healthy changes and that you will restart with a new look. Then try to implement the following ideas.

> Not only did Jesus shatter another pharisaical paradigm, he also gave a prescription for greatness: Be a leader who serves.

Develop Student Leadership Based on Ministry and Lifestyle Qualifications

The model of student leadership I most dislike is the one that identifies student leaders through voting. This type of selection, swayed by influence or attendance, is neither healthy nor biblical. Choosing student leaders on the criteria of popularity and status may be suitable for a social committee but not for a student ministry. If you have a "leadership" group chosen by popular vote, I encourage you to change the name from "leadership" to something like "activity committee" to indicate that it is not biblical leadership and to remove it from the core commitment circle. The group could be viewed as a planning team—making calendar and activity decisions—and be a secondary program for the crowd level rather than a core ministry.

Just imagine if the religious leaders during the time of Christ had taken a vote on who should work side by side with the Son of God. It is safe to assume that many of the disciples wouldn't have made the cut. Serving others through ministry, not popularity, should be the requirement for student leadership. When God sent Samuel to anoint a king for Israel, he told Samuel, speaking of David's brother Eliab, "Do not consider his appearance or his height, for I have rejected him. The LORD does not look at the things man looks at. Man looks at the outward appearance, but the LORD looks at the heart" (1 Sam. 16:7).

Raise Your Expectations for Student Leaders

As you develop—or re-create—your standards for student leaders, raise your expectations. God has revealed high standards for leaders (see 1 Timothy), and it is not wrong to challenge students with high standards if they want to be leaders in the church.

It is not uncommon for school officials, athletic coaches, and music teachers to have demanding expectations of students. Students know that if they want to participate in extracurricular activities, they have to make strong commitments. Why should we require any less from those who want to be leaders on God's team?

Prior to beginning our student leadership program, our core students created a list of lifestyle expectations of a student leader. We asked them to help us create a portrait, based on biblical imperatives, of someone they would respect in the role of student leader (see fig. 10.2). Next, we asked our core students to develop a profile of a student leader's role (see fig. 10.3).

Make Your Expectations of a Student Leader Known

After you have established some student leadership expectations, make sure students and adult leaders understand them. Clearly communicate that leadership isn't for everyone. If some students don't meet the expectations—and not everyone will—carefully communicate to them that they are still special, that you still love them, and that they are no less valuable than anyone else.

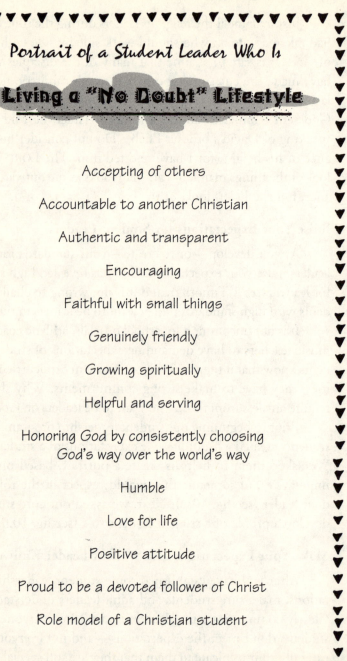

Portrait of a Student Leader Who Is

Living a "No Doubt" Lifestyle

Accepting of others

Accountable to another Christian

Authentic and transparent

Encouraging

Faithful with small things

Genuinely friendly

Growing spiritually

Helpful and serving

Honoring God by consistently choosing
God's way over the world's way

Humble

Love for life

Positive attitude

Proud to be a devoted follower of Christ

Role model of a Christian student

Fig. 10.2

Profile of How a Student Leader Is

Committed to the Student Ministry

Acts as a campus pastor at school

Committed to the unity of our youth ministry

Feels a sense of ownership in the ministry

Follows up on weekend visitors and other students
when on campus

Greets at weekend worship services and other programs

Involved in all our major events

Looks for opportunities to serve

Looks out for loners and visitors

Meets with other student leaders to pray for
their campuses

Models appropriate program behavior

Oversees and encourages at least one ministry team

Solves youth ministry problems without complaining

Speaks highly of staff and other student leaders

Understands the purposes of why we do what we do

Fig. 10.3

> **Why should we require any less from those who want to be leaders on God's team?**

By making your expectations visible, it communicates that your student leadership is open to anyone in the core who qualifies. I have known students who have read the expectations and made decisions to radically change their lives just because they wanted to be a part of something significant. If students still want to be in student leadership after reading the expectations, we give them a short application to complete (see fig. 10.4), and then we interview them.

Interview Potential Leaders

After core students have read the expectations and filled out the application, I meet with them one-to-one to make sure they understand the high calling placed on leaders. We talk through every commitment and expectation, and I give specific examples of what each commitment means. For instance, in the profile of how a student leader is committed to the student ministry (fig. 10.3), one of the expectations is "solves youth ministry problems without complaining." So, I explain that if our Saturday night service is crowded and not enough chairs are set out, a student leader finds more chairs instead of saying, "Doug, we never have enough chairs out."

Because most students evaluate themselves more stringently than I would, some look over the two lists and take themselves out of consideration. By the time I meet with students, they usually do fit the student leadership descriptions. If they do, I "close the deal" by having them sign a student leadership commitment form (see fig. 10.5).

Get Parents Involved in the Process

We require each student's parent(s) to sign the commitment sheet so that everyone is clear on the expectations of our student

Student Leadership Application

Please be as thorough as possible when completing this application. You will be able to explain and expand your answers during the interview section.

1. Why do you want to be in student leadership?

2. How would your non-Christian friends define your relationship with God?

3. How would your Christian friends define your relationship with God?

4. How would your parents define your relationship with God?

5. How is your "friendship evangelism" going?

6. Comment on your spiritual growth and your use of the following tools:
   - Quiet-Time Journal
   - S.A.G. Five
   - Hidden Treasures
   - Bank of Blessings
   - Rootworks

Fig. 10.4

Student Leadership Commitment

Committed to Jesus

- I acknowledge the lordship of Jesus Christ in my life and have a personal relationship with him.

Committed to Spiritual Growth

- I am committing to spiritual growth through involvement with an area Bible study small group.

- I am committing to spiritual growth through the H.A.B.I.T.S. of
  - consistent quiet times (Quiet-Time Journal)
  - accountability with another believer (S.A.G. Five)
  - memorization of Scripture (Hidden Treasures)
  - commitment to the church body
  - giving/tithing (Bank of Blessings)
  - personal Bible study (Rootworks)

Committed to a Ministry Team

- I am committing to leading a ministry or being a member on a consistent basis.

Committed to Living a "No Doubt" Lifestyle

- I am committing to choices and a lifestyle that are godly, knowing that my lifestyle is a model for other students and that it communicates, without a doubt, my commitment to Christ.

Committed to the Friendship Evangelism Challenge

- I am committing to the Friendship Evangelism Challenge and to bring my friends to the appropriate programs.

Student Leadership Commitment (con't.)

Committed to the Student Ministry

- I am committing to attend one of the weekend worship services and to greet other students in order to create a warm environment.

- I am committing to attend classes 101, 201, and 301 before I move into student leadership (and 401 within six months of starting leadership).

- I am committing to attend a nonnegotiable, monthly student leadership meeting.

- I am committing to turn in a monthly accountability sheet.

- I am committing to greet other students at all Saddleback programs I attend.

- I am committing to understand and memorize our purpose statement.

- I am committing to understand the planned values (R.E.L.A.T.I.O.N.S.H.I.P.S.) and the process for spiritual growth (baseball diamond).

- I am committing to become a campus pastor for my school, which includes calling visitors, praying with other student leaders from my school, and overseeing promotion for church outreach events on my campus.

_____
student signature

_____
parent signature

_____
date

Fig. 10.5

leadership program. We tell the parents they can expect five things from our adult leadership.

1. We will MODEL Christian leadership for your kids.
2. We will MENTOR them in their leadership development.
3. We will MONITOR their growth as student leaders.
4. We will MOTIVATE them through encouragement and feedback.
5. We will encourage them to MULTIPLY their effectiveness by sharing their skills with others.

We are especially concerned about the family life of our student leaders. We want parents to know that we don't intend to keep their kids out several nights a week. Spiritual growth does not require sacrificing family time and other key commitments. Bluntly put, we work hard to ensure we have their family's blessing.

Spend Extra Time with Student Leaders

Because of the high requirements for student leaders, there should be a high reward. Student leaders should get more time with you and other adult leaders. I make no apologies that I spend most of my student time with student leaders. I do visit crowd students at their games and on their campuses, but I almost always go with a student leader. I want to spend my time being a leader of leaders. An adult volunteer and I recently took one student leader on a speaking trip across the United States. When we returned, his mother confided in me that, since the death of her son's dad, I had become his father figure. She said, "The trip made a lasting impression on him of Christlike friendship." I might add that he has been a stronger leader in our ministry because of that trip.

Many youth workers have asked me if I take heat from the other students in our ministry because I focus primarily on student leaders. No—mostly because I don't bring attention to it. I don't say, "I was given three free tickets to the Lakers' game, and I'm taking Pat and Robbie because they're student leaders." I just take them. I'm sure some students complain among themselves or to their parents about my apparent unfairness. When they do

> **I want to spend my time being a leader of leaders.**

complain, they have something in common with Jesus' disciples. Remember, they argued over who was going to get preferential treatment and who was going to sit at the right and left of Jesus (see Matt. 20:20–28). Also remember that Jesus always had a crowd around him, yet he was constantly with the twelve disciples. But even among the Twelve, his inner circle was Peter, James, and John. I stop feeling guilty when I realize that I'm following Jesus' model.

Don't be afraid to start with a small student leadership team. It's better to have two high-standard student leaders than fifty students who want to plan activities while they live any lifestyle they please. If you raise the standard, you will start small, but you will be building on strength. A solid foundation will assure healthy growth because spiritual maturity will be a model for future student leaders in your ministry.

> **Better to have two high-standard student leaders than fifty students who want to plan activities while they live any lifestyle they please.**

Programming for Core Students: Saddleback Church Model

Our Primary Core Program: Student Leadership

You have already read about the steps necessary for creating a student leadership program. At Saddleback Church we make it very clear that we raise our expectations for the students we entrust with the title *leader*. We believe that the students we place in roles of leadership need not only be committed to attending (crowd), committed to other believers through a small group (congregation), committed to growing spiritually on their own (committed), and committed to ministry (core), but also committed to a lifestyle that pursues godliness, honors God, and is above question.

We expect our core students to be committed to

- a relationship with Christ
- spiritual growth (small groups and H.A.B.I.T.S.)
- a ministry

We also expect our student leaders to model

- a lifestyle that is above question
- a commitment to our youth ministry
- a commitment to the friendship evangelism challenge

At our student leadership interview we walk through all the commitments on the student leadership form (fig. 10.5). Almost always, the students who complete the process shine as student leaders.

MAKING IT PERSONAL

1. Do you know your spiritual gifts? If so, what are they?
2. What do you like or dislike about the S.H.A.P.E. profile (see appendix E)?
3. How do you respond to the following statement: "Students aren't the future church; they are the present church"?
4. What are you doing to challenge students to do the work of the ministry?
5. What is your process for helping students get into a ministry?
6. How do you presently define "student leader"?

7. What are some nonnegotiable qualities that you expect from student leaders?

8. Name someone on your team who could oversee the implementation and follow-through of your student leader program. How can the rest of your team support this person?

9. What are some specific ministry areas in which students can serve?

NOTES

1. Jim Burns, president of the National Institute of Youth Ministry, and I have written a curriculum called *The Word on Finding and Using Your Spiritual Gifts* (Ventura, Calif.: Gospel Light, 1996). I recommend this book if you need a simple spiritual gifts test and a resource to help you teach on spiritual gifts.

2. For a more complete understanding of S.H.A.P.E., read Rick Warren's *The Purpose-Driven Church* (Grand Rapids: Zondervan, 1995), 369–75.

3. For a copy of this tape series with outlines, contact Making Young Lives Count, 714-459-9517.

4. Using the spiritual gifts test from my book *The Word on Finding and Using Your Spiritual Gifts.*

ELEVEN

Five Characteristics
of Healthy Youth Programs

Now that we have addressed the specifics of developing purpose-driven programing in youth ministry, we will look at five general characteristics essential for all programs regardless of commitment level. Healthy programs need (1) to put relationships first, (2) a fresh source of ideas, (3) strength beyond a personality, (4) an ongoing follow-up system, and (5) clarification of their purpose and potential audience.

1. Programs Need to Put Relationships First

Dave, one of our adult volunteers, wanted to start a Friday afternoon, in-depth Bible study. For whatever reason, this Bible study was poorly attended for about three months. At the beginning of the fourth month, we had our winter camp. During the weekend Dave was able to develop relationships with some students, and these relationships became his impetus for the Bible study. After the camp Dave's Bible study experienced a dramatic attendance increase. The Bible study program didn't become more attractive, but the relationships did. Positive relationships are one of the key reasons a youth ministry grows. A common occurrence is the student who loves being part of a poorly run youth ministry because her best friend is there, even though she could attend her parents' church, which has a strong youth ministry. We see it all the time: relationships are a draw.

A healthy youth ministry is committed to becoming a relational youth ministry. The adult leaders make building relationships with students a high priority, and these relationships quicken the ministry's effectiveness and enhance students' spiritual maturity. This style of youth ministry becomes a ministry *with* students rather than a program-centered ministry *to* students.

Regardless of their level of commitment to Christ, all teenagers need to connect with a caring adult who will take an interest in them and form a mentoring friendship. Personalized care can't be fulfilled by any program, regardless of quality, because programs don't develop relationships; people do. While a program may capture a student's attention, a relationship helps reinforce and strengthen commitments. Programs are important but only after relationships have been developed.

> This style of youth ministry becomes a ministry WITH students rather than a program-centered ministry TO students. Programs don't develop relationships; people do.

It is then that students will be personally nurtured in their faith—especially if the leaders reflect the spiritual maturity described in chapter 1. Obviously, this type of relational youth ministry needs adults who are willing to give their time to care for students. The more students you have in your ministry, the more adults you will need to keep your groups small. While I may be able to recognize my students, I can develop significant relationships with only a few.

Youth Ministry Is Building Doghouses

Several years ago I coined the phrase "Youth ministry is build-ing doghouses." My wife, Cathy, wanted to buy a doghouse, but I thought that buying one was too expensive. After getting a few price quotes, I arrogantly said, "I can build one for much less." Cathy smiled and took me up on the offer. I blocked out an entire Satur-day and called Jeff, a student from my ministry, to help me. I knew he had woodworking skills, because I remembered that he had received a B- in wood shop that semester. (I saw his report card at his house while I was snooping for food during an area Bible study.)

Jeff and I spent an entire day building a doghouse, which some believe looks more like a small version of Noah's ark. At any rate, the day after our construction project, Jeff's mom told me that her son was more excited about Christ after building the dog-house than he had been after any church program he had ever attended. I was puzzled. As it turns out Jeff had given her a detailed description of our time together. He told her about our trip to the supply store and how I had treated the salesman. She heard about all the things Jeff and I had talked about through-out the day. She was informed of our mini food fight in the Taco Bell parking lot, the laughs at my house, my ability not to swear when I hit my finger with the hammer, how I treated my children, and what was not in my refrigerator. (He told his mom, "I've never seen an adult's refrigerator without alcohol.") She heard about everything! Jeff said, "Doug is a normal person. I can tell he has fun being a Christian."

Much to my surprise, our day together made a significant impact on Jeff's faith. After that, Jeff spent more time with me outside the church environment, and we came to know one another better. Not only did Jeff want to build more doghouses with me (I suspect that was just an excuse to spend time together), but he became a better listener during Bible study. I learned never to underestimate the power of spending time with students.

Many of our volunteers feel guilty because they are too busy to relationally invest in students. The self-imposed guilt has even driven some adults away from youth ministry. Since taking time out of a busy schedule to spend with students is so difficult, we need to bring students into our schedules instead. I have learned to create relational time with students while doing home projects or errands. As a relationship develops, students have less need to be entertained and are more appreciative of *any* time together. Here's an easy way to remember this valuable relational principle: Don't create activities to include students in your life; instead, include students in the activities of your already busy life.

In spending much time with both Christian and non-Christian teenagers over the years, I have discovered that there are some things all students need from a caring adult. They need adults to:

Act as Role Models

As adult leaders we need to realize that during our relational time with students we are role models for Christianity, living representations of Christ. In a very real way, we are saying to students what Paul said in 1 Corinthians 11:1: "Follow my example, as I follow the example of Christ." Students watch and listen to everything we say and do. They take notes on how we drive our cars and remember the flippant comments we make about people, life, and situations.

Before my wife and I had children, my wife was an incredible volunteer. When we had one child, she remained at the *incredible* level. At two children, she moved to *great* status. And now that we have three, she describes herself as a *busy* volunteer. She finds it difficult to spend time with students because of the demands of our own children. To remain a relational youth worker, she takes teenage girls grocery shopping. While shopping, she ministers to them as a Christian role model. My three children love these adventures because teenagers are fun. The girls enjoy it because they are spending time with Cathy. Cathy is blessed because she loves teenagers and gets her shopping done in half the time with the girls' help. Everyone wins! Even this seemingly insignificant time becomes a generous deposit in the modeling bank account. Before you go somewhere alone, think twice and call a student to go with you.

Cathy and I recently received a letter from a student who was part of our youth ministry and is now graduating from college.

> Dear Doug and Cathy,
>
> Thank you for everything you've done for me throughout the years. I can't help but think that you have contributed greatly to my successes by giving me such supportive friendship as long as I can remember. The two of you have shown me what it is to have a solid marriage, loving relationships with friends and others, and most importantly, how to live a life that glorifies God. You've definitely made an impact on how I see myself, how I see the world, and how I value God. It's hard to express exactly what I mean, but I just wanted you to know how much I appreciate you.
>
> Love, *Cynda*

I hope you noticed the key phrase in the letter. She didn't say, "You have *taught* me about marriage and life and love through your creative Sunday school curriculum." She said, ". . . you have *shown* me. . . ." We model God's ways when we spend time with students.

Be Revealing

One of the true marks of good youth workers is authenticity with students. These workers aren't afraid to be transparent and show signs of weakness. They might teach on prayer and admit that their prayer life isn't all that it should be. They might express some of their failures and fears because they know their honesty can help students and give them hope when they feel like giving up.

Most students have false perceptions that their leaders, if not perfect, are close to perfect. I know this because they say things like, "You wouldn't understand what I'm going through" and "You've probably never struggled like this before." Students can be empowered to keep going in spite of their mistakes by rubbing shoulders with leaders who honestly share some of their own struggles. You don't need to expose all your sins for public viewing, but do be honest when you talk about life and the faith process. If a spiritual discipline is difficult for you, be open about it.

> You don't need to expose all your sins for public viewing, but do be honest when you talk about life and the faith process.

Express Acceptance

If a student arrives at church with a nose ring, green hair, and tattoos, and you find out that he has a broken family, an abusive background, and an addiction to cigarettes, he needs to be loved and accepted as God loves and accepts him. His actions do not need to be accepted, but he should be accepted for who he is—God's creation.

I have developed a fairly close relationship with a student in our ministry who is a "party animal." He enjoys our conversations, but he isn't ready to commit his life to God. He gets drunk almost every weekend, but for some reason, he likes coming to church. When I see him on Sunday morning, I put my arm around him and tell him I'm glad to see him. (I say it loud in his ear to enhance the pain of his hangover!) I also tell him that I hate what he is doing to himself. In his search for truth, he can see me as someone who loves and accepts him for who he is while rejecting what he does. He would be the first one to tell you that I am praying for him to turn away from sin.

Help Them Depressurize

Students are stressed out! And their stress level is getting worse, not better. Students need to learn to relax, take breaks, and not grow up so fast. They need to learn that everything in life doesn't have to be serious.

To help students battle their stress, you may want to cancel a week-night meeting every so often to help them remove one *serious* commitment from their calendar. Once a month we cancel our midweek area Bible study small groups and replace them with a fun night out. Each of our groups chooses its own version of fun. Not only does this time help relieve some of the students' stress, but it also builds community within the area Bible study.

Challenge Them Spiritually

When we develop relationships with students, we earn the right to be heard on spiritual matters. Thus, this is prime time to start talking about God. Teenagers want to make sense of God and figure out how he fits into their worldview. As our world's moral decay becomes more prevalent, our teenagers' quest for answers becomes more desperate.

> **As our world's moral decay becomes more prevalent, our teenagers' quest for answers becomes more desperate.**

As you connect with students, don't be afraid to ask them how they are doing in their relationship with God. Boldly ask the students in your small group if they are reading their Bible. Students understand that you want them to know God, and they won't be overwhelmed by questions directed at their faith. No matter where they are in their commitment, they can be nudged and coached into taking bigger steps into God's ways. When they do, celebrate every step of growth.

I recently asked a typical crowd student if he prays. He said, "Not really, I never know what to say to God." I said something like, "Yeah, I've been there before. Sometimes I don't know what to say either. You might try talking to God as if he is a friend sitting right next to you. Why don't you try talking to God for at least thirty seconds every day, and I'll ask you about it next week, okay? The more you do it, the more normal it will feel." As you can see, a spiritual challenge becomes a natural part of a relational conversation.

2. Programs Need a Fresh Source of Ideas

As a youth worker you probably love creative, new ideas that you can use to supplement your programs. Once you know what you're about (fulfilling the five purposes) and who you're trying to reach (potential audience), new ideas will help you design more effective programs. But without the purposes and potential audience, ideas are empty and have no foundation.

> Without the purposes and potential audience, ideas are empty and have no foundation.

When creating purpose-driven programs, it is always helpful to have resources for ideas. Here are three ways you can find more ideas than you will ever need.

Ideas Library

Since 1969 Youth Specialties has been publishing volumes of *Ideas* books filled with field-tested program ideas. These extraordinary books are written by creative youth workers who want to share their successes. More than 3,500 ideas are categorized under such topics as games, special events, meaningful discussions, skits, crowd breakers, publicity, worship, camps, missions, outreach activities, creative learning games, fund-raisers, scavenger hunts, parents, Bible studies, creative communication, and student leadership.[1]

If you don't have a set of *Ideas* books, you may want to make it your next primary investment. When you get the books, glance through them with the filter of the five purposes. For example, if an idea will help fulfill the purpose of evangelism, it is worth noting. As I read through the volumes, I mark the material I find helpful or interesting and photocopy it. Then I categorize the ideas into one of seven files: (1) evangelism, (2) worship, (3) fellowship, (4) discipleship, (5) ministry, (6) parent/family, or (7) leadership.

The essence of creative programming is simply your ability to find an idea and adapt it to your situation. Even a bad idea can trigger a new thought. Don't feel pressured to use all original concepts. I have met too many youth workers who were creative but not effective. If I were to place a priority on creativity or effectiveness, I would choose the latter.

Youth Ministry Mailing Lists

Get your youth ministry's name and address (not your phone number) on every youth ministry mailing list that you can. You will soon receive so many advertisements that, besides filling your trash can, you will also have some good resources. Even if a piece of mail doesn't give me a program idea, it may give me a layout and design sample.

Surf the Internet

I am amazed at how many youth ministry ideas are floating around in cyberspace. Nearly every time I access the Internet I find new youth ministry sites filled with great ideas. You can check out my home page (www.dougfields.com) because I keep a current list of youth ministry Internet addresses.

3. Programs Need Strength Beyond a Personality

A healthy youth ministry must have strength beyond a leader's personality. If a leader with a charismatic personality leaves a youth ministry that is built without a strong foundation of additional leadership, the ministry will soon diminish. Your youth ministry programs are only as strong as your support team.

We've all heard that successful managers "work themselves out of a job." Well, I like my job! While I don't want to work myself out of a job, I do want others to share in significant aspects of my job so I can reinforce struggling areas of the ministry and/or spend time where I am most effective. Three actions we can take to become healthier leaders are to dispense responsibility, schedule planned absences, and train successors.

Dispensing Responsibility

I have grown tired of the word *delegate* because it has become synonymous with *dump*. Delegation often communicates, "I don't have time to do something myself, so I'll dump it on you." No one likes to be dumped on. A better concept is *integration*, which communicates, "I want to help you get plugged into the life of the ministry. Let's do this task together, with the idea that you won't need my assistance next time; you will be able to do it on your own." If you don't share your work load, you will damage the foundation of your ministry and quench the possibility of workers expressing their giftedness.

> If you don't share your work load, you will damage the foundation of your ministry and quench the possibility of workers expressing their giftedness.

Scheduling Absences

To find out if your ministry is based on your personality, plan a spontaneous absence. Confide in one of your leaders that you are not going to lead or be at a particular event. Give her a little direction, but tell her she is on her own. If the program bombs, it may be because you have too much of your personality in the program. If the program goes as planned, congratulate yourself on developing a team of capable leaders who aren't dependent on you, then congratulate your leaders.

Train Successors

I feel a heavy responsibility and privilege to mentor potential leaders who could take my place at Saddleback in the event that the Lord "calls me home" or commands me to serve elsewhere. One of the most profound joys in my ministry is witnessing the spiritual and leadership growth of those anointed for youth ministry that I get to have a hand in training. Until you see this fruit of your labor and of God's gracious leading, you haven't fully lived.

4. Programs Need an Ongoing Follow-Up System

If God has entrusted you with the leadership of students, make sure you know when they are absent, because their physical presence often gives an indication of their spiritual condition. Proverbs 27:23 says, "Be sure you know the condition of your flocks, give careful attention to your herds." If you tell your students that you want them to feel that your youth ministry is their "home away from home," you need to back up your words with a follow-up system. If one of my three children were missing from home for even one night, I would frantically notify the police and search for them. Two program follow-up questions to consider are: Do you know when a student is absent? If a student is missing, do you do anything about it?

The larger your ministry becomes, the more difficult these questions are to answer. We expect our small-group leaders to follow up on the specific students in their small groups at the congregation level. For the crowd students who aren't in a small group, we utilize a general follow-up strategy. Students who attend our church for the first time are encouraged to fill out an information card. Their name is then typed on an attendance list. A revised copy of this list is located at every table during our weekend worship service (crowd program). When students sit down, they locate their name on the list and circle it. Every Monday one of our volunteer moms comes to the church office and transfers the circled names to a master list. Each student's name has an assigned bar code that she then scans into the computer. The result of the scanning is a printout of each student's attendance. If a student misses two consecutive weeks, he or she receives a short, hand-written note from a staff member. If a student misses three weeks in a row, he or she receives a phone call from one of our student leaders.

If your group isn't set up for a bar-code scanning system (mine never was prior to Saddleback), you can use a mailing list. Have the students who attend fill out information cards, and then compile a mailing list. Spend a few minutes each week simply looking through the names, figuring out who was missing, and respond appropriately. As you grow, you will need to discover a more efficient method.

5. Programs Need Clarification of Their Purpose and Potential Audience

Within a healthy youth ministry, there should never be any question as to why your programs exist. You should know what primary purpose your programs fulfill, for whom they are intended, and what usually happens at each program. (See Appendix D for an overview of each program and its key values.)

When you write out this information, you will provide your church with the "big picture" of your youth ministry. As your programs change, update the information and make it available to your pastor, as well as your youth ministry volunteers, parents, and students. Your workers are your ministry's life blood, and the better informed they are, the more they will support you. Unsupportive people are often simply uninformed people.

MAKING IT PERSONAL

1. On a scale of 1 to 10, what rating would you give your ministry for developing relationships with students? What examples support your score?

2. What have been some of your favorite relational experiences with students?

3. After you have earned the right to be heard (through relationships with students), how do you challenge students spiritually?

4. Are any of your programs dependent on a personality? If so, which programs and personalities? What course of action can be taken to help strengthen the program and lessen the role of the personality?

5. How do you know if a regular attender stops attending or is absent for a few weeks? If a student is an irregular attendee, how do you know he or she is missing? Do you have a consistent follow-up plan for contacting absent students?

6. Name some students in your youth ministry who are unconnected and in need of a relationship.

7. What can you do to be more aggressive in pursuing relation-ships with unconnected students?

8. Do you have a short, written description of all of your pro-grams?

NOTES

1. You can order the *Ideas* set by writing to Youth Specialties at 1224 Greenfield Drive, El Cajon, CA 92021, or you can get it from me at Making Young Lives Count (see page 397).

COMPONENT FIVE

PROCESS

TWELVE

Using a Visual Process to Communicate Your Spiritual Growth Plan

Imagine that you have been dumped in the middle of a desert and have been challenged to walk home. You have been given supplies, a map, and a compass. To walk straight home without stopping would be impossible—the journey is too long. You study the map and find places along the way to eat, rest, and prepare yourself for the next leg of the trip. Once you've established your route, you begin to head home. It's not an easy journey, but you can envision the end. Each day is filled with adventures that are extraordinary learning experiences. Finally you make it home.

I use this illustration to explain how a visual process acts as a map to help your students reach home—that is, spiritual maturity. By plotting your programs—which represent the resting places in your students' journey toward home—you logically and visually communicate their route of spiritual growth. Just as traveling in the desert illustration wasn't easy, so the spiritual journey isn't easy either, but the end can be seen.

Before we jump into this chapter, let's take a quick review of components two, three, and four. God's purposes expressed through a purpose statement reveal *why* your ministry exists (component two), the potential audience defines *who* you want to target (component three), and the programs determine *how* you will attempt to reach your target and fulfill a purpose (component four). A process (component five) will help you communicate *where* you want your students to go on their spiritual maturity path.

At Saddleback Church we use the circles of commitment (see chapter 5) to define our potential audience, and we use a baseball diamond as our process to help communicate the sequence of our programs and our plan for spiritual growth.

An Overview of Saddleback's Process

If a process illustrates the path toward spiritual growth, you may be thinking, based on what you've read, "Aren't the circles a process? Don't you use them to show your plan to move students from the community to the core and the core back out to reach the community?" That's a good question.

Though the circles *can* serve as a process, at Saddleback we chose the baseball diamond as a simple and universal way to communicate movement. It portrays a very familiar process. Almost everyone understands that the diamond is a path for runners to follow in order to score. In our ministry, the students are the runners, and we are coaching them to follow our programs around the base path. We communicate that we want to move students from being a community spectator in the stands, to runners making their way around the bases, to core students sliding in for a home run. As in baseball, we don't get credit for runners left on base, so we challenge students to run for the prize (Phil. 3:14) and help them rid themselves of anything that might slow them down (Heb. 12:1–2).

This baseball diamond process also aligns with the five circles of commitment. Figure 12.1 shows the location of the potential audience when the circles and the diamond are combined.

For students, a process serves as a spiritual growth map they can follow. By connecting a program to a spot on the process, students can easily see where they are in the youth ministry's strategy for growth (see fig.12.2). It is like looking at a mall map and finding the "you are here" dot. When students see where they are

Fig. 12.1

in the spiritual growth process, they can be challenged to take the next step and attend a program sequentially designed to further their faith. When students realize you want to produce home-run followers of Christ, they understand that a home run doesn't happen when they stay at second base.

The primary programs discussed in chapters 6–10 are plotted on the baseball diamond (see fig. 12.2). As you see the primary programs around the baseball diamond, note that students can jump into the process wherever they want. They aren't required to start at the weekend worship service and work their way around the bases. Most students do enter our ministry through our weekend worship services, usually because of a friend participating in our friendship evangelism challenge, but they don't have to start there.

Discipleship
Tools

Area Bible Study
Small Groups

Student
Leadership

Weekend
Worship Service

Friendship Evangelism
Challenge

Community

Fig. 12.2

A Detailed Look At Saddleback's Process
Secondary Programs: Designed by Need

In addition to our five primary programs, we have designed thirteen other programs that assist in moving students around the bases. We call these assisting programs our *secondary programs*. Each one of these is designed to fulfill one of the five biblical purposes *and* target one of the five potential audiences—just like our primary programs.

For you to get the complete picture of our entire process of moving students around the bases, I need to introduce you to our secondary programs. These secondary programs don't receive as much attention as our five primary programs for at least three reasons: they don't meet as often, they don't reach as many students, and since everything can't be primary in our ministry, they don't get as much time, publicity, and resources. They are not lousy programs (we would never keep them if they were), they just take a back seat to our five primary programs.

One of the key factors in all of our secondary programs is that they meet specific needs of our potential audience that the primary programs don't meet. For example, our weekend worship service targets the crowd student, but because our crowd has grown so large we needed to create a smaller secondary program to reach the crowd student who was intimidated by a large group.

One answer to this need became a secondary program we call "dinner for ten," which you'll soon read about.

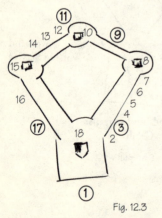

We sequentially organize all our programs, both primary and secondary, along the baseball diamond to communicate our process for spiritual growth (see fig. 12.3 and also appendix D for an overview of all our programs and the purposes they fulfill).

Fig. 12.3

1. Friendship evangelism challenge (see chapter 6)
2. Hot-night events
3. Weekend worship services (see chapter 7)
4. New believers' class
5. Dinner for ten
6. TNT: teens 'n' temptation
7. Ministry teams
8. Class 101
9. Area Bible study small groups (see chapter 8)
10. Class 201
11. Discipleship tools (see chapter 9)
    - Quiet-Time Journal
    - S.A.G. Five
    - Hidden Treasures
    - Rootworks
    - Bank of Blessings
12. Praise and worship
13. Missions monthly
14. Bible Institute
15. Class 301
16. Ministry team leader
17. Student leadership (see chapter 10)
18. Class 401

A brief description of each of our secondary programs follows.

1. Friendship Evangelism Challenge

See chapter 6 for a description.

2. Hot-Night Events

One of the best ways to complement the Friendship Evangelism Challenge and reach community students is to help your community during times when teenagers most likely need a place to go. I call these "hot nights," and they are times like New Year's Eve, prom night, graduation night, and Halloween—any night when community students will be on a party hunt. The church can provide a great ministry to the community by sponsoring an event that will draw unchurched students away from unwholesome parties and/or trouble to a safe, fun place.

Hot nights serve as the perfect alternative for our regular students who have a tough time bringing community students to our crowd program (see chapter 6, step two in our five-step Friendship Evangelism Challenge), at which we present the gospel. Over the years I have taken criticism from other youth workers because we don't preach the gospel at all of our community events. I absorb the criticism because I understand the big picture of what we are trying to do with hot-night events. These nights don't represent our primary evangelistic strategy. Friendship evangelism through our regular students is our evangelistic strategy. (See fig. 12.4 for a sample of the handout we give to the kids who come to hot nights.)

Our junior high and high school ministries each try to have three community programs during the year. Both ministries do something on New Year's Eve, during the graduation season, and occasionally on Halloween. Our junior high ministry rents out an entire water park for junior high students after graduation. Our high school ministry turns our church property into a carnival-type setting on the night of graduation so that students will have a safe place to party. For a few dollars, students experience a night of food, a place to hang out, free haircuts (just for fun), and wild games (sumo wrestling in inflatable suits, Velcro wall jumping, modified (sissy) bungi jumping, and anything else we can rent that is attractive and fun—and covered by our insurance!

If your resources are limited, you can use these hot nights as opportunities to combine resources with other churches' youth ministries. By networking with other ministries you will not only have more resources to create an attractive event for community students, you will also provide a great opportunity for the unified body of Christ to influence the community. Remember, there should never be any competition within the body—there are plenty of unchurched teenagers without a church to call thier home.

3. Weekend Worship Services
See chapter 7 for a description.

Thanks for joining us at Undergrad Night

Why? THROW THIS PARTY?

Because we care about **YOU**, **LIFE**, and **GOD!**

▲ **YOU** . . . as a person
▲ **LIFE** . . . as a journey
▲ **GOD** . . . as a creator of both

EVERYONE
is looking for **LIFE**
& personal **FULFILLMENT**.

MANY
people believe this
LIFE & FULFILLMENT
can be found in ▶ ▶ ▶ ▶ ▶ ▶

▲ relationships
▲ sex
▲ alcohol
▲ partying

YOU NAME IT . . . people have **TRIED IT** in their search for life. All the answers they find only bring **TEMPORARY** satisfaction.

THERE IS AN ANSWER

At Saddleback Church we try to help **HIGH SCHOOL** students **GRASP** that

▲ 1. **GOD** loves us and wants us to **ENJOY** a personal relationship with **HIM.**
▲ 2. A **RELATIONSHIP** with God is **POSSIBLE.**
▲ 3. **GOD'S** way of **LIVING** really leads to **LIFE.**

Jesus said,

"The thief's purpose is to steal and kill and destroy. My purpose is to give life in all its fullness." *John 10:10*

If you're not plugged in to a church and are interested . . . we would **LOVE** to have you **JOIN** our high school group. We have three identical services you can **ATTEND:**

Saturday @ 5:00 p.m., Sunday @ 8:45 a.m., Sunday @ 11:00 a.m.

Every weekend hundreds of high school students gather for a program that includes a great live band, funny videos and games, entertaining dramas, and messages of hope for life. Join us in Room 404 this weekend! If you have any questions, you can call us.

Fig. 12.4

4. New Believers' Class (Discipleship)

Once a month we have a class for new believers that covers some of the basics of the faith. Our new-believer curriculum has six sessions, and we teach one session per month and encourage new Christians to return for the other five classes. These classes are taught by one of our volunteers who has a heart for new believers. He teaches a little, answers questions, and helps students take some foundational steps in the right direction. We view these classes as supplements to our weekend services and midweek Bible studies. We also have these classes in a workbook form for students to do on their own and then discuss in their small groups.

5. Dinner for Ten (Fellowship)

At Dinner for Ten, we invite crowd students who are visiting or feel unconnected to my house for dinner. We used to serve pizza until one of our core students started a cooking ministry. Now the meal includes delicious lasagna served on paper plates. From 4:00 to 5:30 on a Sunday evening we eat together, tell stories, and try to help the unconnected connect. Besides praying before the meal, there is nothing overtly spiritual about the program.

This is a perfect opportunity for some of our new volunteers to meet students who are desperately searching for someone to take an interest in them. The larger your ministry becomes, the more necessary these types of small-group contacts become.

6. TNT: Teens 'n' Temptation (Fellowship)

This is a weekly meeting for students struggling with all different types of temptations—often chemical related. Our church has a strong, Christian recovery program with enthusiastic volunteer leaders who have brought the recovery concept to the student level. I really don't have much to do with this program other than encouraging struggling students to be a part of this group. Students who attend TNT are typically students who don't choose to be involved in any other areas of our ministry. This group often represents their total youth ministry experience.

7. Ministry Teams (Ministry)

Any student can join a ministry team at any time. Each team is overseen by a student ministry team leader. We presently have twenty-nine ministry teams which serve others in some capacity.

- art
- audio
- band
- baby-sitting
- big church transition
- camping
- cancer support
- cooking
- computers
- drama
- encouragement
- greeting
- incoming transition
- jackets for Jesus
- meals for the needy
- missions
- mountain biking
- office work
- photography
- prayer
- recycling
- sign language
- singers
- skateboarding
- Sunday school children's teacher
- surfing
- video
- weekend setup
- world shoe relief

Some of the ministry teams, such as drama, meet on a weekly basis (Saturday morning), while others meet whenever they need to prepare for an event or task, such as the camping team prior to a trip. These teams offer a fun and easy way to get students involved. Honestly, not all of these teams are smooth-running machines. Some of them function well on their own and others need routine checkups. Some of them have adult supervision, while others are led by our core students.

8. Class 101 (Fellowship)

This is our membership class and one of four classes in our life-development process. It is actually the youth version of our church's membership class. During this class we teach on the basics of salvation and the beliefs of our church. We explain the five purposes, the programs, and how a member can support our ministry. At the end of the class, we give students an opportunity to commit to becoming a member of our church.

We have created Class 101 to be our official door from the crowd commitment level to the congregation level. It is not mandatory for students to take this class before they attend an area Bible study small group but it is always encouraged. Pages 225–26 give an overview of all four classes we offer and how they serve as markers of commitment.

9. Area Bible Study Small Groups

See chapter 8 for a description.

10. Class 201 (Discipleship)

After students have taken Class 101, we offer Class 201, which focuses on the habits Christians need to develop in order to grow in their faith. During this class we teach about the habits discussed in chapter 9. At the end of the class, students are given an opportunity to commit to the habits of spiritual growth and are given some of the tools that will help them grow.

(Congregation students can move into the committed level simply by asking for the discipleship tools we provide committed students. We do encourage them to go through our *official* door—Class 201—into the committed level, but as with Class 101, it is not mandatory.)

11. Discipleship Tools

See chapter 9 for a description.

12. Praise and Worship (Worship)

Besides our weekend worship services (crowd) and our midweek area Bible study small groups (congregation), Praise and Worship is our only other weekly program. Every Sunday night from 6:00 to 7:00 we have a time when our entire agenda is to honor God through praise and prayer. It's not heavily promoted, but many committed students who want to express themselves to God through an extended time of singing do attend. Since our singing time is limited at our weekend worship services and we don't sing at area Bible studies, some students hunger for a longer time of worship in song. At Praise and Worship a short thought or challenge from the Scriptures is given, but the emphasis is on singing.

We have this service early on Sunday evening so that our students aren't out late two nights a week (the other night being area Bible study small groups). If students can be out only one night a week, we ask that they consistently attend their area Bible study small group but come to Praise and Worship whenever they can. The last Sunday night of every month is our family Praise and Worship to which we invite the students' family members.

13. Missions Monthly (Ministry)

On a monthly basis, we conduct some type of formal or informal missions project in our community or in nearby Mexico. When we are not taking a missions trip to Mexico, we are participating in two student-run ministries called World Shoe Relief and Jackets for Jesus. Students bring used shoes and jackets to church anytime, and our student ministry teams organize occasional shoe and jacket parties, during which the students clean, sort, and lace shoes as well as mend jackets. Then they take the items to homeless shelters or send them to an overseas missions organization. Often, an area Bible study small group will host a shoe or jacket party as a group project.

While most of our missions opportunities are geared for committed students, we will take just about any student on a missions experience regardless of spiritual commitment. If students aren't committed before they leave, they usually are when they return.

Some of our missions opportunities are more demanding than others. The easier tests of serving are our local missions days. We also schedule Mexico work parties twice a year, which require a stronger degree of interest. Once a year we travel to a Third World country (usually Haiti). We would love for all our students to go to Haiti and serve for two weeks, but most need to first experience the responsibilities of a one-day local trip.

14. Bible Institute (Discipleship)

We created the Bible Institute to provide our committed students with more in-depth education. Once a month, we teach one three-hour class on the Bible, theology, or apologetics. We have twenty-four classes under those three main headings.

In the Bible classes, we teach an overview of all of the books and major passages in the Bible:

Introduction to the Bible
Old Testament Overview
The Pentateuch
The History Books
Poetry and Wisdom Literature
The Prophets and Prophecy
New Testament Overview
The Life and Teachings of Jesus
The Book of Acts
The Pauline Epistles
The General Epistles
Hermeneutics

In the theology track, we teach six classes:

Introduction to Theology
Good vs. Evil/Heaven vs. Hell
The Resurrection
Sin, Salvation, and Sanctification
The Church
Eschatology

In the apologetics (defense of the faith) track, we study truth that will help students tell others why they believe what they do. The classes include

Introduction to Apologetics
The Authority and Authenticity of the Bible
Creation and Evolution
Mormonism
Cults
Advanced Evangelism

15. Class 301 (Ministry)

After students take classes 101 and 201, they take Class 301, in which we help them identify their spiritual gifts, temperaments, and talents to see how God has shaped them for ministry. This is the class they must take if they want to begin their own ministry in our church. Anyone can join a ministry team, but if students want to start a ministry, we first help them identify their personal S.H.A.P.E. (Appendix E, see chapter 10). Class 301 is also a requirement for student leadership.

16. Ministry Team Leader

When students complete Class 301 and fill out a S.H.A.P.E. profile (see chapter 10), they usually either start a ministry or become the leader of an existing ministry. This designation was based on a need to help us oversee and care for our expanding ministry teams. Ministry team leaders are core students who, for whatever reason, are not a part of our student leadership team. Their main responsibility as a ministry team leader is to ensure the ministry team functions and to make sure the other students on the particular team are being cared for. These leaders also become the liaison for communication between the students on ministry teams (see number 7) and our adult leadership. For example, when one of the adult leaders wants to know what's going on within a ministry team or needs to access a ministry, we will get in touch with a ministry team leader, and he or she will give us feedback. Many of our quality students who don't have the time or desire for student leadership are ministry team leaders. As with student leadership, leaders in our ministry take the role of servants.

17. Student Leadership

See chapter 10 for a description.

18. Class 401

This is the last stop in our process. In this class, we begin by reviewing all the basics from the other three classes (101, 201, 301). We give students some practical tools to write a life mission statement that will characterize their walk with Christ as well as their call to make a difference in the world. Most of the students who take Class 401 have already made a commitment to the friendship evangelism challenge somewhere along the way, therefore we focus most of the teaching time to understand world missions, the needs, and the opportunities for missions' trips. At the end of the class, students are given an opportunity to commit to one of the extended mission trips our church provides. Most of the students that complete Class 401 don't have an "I've arrived attitude" in regards to our spiritual growth process. These are the students who are eager to get community students involved in the ministry and help their friends through the process.

Now that you've read the descriptions of these secondary programs I want you to keep in mind that nine programs happen on the same day, once a month. We do not accomplish all these programs on a weekly basis. Also, these secondary programs don't all take a lot of programming effort, but they do become an instrumental part of our strategy to move students from the community to the core. A sample schedule of our once-a-month "Super Sunday" follows (see page 224).

REACH
"Go and make disciples"

Evangelism
(mission)

CONNECT
"Baptize them"

Fellowship
(membership)

GROW
"Teach them to do"

Discipleship
(maturity)

DISCOVER
"Love your neighbor"

Ministry
(ministry)

HONOR
"Love the Lord your God"

Worship
(magnification)

THE GREAT COMMANDMENT

"Jesus replied: 'Love the Lord your God with all your heart and with all your soul and with all your mind.' This is the first and greatest commandment. And the second is like it: 'Love your neighbor as yourself.' All the Law and the Prophets hang on these two commandments."

Matthew 22:37-40

THE GREAT COMMISSION

"Therefore go and make disciples of all nations, baptizing them in the name of the Father and of the Son and of the Holy Spirit, and teaching them to obey everything I have commanded you. And surely I am with you always, to the very end of the age." *Matthew 28:19-20*

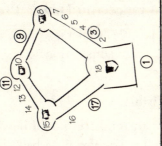

1. FRIENDSHIP EVANGELISM
2. hot-night events
3. WEEKEND WORSHIP SERVICES
4. new believers' class
5. dinner for ten
6. TNT: teens 'n' temptation
7. ministry teams
8. class 101
9. AREA BIBLE STUDY SMALL GROUPS
10. class 201
11. DISCIPLESHIP TOOLS
    quiet-time journal
    S.A.G. five
    hidden treasures
    bank of blessing
    rootworks
12. praise and worship
13. missions monthly
14. Bible institute
15. class 301
16. ministry team leader
17. STUDENT LEADERSHIP
18. class 401

Fig. 12.5

Super Sunday

1:00–3:00 p.m.
- New believers' class
- Class 101
- Class 201
- Class 301
- Class 401
- Student leadership meeting

3:00–5:30 p.m.
- Bible Institute

4:00–5:30 p.m.
- Dinner for Ten

6:00–7:00 p.m.
- Family praise and worship

What to Do Once You Have a Process

A process that sits in a file cabinet is worthless. You will need to take some strategic leadership action to make sure people understand your process.

Make Your Process Visible

The students in your ministry should be visually familiar with your process. Whether you use a baseball diamond, a series of concentric circles, a pyramid, a funnel, an armadillo, or a staircase, students need to see the image on a regular basis.

All of our crowd students have seen our process. Not all of them care about or understand it, but they see it every week. Not only is it hanging on the wall in our meeting room, but it's printed on the back of their weekly message outline (see fig. 12.5).

Identify Key Spots Along Your Process
Where You Ask for Commitments

Classes 101–401 are identified as bases—that is, first base is 101, second base is 201, third base is 301, home plate is 401. When the classes are emphasized on the process chart, it looks like figure 12.6. These four classes serve as the different points within our youth ministry process where we challenge students with various life commitments.

Students only need to take each class once, and all four classes are optional. Students can attend our primary programs without taking the classes (with the exception of student leadership; student leaders must take classes 101 through 301 [see chapter 10]). An outline of the classes follows.[1]

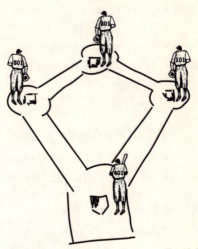

Fig. 12.6

Classes 101 Through 401

First Base: Class 101

What We Teach:

Our salvation (What God has done for us)

- baptism
- the Lord's Supper
- what we believe

Our statement (Why we exist as a church)
Our strategy (How we attempt to fulfill the purposes)

What We Challenge Students to Commit to

- living in Christ
- joining the church (membership)
- connecting to a small group

Second Base: Class 201

What We Teach

Spiritual maturity
Habits necessary for spiritual growth

- quiet times
- accountability
- Bible memorization
- church involvement
- tithing
- Bible study

What We Challenge Students to Commit to

- the H.A.B.I.T.S. of maturity
- using our discipleship tools

Third Base: Class 301

What We Teach

How to discover their God-given S.H.A.P.E.

- spiritual gifts
- heart
- abilities
- personality
- experiences

What We Challenge Students to Commit to

- discovering their ministry
- beginning to serve

Home Plate: Class 401

What We Teach

- Developing a life mission statement
- Developing a world mission (missions)
- Developing a friendship mission (evangelism)

What We Challenge Students to Commit to

- an extended mission experience
- friendship evangelism

Provide Appropriate Promotions Throughout the Process

When you lay out your programs, think through how you will encourage your students to continue taking new steps. For example, we are always promoting Class 101 and area Bible study small groups for the crowd students who attend weekend services. Those programs would be the next logical step for a student to take in our process. There's no need for us to promote Class 301 to crowd students since that is not the next step for them.

We refer to our next step attempts as *gateway promotions*. We ask ourselves, "How do we open the gate to the next program?" For example, when we have a hot-night event, we need to provide a gateway promotion to make sure all unbelievers at the outreach get a flyer inviting them to our weekend services (like the one mentioned on page 214, see fig. 12.4). At our weekend worship services, we promote area Bible study small groups. And at area Bible study small groups, we promote our discipleship tools. For those who have the tools and have taken classes 101 through 301, we encourage student leadership.

Recognize That the Process Doesn't Always Produce the Product

A process will not guarantee spiritual maturity for those who complete it. It's possible for a student to make it through your process and not have the spiritual depth you anticipated, because commitments to programs don't necessarily indicate growth. Jesus faced that same issue with the Pharisees—their feet followed a process but their hearts didn't follow their footsteps. We need to look for signs of maturity measured by a commitment to Christ, spiritual growth, serving, and expressing faith through everyday circumstances.

I encourage you to lay out your programs and plan for movement. Figure 12.7 is a way we lay out our process before placing them around the baseball diamond. Use ours, find another one, or create your own. Begin to show your students that you have a plan to help them with their growth, a plan they can envision through your ministry process.

WHO are we trying to target?	WHAT is our purpose?	HOW will we attempt to do this?	HOW else will we assist movement?
Potential Audience	Primary Purpose	Primary Program	Secondary Program
Community	Evangelism	Friendship evangelism challenge	Hot-night events
Crowd	Worship	Weekend worship services	Special events Ministry teams Dinner for Ten TNT: Teens 'n' Temptation New Believers' study Class 101
Congregation	Fellowship	Midweek area Bible study small groups	Class 201
Committed	Discipleship	Self-initiated discipleship tools • Quiet-Time Journal • S.A.G.Five • Hidden Treasures • Bank of Blessings • Rootworks	Praise and Worship Bible Institute Missions Monthly Class 301
Core	Ministry	Student leadership	Ministry team leader Class 401

Fig. 12.7

MAKING IT PERSONAL

1. Do your programs move students in a sequential order from the community to the core?

2. Do you think a process would be helpful in your youth ministry? What visual symbol could you use to show student progression in your ministry?

3. What are the pros and cons of having commitment classes such as 101, 201, 301, and 401?

4. Evaluate your gateway promotions from one program to the next. Do students know the next step they should take?

5. What would a spiritually mature graduate "look like" when he or she leaves your ministry? Five years after graduating from your youth ministry? Does your program strategy promote and support that picture of spiritual maturity?

6. Do your students understand what a spiritually mature person looks like?

7. What are some ways you can communicate your process for spiritual maturity?

NOTES

1. If you are familiar with the life-development classes from Rick Warren's book *The Purpose-Driven Church*, you will recognize the similarity between the classes. Rick and I have taken the material that we use for our adult classes and rewritten it for students. The edited version of these classes for teenagers takes about two hours to teach rather than the four hours spent with adults. It is available through Making Young Lives Count (see page 397.)

COMPONENT SIX

PLANNED VALUES

THIRTEEN

Defining and Communicating Important Values

As you build for health in your youth ministry, spend time with your leadership team considering what values are important. I refer to these as *planned values* because they won't appear in your ministry spontaneously. For your values to influence your ministry, they must be strategically planned.

In the PDYM model, planned values answer the *what* question in the series of who, what, where, when, why, and how.

- The purposes reveal *why* your ministry exists.
- Potential audience defines *who* you plan to target.
- Programs determine *how* you attempt to reach your target and fulfill a purpose.
- Process communicates *where* you want students to go for spiritual growth.
- Planned values reveal *what* is important to your ministry.
- The power of God determines *when* growth is going to happen.

If you can imagine the above components (purposes, potential audience, programs, and so on) as ingredients of a cake, you will notice that all of them are essential to the recipe. Not one of them is simply icing on the cake. Like the other ingredients, your planned values are a key to the success of your ministry because they influence everything you do. Specifically, planned values are *descriptive words that communicate the values you want to reflect throughout your entire youth ministry.*

Why Are Values Important to a Ministry?

A healthy youth ministry develops a leadership base larger than one person. As leadership expands, planned values need to be expressed to all leaders. Not only must they know why the ministry exists (the five purposes), but they also must understand the values that are to be reflected when pursuing the purposes.

At Saddleback Church we want our adult and student leaders to know our planned values so that each can express them in his or her particular sphere of influence in our youth ministry. For example, a student attending the Trabuco Hills area Bible study should be treated by the leaders there the same as if attending the El Toro area Bible study. Each leader's personality will be different, but the expressed values should be the same.

> Each leader's personality will be different, but the expressed values should be the same.

Where Do Planned Values Come From?

Saddleback Church's youth ministry values were generated by our adult and student leadership teams. First, I asked our adult leaders to tell me what values were important to them. As they talked I made a list of the values they expressed as well as the illustrations they used to define their values. After everyone was finished talking, I affirmed the importance of their values.

Next I met with the student leaders. It was not a good meeting! They didn't seem to understand what I was trying to get from them, but once again God was kind to me when I was in a bind. In a stroke of inspiration, I asked each of them to attend another church! I made it clear that I wasn't kicking them out of our ministry, I simply wanted them to visit other youth ministries where they weren't the center of attention or weren't even known. I assigned each of them to a church and instructed them to go alone so that they wouldn't use a friend as a security blanket.

At our next leadership meeting, these students had much stronger feelings about values. Their visits had caused some of them to feel uncomfortable, alone, and embarrassed. They remembered what it felt like to be a visitor, and they returned with new insights into the values our ministry should hold.

To arrive at a realistic number of values that we could memorize, I combined similar values and prayed for godly wisdom in prioritizing them. I disclosed the final list at our staff and student leadership meetings, and everyone seemed to be proud of the final product. Because they contributed to the list of values, they were eager to commit to them.

Our Planned Values Spell R.E.L.A.T.I.O.N.S.H.I.P.S.

We value relationships in our youth ministry at Saddleback Church. We want students to have a vital relationship with God through Jesus Christ. We want leaders to have solid relationships with one another, with students, and with students' parents. We want students to have accountable relationships with other students and with their own parents; and we want the church body to have a good relationship with the youth ministry. Relationships are the backbone of all our values. Thus, we use the word *relationships* to help us remember our planned values.

R ELATIONAL APPROACH
E NCOURAGEMENT
L AUGHTER AND CELEBRATION
A CCEPTANCE
T RANSPARENCY
I NVOLVEMENT OF STUDENTS
O UTREACH ORIENTATION
N UMERICAL GROWTH
S PIRITUAL GROWTH
H OME-LIKE FEELING
I NTIMACY
P ROFESSIONALISM
S TRATEGIC FOLLOW-UP

Relational Approach

At Saddleback our approach to working with students is to spiritually impact them through relationships, because we know that is the best way to help them grow in their faith. Our leadership style has been greatly influenced by the relational philosophy of the parachurch ministry of Young Life. For several decades, Young Life has successfully modeled the importance of relational youth ministry. Jim Rayburn, founder of Young Life, realized that "a life speaks louder than words" and that "discovery, as well as growth, happens best in the context of relationships." Today many churches and youth ministries are relational by design because they realize that they earn the right to be heard by first caring about people.

> **Leaders earn the right to be heard
> by first caring about people.**

Encouragement

We want our church body to understand the power of words and to use them wisely. The Bible tells us that the tongue is a powerful tool (see James 3:1–12) and that the words that come from our mouths are a reflection of what is in our hearts (Matt. 12:34–35). Relying on the power of God to refresh our hearts enables us to use words that will build people up rather than tear them down (see Eph. 4:29).

Students don't receive much encouragement. School is often a negative environment filled with biting and damaging words, and the home, for many teenagers, is void of genuine affirmation. We want our church to be a place where students are encouraged.

Laughter and Celebration

We also want students to have fun. They are so stressed that church ought to be a place where they can laugh and sense an attitude of joy and celebration. Although we intentionally plan for laughter during our weekend worship services (crowd students), we want a hearty attitude of laughter and celebration to be apparent everywhere within our ministry. We don't require our leaders to be stand-up comedians, but we do look for people who have a good sense of humor and enjoy laughter. We believe we can be serious about God and still joyously celebrate life.

This value is especially significant to me because I gave my life to God at the age of fourteen after hearing a comedian give his testimony. He said that the source of his joy and laughter was God. That was the turning point in my life. God used what was important to me (laughter) to get my attention. To this day, it remains a strong personal and professional value.

Acceptance

If we want to reach students, we must accept them. We value acceptance and want everyone to feel accepted in our youth ministry regardless of looks, grade-point average, campus status, or sports accomplishments. Because of that, we spend a significant amount of time trying to make students feel welcome at our programs.

We want to express acceptance during a student's spiritual journey as well. While we want to challenge students to grow, we realize that each student's spiritual movement will be different. We don't want to turn our backs on students when they struggle; struggle can be a sign of growth. The prodigal son had to leave home and flounder in order to return home. Part of his journey included turning his back on his father. While we don't encourage disobedience in order to prompt growth, we do express acceptance when a student is questioning and struggling. Acceptance doesn't say, "Where have you been?" It says, "Welcome back." This type of unconditional love is at the heart of the Father.

Acceptance doesn't say, "Where have you been?" It says, "Welcome back."

Transparency

We value honesty. We want our leadership to be *real* with students. The old cliché "You can't kid a kid" constantly reminds me that teenagers can easily spot a fake. As our culture increasingly romanticizes fraud, deceit, dishonesty, and cover-ups, it amazes me that our students are increasingly attracted to adults who are transparent. We want to model Christianity for students yet be honest and vulnerable about our journey. We want them to see that struggle and failure are a part of growth and that they are not the only ones who fail. We want transparent students in our ministry, who have learned from transparent adults.

Involvement of Students

We are always asking, "How can we get that student involved in our ministry?" We don't want students just to attend our programs; we want them to be involved through the expression of their gifts. We tell them, "We'd love for you to participate rather than spectate." We try to make it as easy as possible for students to get involved in any area of our ministry.

Outreach Orientation

We place high value on our outreach orientation, and we want to communicate this as many ways as we can so that everyone hears and understands. We don't want leaders to settle into a "maintenance mentality." We want them to be passionate about our mission: to reach the world with the hope of Jesus Christ.

Numerical Growth

Numerical growth is not our only value. We are much more interested in health than numbers. But because health precedes growth, we *expect* our youth ministry to grow numerically as it grows spiritually. We want to grow, not because we want to be the largest youth ministry in the community, but because students need Christ. Numerical growth may also signify that we are meeting needs and fulfilling all the purposes.

We want every youth ministry to grow—not just ours! We don't want to increase by taking in students from other youth ministries. That's not growth; that's swapping sheep. True numerical growth communicates that our students are maturing in their faith and catching the vision for friendship evangelism.

> **We don't want to increase by taking in students from other youth ministries.**

Spiritual Growth

The fact that we value spiritual growth may seem obvious, but we want to make sure everyone knows that our goal is to produce lifelong followers of Christ. We want all our students to grow spiritually. Furthermore, we want students to grow in the way God has planned. Although we have a pathway for spiritual growth, we don't expect everyone's faith to look the same. Spiritual growth is unique and difficult to measure. It can't be franchised, but it can be nurtured.

> **Spiritual growth ... can't be franchised, but it can be nurtured.**

Home-Like Feeling

We want students to feel at home in our church, so we work at developing a family atmosphere within our ministry. We want our leadership to reflect the value that students are important and that church is a place where they belong. We want to know students by name and show we care for them. No matter how big the church gets, we want them to feel like it is their home.

Intimacy

One of the common goals for our entire church is to grow larger and smaller at the same time. We want to grow larger as we express evangelism and smaller as we express fellowship in small groups. Small groups are where students are known and cared for, and where they can develop a close relationship with a leader.

Professionalism

We want people in our church and community to take our youth ministry seriously. We don't want to be perceived as an out-of-control teenage baby-sitting service. We know we have a vital ministry in the church and in the kingdom.

Besides that, respect often precedes resources. If adults in our congregation sense a professional youth ministry and respect us, they are more likely to get involved with their time and resources. If our church elders see that we know what we are doing, they are more likely to advance us financial support to help our ministry.

Strategic Follow-Up

If we say we want our youth ministry to be home-like, then we had better know where our teenagers are. If they don't come to church, we need to follow up on them. Because we hold this value dear, our leadership teams work hard to keep in touch with the students God has entrusted to our care.

After learning about the planned values of Saddleback Church's youth ministry, you may want to consider what values you want reflected in your youth ministry. Take time now to begin a list.

What to Do with Your Planned Values

After you compile a list of values, it takes a significant amount of leadership to make sure they are expressed, known, and evaluated. The following steps may be helpful:

Make Your Values Known

After we stacked hands on our list of planned values (we made guttural teamwork noises) and committed to express them as a team, I had to encourage our leaders to learn them. The steps I described in chapter 4 for helping to make your purpose statement known also apply to planned values. (You may want to review the steps on pages 74–5.) Making our values into an acronym was a memorization technique. If you have difficulty fitting your values into an acronym, you may try another method, such as giving them to your leaders with Bible verses as in figure 13.1.

Model Your Values to Your Leadership

In addition to making the values known, I must model the values if I expect other leaders to express them. When I write notes of encouragement to my leaders, they have a model for the value of encouragement. When I follow up on other leaders, they get an idea of how to do the same with the students in their small groups. Any value can be modeled.

Show How Your Values
Affect Different Areas of Your Ministry

In an attempt to put our values into practice, our leadership team came up with specific ways our planned values could be expressed through leading a small group (see fig. 13.2).

Create Questions to Assess the Effectiveness of Your Values

If your values exist only on paper, they won't do you any good. And even if your leaders memorize your values, the values can become ineffective if they are not evaluated. So have your leadership team create questions that will aid you in reviewing and enhancing the implementation of each value.

RELATIONSHIPS in small groups

FROM GOD'S WORD

Relational approach

"We loved you so much that we were delighted to share with you not only the gospel of God but our lives as well, because you had become so dear to us." *(1 Thessalonians 2:8)*

Encouragement

"Therefore encourage one another and build each other up, just as in fact you are doing." *(1 Thessalonians 5:11)*

Laughter and celebration

"The thief comes only to steal and kill and destroy; I have come that they may have life, and have it to the full." *(John 10:10)*

Acceptance

"My brothers, as believers in our glorious Lord Jesus Christ, don't show favoritism." *(James 2:1)*

Transparency

"I came to you in weakness and fear, and with much trembling. My message and my preaching were not with wise and persuasive words, but with a demonstration of the Spirit's power." *(1 Corinthians 2:3–4)*

Involvement of students

"Now the body is not made up of one part but of many." *(1 Corinthians 12:14)*

Outreach orientation

"Therefore go and make disciples of all nations, baptizing them in the name of the Father and of the Son and of the Holy Spirit." *(Matthew 28:19)*

RELATIONSHIPS in small groups con't.

FROM GOD'S WORD

Numerical growth

"Then the church throughout Judea, Galilee and Samaria enjoyed a time of peace. It was strengthened; and encouraged by the Holy Spirit, it grew in numbers, living in the fear of the Lord." *(Acts 9:31)*

Spiritual growth

"Therefore let us leave the elementary teachings about Christ and go on to maturity." *(Hebrews 6:1)*

Home-like

"In him the whole building is joined together and rises to become a holy temple in the Lord." *(Ephesians 2:21)*

Intimate

"Therefore confess your sins to each other and pray for each other so that you may be healed. The prayer of a righteous man is powerful and effective." *(James 5:16)*

Professional

"A good name is more desirable than great riches; to be esteemed is better than silver or gold." *(Proverbs 22:1)*

Strategic follow-up

"Be sure you know the condition of your flocks, give careful attention to your herds." *(Proverbs 27:23)*

Fig. 13.1

RELATIONSHIPS in small groups

Relational approach

Make it a goal to have a serious conversation with every student in your small group at least once a month.

Encouragement

Praise good questions, answers, and sincere sharing.

Laughter and celebration

Although you don't need to pursue laughter like we do at our weekend services, your small group shouldn't be a funeral.

Acceptance

Remember that spiritual growth won't look the same for everyone in your group.

Transparency

Don't be afraid to openly admit your confusion to some questions and to share your struggles.

Involvement of students

The students in your group should be doing 90% of the talking, which means you should be doing 90% of the listening.

Outreach orientation

Make sure you pray for nonbelievers and that you constantly talk about friendship evangelism.

RELATIONSHIPS in small groups con't.

Numerical growth

Good small groups grow by word of mouth, but they stay small by dividing into more groups. Pray that our leadership base will grow.

Spiritual growth

Your relational investments will pave the way for students' spiritual growth.

Home-like

When a student returns from being absent say, "Welcome back," rather than "Where have you been?"

Intimate

Make small groups happen every week; be consistent.

Professional

Be conscious of parents' perceptions and host families' homes.

Strategic follow-up

Write a letter or make a phone call when a student is absent from your small group.

Fig. 13.2

Our adult and student leadership team came up with three to five questions used for assessing each of our values. We did this by breaking into groups of three people and spending five minutes creating questions for each value. At the end of the hour, I collected the questions, and we used the best ones to compile an evaluation form for our planned values. Below are five questions, for example, that we use to assess our value of acceptance.

ACCEPTANCE

1. Do students feel accepted before, during, and after the meeting? Are all students greeted in the same way regardless of their dress, looks, or attendance record?
2. Does the spoken message isolate students of a particular group, race, or school?
3. Do students leave the meeting with the impression that their presence was appreciated by somebody?
4. Do the leaders express an attitude of concern for each student's personal life?
5. Do adults purposefully meet students, ask their name, and inquire about their personal lives?

The first question was developed by one of our student leaders who is overweight. She said, "I feel like I'm not accepted because of my weight. Everyone else gets a hug, but I get a handshake." She makes a good point. Have you ever noticed how we tend to greet people? Expressive people usually get hugs, while unexpressive people receive a "Hi" and a handshake. The cute, fun, popular students get warm greetings, while the homely, reserved, or unsociable students are often ignored. When we do this, we violate the value of acceptance.

The second question was also developed by one of our student leaders. He noted that I always referred to El Toro High School during my teaching illustrations. Even though we draw

> The cute, fun, popular students get warm greetings, while the homely, reserved, or unsociable students are often ignored.

students from several schools, my stories created the feeling that our ministry is mostly made up of El Toro High students. He said, "You never give illustrations of things that happen at our school." He was right. Hearing that input forced me to be more inclusive in my communication so that students from all schools feel accepted.

We spend a few minutes at each of our monthly leadership meetings reviewing all our values. Then we spend about fifteen minutes focusing on one. This is always a refreshing time of new ideas and a time of challenge to hold our values high.

The thirteen specific planned values I have discussed in this chapter are not an exhaustive and definitive listing for every ministry; they are simply an example. Your planned values will flow from the passions God has implanted in the hearts of your leaders. Discover them, communicate them, evaluate them, and watch God strengthen your ministry because of them.

MAKING IT PERSONAL

1. What are some of your most deeply held values?

2. Would identifying some key values be helpful for your youth ministry? Why or why not? If yes, what are some values that you feel should be represented in your youth ministry?

3. How would these youth ministry values impact your personal ministry to students?

4. What process can you use to discuss and implement an appropriate number of values for your ministry?

5. If you were to start with three values (for example, the ABCs—acceptance, belonging, and cared for), what few questions would best evaluate their effectiveness?

6. Do you feel that your ministry violates some of the important values mentioned in your discussion? If so, which ones and how?

COMPONENT SEVEN

PARENTS

FOURTEEN

Teaming Up with Parents for a Family-Friendly Youth Ministry

Youth workers are becoming increasingly aware that a student-only youth ministry is less effective than a family-friendly youth ministry. Because we rarely see students in their family context, we often underestimate the power of the family. Each student in our youth ministry is the product of a unique family system, a system responsible for forming beliefs, values, and actions. If we plan to effectively minister to students over the long haul, we must sincerely desire to minister to entire families, because a youth ministry that excludes parents is about as effective as a Band-Aid on a hemorrhage.

If you're anything like me, you understand that a family-friendly youth ministry is vital, but you live with guilt because you've been slow to move in that direction. You're probably already overwhelmed by what it takes to develop a ministry to students, let alone to their families. Plus, there are very few models, resources, and practical ideas on how to minister to both parents *and* students. The youth ministry *world* has been quick to challenge us to change our focus from *youth ministry* to *ministry of youth and their families*, but it has been slow to show us the practical side of this new paradigm.

The complexity of the family and our ability to minister to it can't be captured in one chapter. This subject is broad, and besides, I'm not the best one to provide ground-breaking ideas for effective family-based youth ministry. Of all the chapters in this book, I write this one more out of necessity than credibility. Prior to coming to Saddleback, I had a healthier youth and family ministry than I presently do, mostly because I worked at that church for eleven years. A youth *and* family ministry takes time to develop.

If, during the formative era of youth ministry, youth worker pioneers had created an integrated family ministry, we might have a more holistic youth ministry approach today. Since this didn't happen, we must start over, developing a philosophy of youth ministry that promotes taking intentional steps to be more involved in family life. I pray that some courageous churches in the twenty-first century will give us new models for youth and family ministry (I pray Saddleback will be one of them). I challenge you to begin integrating your youth ministry, the church, and the family in a more effective manner. I believe the biggest change will be in attitude rather than in direction or program components.

Be advised that neither parents nor students want a totally integrated parent-teen youth ministry. Although parents are more open to a family-friendly youth ministry than students, most appreciate a youth ministry *for* their kids and not *with* their kids. And it is no surprise that most students prefer the traditional compartmentalized youth ministry where they can have an autonomous church experience away from their parents. Some of this can be explained as adolescents' natural desire for independence from their parents. In addition, most students have only been exposed to age-segregated youth ministry.

A family-friendly youth ministry is based on a series of progressive steps that build on one another and lead toward a stronger family focus. These steps go from the general, requiring little time, to the specific, requiring more time, energy, and resources for implementation. The steps we have taken at Saddleback Church follow.

Step 1: Create a Teamwork Mentality

A family-friendly youth ministry begins when leaders are mature enough to realize that parents are not the enemy. When we understood that students would be healthier if they were ministered to with their families, we moved toward a family-friendly youth ministry. We saw the win-win-win potential for students, parents, and us.

For some youth workers, this reality comes with age, experience as a parent, or spiritual maturity. It did with me. Prior to becoming a parent, I was intimidated by parents of teenagers. Although unspoken, I felt an element of competition for students' time. I didn't view parents as partners, but as enemies who slowed down my plans to produce disciples. I had a bit of a boot-camp mentality regarding youth ministry. I wanted parents to give me (as the omniscient guru of youth ministry) their kids when they were in junior high. I planned to have them converted, baptized, educated, sanctified, dry-cleaned, and ready for pick up when they were eighteen. I maintained this attitude until I realized that my role and influence in a student's life were limited and that our youth ministry was superficial without a focus on the family.

Figure 14.1 shows the image I now have of teamwork. Three major influences work together to help a student grow in faith. The more the three parties can work together and move toward one circle, the more powerful the results of the team-work. It is not the intent of this chapter, however, to explore the church's role and the parents' role. Instead, let's focus on our role as youth workers and see what we can do to strengthen our part of the team.[1]

Fig. 14.1

Recognize Your Limited Role as a Youth Worker

I was able to develop a teamwork attitude when I finally realized that God expects parents to take primary responsibility for their children's spiritual maturity. Moses gave this instruction in Deuteronomy 6:5–7: "Love the LORD your God with all your heart and with all your soul and with all your strength. These commandments that I give you today are to be upon your hearts. Impress them on your children. Talk about them when you sit at home and when you walk along the road, when you lie down and when you get up."

This passage doesn't ask parents to shift their spiritual responsibility to youth workers. Our role in a student's spiritual development is helpful, but a parent's role is crucial. The more I understood this Scripture, the more I recognized what had been arrogant control on my part. I released the primary obligation back to parents, and I saw my position as parents' assistant in the spiritual development of their teens. Obviously, a youth worker's role increases if students come from unchurched families.

> Our role in a student's spiritual development is helpful, but a parent's role is crucial.

Develop Relationships with Parents

It is impossible to create healthy teamwork with people you don't know. Chapter 11 refers to relational ministry with students as the backbone of a healthy youth ministry. That same relational principle applies to parents. For me, it means that I conscientiously attempt to meet parents and memorize their names. It also means that I find ways to spend time with parents. For example, when I go to a high school football game, I spend one half sitting with students and the other half with parents. I also occasionally try to meet parents for lunch at their place of work and show an interest in their occupation. I once spent an entire day shadowing a dad who is a doctor. He gave me a white gown to wear, a stethoscope, and a clipboard. Not only was it a fun day for me, but I also gained a new friend, supporter, and a few gross stories.

Remember that youth workers don't get together with parents to teach them parenting skills, but to develop relationships with them, to learn from them, and to talk about their kids and the roles we each play.

Ask Parents About Their Fears

My teamwork mentality strengthened when I understood what parents of adolescents go through. When I stopped *pretending* to care about parents and started listening to them, I heard intense feelings of pain, fear, and inadequacy. Some of these feelings stemmed from the fact that their kids were growing up and their parental role didn't seem to be needed as much anymore. Their adolescents' independence was troubling. I heard deep emotion when parents spoke of their loss of communication and attachment. The most expressive feelings were rooted in the fear that their children would no longer embrace their faith and values. When we take time to understand parents' feelings, we will be impassioned to help them and inspired to work with them.

Be Sensitive to Family Priorities

Teamwork mentality minimizes a youth ministry calendar so parents can maximize their family priorities. You can't be a family-friendly youth ministry and demand that students be out of the home several nights a week. Teach your students to always check with their parents to decide what programs they will attend. Consistently ask parents to give you their honest evaluation of your youth ministry schedule. Your calendar may be pleasing students while frustrating parents. (Remember, spiritual growth shouldn't be dependent on program attendance. See chapter 9.)

> **Your calendar may be pleasing students while frustrating parents.**

Support Parental Teaching

If you want parents to know your youth ministry's purpose and to support your programs (as we discussed in chapter 3), be an advocate of their important messages as well. Some students will listen to family messages from youth workers that they won't tolerate hearing from their parents. During your teaching time you can reinforce decent family values along with the biblical messages of obeying and honoring parents.

At least once a year, invite parents to tell you what they are teaching at home. You will get a wealth of feedback that can enrich your teaching. While I won't teach a lesson on the biblical view of keeping a bedroom clean, I will teach basic family messages like respect, responsibility, and concern for others.

Step 2: Keep Communication Clear

Most parents don't like to be surprised by spontaneous program plans. They like to be informed about youth ministry events well ahead of time so they can schedule priorities into their family calendar. If you want parents on your team, you must communicate.

Communicate Regularly

In addition to your calendar of programs and events, send parents an information letter (monthly or quarterly depending on your time, help, and resources). This will keep them updated in case they have misplaced your ministry calendar, have forgotten the announcements from the last parents' night, or aren't being informed by their teens. See a sample update letter in figure 14.2. (My monthly letters aren't fancy, but they are effective communication pieces.)

As a general rule, the earlier parents know about event dates and costs, the better. One example of family-friendly communication is having the dates of your major events published six to nine months in advance and your summer calendar completed and available by Easter Sunday at the latest. You don't need to have all your events planned this early, but you should at least have the dates blocked out so families can plan their vacations.

PARENTS' UPDATE

Doug's Top 10 Things Every Parent Should Know

January

1. MEXICALI

During Easter break we join over 4,000 high school students from across the country to work in Mexicali, Mexico. The name of the trip is MEXICALI, and it's a life-changing week. We work in poverty-stricken villages and help the local churches by organizing lessons and activities for the children. It would take 1,000 words to describe this trip, so if you would like more information, please let us know and we'll send you a brochure right away. The dates are April 6–12 and the cost is $199.

2. DINNER FOR 10

Every month I have ten students over to my house for dinner. It's one way to make our big group small. It's also a perfect way for those who don't know many (or anyone) to make some good contacts. Please call for reservations.

3. 12–HOUR BLITZ

On Friday, March 17, at 7:00 p.m. to March 18 at 7:00 a.m. we will take a bus to several fun spots throughout Orange County. This is our third year for this all-niter and it has always been a great night. The cost is $39 and space is limited.

4. CAN WE HELP YOU FIND AN AREA BIBLE STUDY SMALL GROUP?

They are in full swing! We have twenty different ABS groups that meet Monday through Thursday nights. This is a great time for your student to connect with students from their campus or their neighborhood. It is one of the best ways we make our large group small with Bible study, small groups, and prayer. We'd love to have one of our leaders call and invite your son/daughter to an ABS. Please call and let us know if we can help.

5. ROOTWORKS

We have a take-home Bible study called Rootworks that is intended to help students study the Bible. The first volume is a verse-by-verse study of Philippians. Encourage your son/daughter to give it a try. (We also have Hidden Treasures, Bank of Blessings, and a Quiet-Time Journal to help develop spiritual disciplines.)

Fig. 14.2

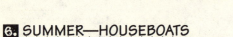

PARENTS' UPDATE

Doug's Top 10 Things Every Parent Should Know con't.

6. SUMMER—HOUSEBOATS

August 12–17: Mark your calendars. Save your money. An incredible camping experience!

7. VALUE INPUT

I know you are swamped, but I would love to share any input you have with our youth ministry staff. I want to hear family success stories and how we can better serve your family. Anything you put in writing can be shared with our volunteer staff and become an ongoing encouragement. We'd really like to hear from you!

8. PARENTS' NIGHT

On Wednesday, January 29, we are having a Parents' Night for all parents and their teenagers. We have a great night planned! Please set this night aside and we'll see you at 7:00 p.m. in room 500. (Also, don't forget parents' Praise and Worship on January 26 at 6:00 p.m. in the green room.)

9. STILL NEED MORE PARENTS ON PRAYER TEAM

If you are one of those parents who has read my last two letters and said, "I'm sure there are a lot of parents to pray; surely they don't need me," we do need your prayers! I want our ministry prayed for on a continual basis. We will send you prayer requests from within our ministry if you will commit to pray for them. Drop us a note or call us if you're interested.

10. MEMORIZED IT YET?

Our youth ministry exists to REACH nonbelieving students, to CONNECT them with other Christians, to help them GROW in their faith, and to challenge the growing to DISCOVER their ministry and HONOR God with their life.

Communicate Encouragement

When my first child, Torie, was in kindergarten, I learned the value of being affirmed as a parent. What a great feeling! During our parent-teacher conference, the teacher spent a great deal of time telling Cathy and me wonderful stories about Torie. She told us that Torie was a delight to have in class and that she was amazed at Torie's kindness and compassion for other students. We couldn't have been happier parents! We left the meeting appreciating the school and thanking God for the teacher and the fact that Torie was in her class.

Take advantage of every opportunity to brag about kids to parents. Write them letters, leave them messages at their work, or find them in the church parking lot and bless them with a story or an example of what you appreciate about their child. I know a youth worker who races to the phone after his Wednesday night junior high meeting so he can call parents and brag about their child's behavior, participation, and input. He is a great example of a family-friendly youth worker!

> **Take advantage of every opportunity to brag about kids to parents.**

Communicate Professionalism

One of the ways to keep parents on your team is to present yourself and your ministry in a professional manner. If you follow your own best instincts, as well as some of the ideas in this book, you will convey the image of a professional, purpose-driven youth ministry that communicates to parents that you know what you are doing. Professionalism includes handling yourself well around parents. They watch how you dress, how you talk, and how you respond to them on an adult-to-adult level. Although I would rather be throwing a football in the church parking lot with students after a program, I choose to greet the parents as they arrive to pick up their kids. It isn't as much fun, but parents value the gesture.

Encourage Two-Way Communication

A professional youth ministry encourages and creates an atmosphere for two-way dialogue. Since you usually do most of the talking and informing, provide parents an opportunity to give you constructive input on how you can better serve their families. I would much rather have parents talk directly to me when they have a question about or problem with something in our ministry than to hear it through the rumor mill. When parents come to me, I can provide answers and address issues before gossip starts.

Recently, a father and son were discussing the topic of inappropriate music. The dad was objecting to certain lyrics and told the son that he didn't want him listening to that type of music. The son said, "At church Doug teaches that it's okay for us to listen to any type of secular music we want." The family debate increased as the convincing boy said, "You want me to go to church, so I go to church. I try to follow my youth pastor's teaching, but now you don't want me to follow it when it offends you." The dad was confused because he couldn't believe I would teach what his son said I was teaching. He became angry when his son used the church to support his music selections. Instead of calling me—which would have been good two-way communication—the dad shared the situation with his small group and asked them to pray about my "heretical" teaching. These men passed the story on to their wives. Soon my youth ministry leadership was being criticized by people I didn't even know.

Before long the entire planet thought I was a wolf in sheep's clothing. As soon as I heard about the rumor, I called the boy's father. During our discussion I assured him that I didn't say what I was quoted as saying. I explained what I had said: "Most non-Christians aren't going to change their music until their hearts have been changed." That was a totally different message than he had heard from his son. I mentioned that he might want to listen to the message, which I had recorded (for such reasons). Although this situation wasn't fun, it did give the dad and me an opportunity to talk, learn from each other, and discuss ways we can work as a team the next time something like this happens. Healthy two-way communication can stop potential problems.

Step 3: Find Family Resources

One way to build a family-friendly youth ministry is to have quality family resources, such as books, magazines, and videos available to parents. This is an ongoing task because there are new family resources coming out all the time. Providing informative material shows your concern for families and your desire to offer practical solutions for the issues they are facing. If you don't have the time or ability to track down resources, contact a local Christian bookstore and ask them to help you keep current on parenting resources. You can also ask a larger church if they have a list of resources you may copy for your parents.

As you gather new resources, notify parents in your update letters. Allow parents access to your audiocassette and video library, and ask them to share with you resources they find. You may not have all the answers for parents, but you can still minister to them by pointing them in the right direction.

Find "Been There" Parents

Because my parenting experience is limited to small children, I often feel inadequate when parents of teenagers ask me what I should do about their drug-addict son, for example. I generally have some ideas, and I can pray for them, but I've found that I can really help these hurting parents when I put them in touch with other parents, in the church, who have "been there."

During a parent night, I will ask parents if they would feel comfortable talking to a hurting family about a specific pain they may have experienced. If they are open to sharing, I ask them to list what they're willing to talk about. I found parents who will talk about their child's death, teenage pregnancy, rebellion, occult involvement, use of Internet pornography, drug abuse, you name it. I simply gather the names and keep them in a file for when struggling parents call.

When I get these calls, I direct them to our "been there" parents who can offer ideas and hope. I usually say, "I can't guarantee you're going to get incredible counseling, but I can assure you this person is willing to talk about what she went through with her son when he was heavily involved with drugs," or whatever the case may be.

Step 4: Facilitate Family Learning

Family resources are often a quick fix that need to be followed up with something more personal than a book or tape. A family-friendly youth ministry offers educational opportunities for parents to ask questions and look for personalized answers. If you aren't experienced at successfully parenting teenagers, don't pretend that you are. Find some mature Christian parents to assist you.

Use Experienced Parents As Teachers

I caution youth workers not to teach on parenting if they haven't been a parent of teenagers. Parents of teenagers realize that my three children give me some insight into the roles and tasks of parenting, but since my children are not yet teens, they don't enhance my credibility as a parent of teenagers. To be honest, I don't know how to parent teenagers.

> **I caution youth workers not to teach on parenting if they haven't been a parent of teenagers.**

What I can do, though, is find men and women in our church who have parented adolescents and ask them to share their ideas. The most successful educational experience we offer is our parenting panel—four or five experienced parents sit on a panel and answer questions. I play the role of facilitator and direct the questions from parents to the appropriate "experts." By doing this, I don't have to have all of the answers, and my presence shows my teamwork, support, and concern.

Share Your Cultural Expertise

Just because you don't have teenagers doesn't mean that you have nothing to offer parents. As a youth worker, you probably know more about adolescent culture than most parents in your church and can keep parents abreast of cultural trends. As you educate parents on teenage culture, you can also express what you believe today's students need from their families. You don't have to give specific parenting advice, but you can give general family principles. For example, you might teach on culture for a little bit and then say something like, "I'm not a parent of a teenager, so my parenting experience is limited. I am a student of culture, however, and I spend much of my time with your teenagers. Based on what I understand about culture, what I know about today's students, and what I hear your kids saying, it is my belief that students need the following three things from their parents. The first thing is ..."

Create "I'm Normal" Meetings

Parents need to feel that what happens in their home is normal. Parents find it liberating when they realize they are not alone in their situation. This "I'm normal" experience can happen when you bring parents together to talk or when you organize parents' small groups. Several years ago we held a parents' night that focused on youth culture and the latest musical trends. About fifteen minutes into my presentation, a parent interrupted, "My daughter has an 11:00 P.M. curfew but never comes in until after 11:30 P.M. I want to know what I should do." (To this day, I still don't get the connection between my explanation of the song "Hotel California" by the Eagles and her question.) I didn't know what to say to her.

> **Parents find it liberating when they realize they are not alone in their situation.**

I knew what I'd do with my three-year-old, but I didn't think it would be appropriate to answer, "Take away her tricycle," so I said, "Does anyone else in here have a curfew problem?" Several hands shot up! I asked, "What would you suggest for her situation?" Discussion exploded immediately. The parents rearranged chairs, turning them from the front to face one another, and I never got to finish my fabulous dissertation on the cultural influence of music.

That night I learned an important lesson: Parents can minister to parents. They left the meeting thanking me for my help, and I hadn't done anything! Their comments affirmed to one another that each of them was not the only one struggling. One mom said, "I came here feeling a little depressed about my situation. Now I feel pretty normal." After this particular parents' night, I asked one of our youth staff, a father of a teenager, to facilitate a similar parents' meeting every other month. He was thrilled. I never went to another meeting, and the attendance stayed consistent. Parents weren't coming to hear me; they were coming to talk and listen, to find out if they were normal.

Step 5: Design Family Programs

This fifth family-friendly step may require you to venture into some new territory for programming. Ask yourself, "Do we have a current youth ministry program that we can convert into a family program?" This family program might be yearly, quarterly, monthly, or weekly. If you plan to team up with parents, you have to look at your programs and evaluate realistic opportunities for including families.

We took our weekly Praise and Worship, a secondary program geared for committed students (see pages 218–19, chapter 12), and made it a once-a-month family Praise and Worship. The students weren't too excited about sitting with ol' Mom and Dad! Some parents were mildly interested, but they were questioning the value of this time. The first month we tried it, our attendance dropped eighty percent. The majority of our regular students didn't show, and the parental response was weak. During the next month we made individual contacts with several parents and personally invited them to "round two." The second month was much better. Not only did we have a great turnout, but we had a great time.

The response to this family program has been extremely positive and has spread to more families in our church. We even have some parents begging for more frequent times of worship together. Because our students don't regularly attend the weekend church service with their parents, we felt it was important to create opportunities for our students to worship with their parents. This monthly time of praise and worship has been a great addition to our attempt to develop a family-friendly youth ministry.

Use Your Crowd Program for a Regular Parents' Night

Constantly invite parents to be part of your crowd program so they can see and experience what *really* happens behind closed doors. Parents are always welcome, but we extend a formal invitation three times a year. We use these open houses to show off our student ministry teams and the quality of our program. During the teaching time, we usually address the parent-child relationship and focus on communication or conflict management. This also is a good time to share our vision for a parent-youth ministry approach.

Create Table Talk Through Your Congregation Program

Every week we send our students home from their area Bible studies with some discussion questions for the entire family. We also ask students to initiate dialogue that focuses on their Bible study lessons during a weekly dinner. In addition to discussing the table-talk questions, every week we urge our students to share the information from their Bible study notebooks with their parents. We suggest they reteach the lesson to their parents so that the parents know what they are learning. We realize that many of our students don't do this, and we don't even attempt to enforce it, but we do mention it often. Below are some examples of our table-talk questions.

TABLE-TALK: BIBLE STUDY ON JAMES 1:2–18

1. What are the two biggest trials we are facing as a family?
2. Why do you think Paul said we should consider our trials a joy?
3. What benefits do you think might come out of our family trials?
4. What does wisdom have to do with experiencing trials?
5. How should our family respond when we are faced with trials?
6. What is an example of a past trial that we have gone through, and what did we learn from it?

Facilitate Family Fun

Healthy youth ministries plan fun times for families throughout the year. These times might include a talent show, a scavenger hunt car rally, a weekend retreat, a one-day picnic filled with wacky games, or a food feast Super Bowl party. The ideas are negotiable, but the principle of facilitating family fun is vital.

Step 6: Add Parents to Your Volunteer Team

Bringing parents into your leadership team can be one of the wisest moves you make as a youth worker. If you enlist the right parents for your team, you will discover a new level of support and enthusiasm. Having parents on the staff builds a family-friendly youth ministry and brings a strong sense of ownership to the ministry because the parents are each committed to their own teen's spiritual growth. These parents are a unique channel of positive support and communication to other parents since they represent the youth ministry from an insider's perspective. Parent volunteers also often have compassion for hurting parents, and they serve as role models for students who don't have spiritually healthy parents.

Make sure your students have input as to how they feel about their parents being involved in the ministry. (This is discussed further in chapter 15.)

Step 7: Offer Parents a Spiritual Life Plan

When I started attending parent-teacher conferences at my daughter's school, I was impressed by the teacher's desire to include Cathy and me in the overall plan of our child's education. The teacher asked us what we thought was important for our daughter to learn. She explained her desire for us to work as a team so both the school and home environments would be aiming toward the same goals. I was inspired to try this same type of formal plan with parents in our youth ministry. We call it a spiritual life plan.

A spiritual life plan is based around the five purposes of our ministry. When parents express an interest, one of our leaders meets with them at least one time during the year for a parent-youth worker conference. The primary purpose of a spiritual life plan is to determine how parents and ministry can work as a team to encourage the teenager's spiritual life. At the meeting the youth worker reviews the five purposes from the Great Commandment and the Great Commission (see chapter 2). The worker shows the parents our youth ministry's process (chapter 12), and then they discuss how to work together to coach the teenager in evangelism, worship, fellowship, discipleship, and ministry. They use the meeting time to arrive at some specific actions, and the leader documents these actions. The leader also writes down any special requests and/or concerns parents might have for their teenager. They end the meeting with prayer. The leader makes a photocopy of what was discussed and gives the original to the parents. This time is most effective when a student knows that a youth worker is meeting with his or her parents.

Since our youth ministry already has a strategy based on the five purposes, our role in a student's life doesn't change much as a result of a spiritual life plan. We walk alongside a student through the maturity process regardless of whether he or she has a spiritual life plan. What does change is our understanding of the family and our sensitivity to the student.

At Saddleback we make spiritual life plans available to all parents of teenagers. I did the first few by myself and then trained other leaders to facilitate the meetings. Our ideal is for the student's small-group leader to do the spiritual life plan because it results in more contact and stronger accountability. Parents who take time to pursue a spiritual life plan typically leave with a greater understanding of our ministry and a new appreciation for how our youth staff wants to team up with them.

If you try spiritual life plans in your youth ministry, don't get discouraged if parents lack interest. It is a fairly intimidating experience. I don't push parents to meet with me; I make the time available, communicate my teamwork mentality, and recommend that they begin the plan when they are ready.

Working with families isn't easy, but it is rewarding for you, your families, and your church body. This type of family-friendly spirit is essential for healthy youth ministry.

As you develop your own steps or personalize the seven from this chapter, make them available to parents. Let them see that you are trying to create a family-friendly youth ministry. We send a letter to every parent every year to communicate our desire for a family-friendly youth ministry.

MAKING IT PERSONAL

1. What are some reasons a family-friendly youth ministry has been difficult to achieve?
2. What do you perceive as parents' fears of parenting?
3. Has your youth ministry been insensitive to families in the past? If so, how?
4. What are some ways you can better communicate with parents?
5. How do you think church members and/or parents perceive your youth ministry?
6. Who are some godly parents who could serve as experienced teachers of parents?
7. What is one program you currently host for students only that you could modify to do with students and their families?

NOTES

1. Chap Clark, in his book *The Youth Worker's Handbook for Family Ministry* (Grand Rapids: Zondervan, 1997), suggests practical ways for youth ministry teams, church bodies, and families to work together.

COMPONENT EIGHT

PARTICIPATING LEADERS

FifTeen

Finding the Leaders
Your Students Deserve

L eaders can make or break a ministry. A youth ministry without adequate leadership can never be healthy, but one with an abundance of quality leaders will always have the potential for health. Proverbs 11:14 readily applies: "For lack of guidance a nation falls, but many advisers make victory sure."

Understaffed youth ministries are often overburdened, stressed, and too tired for new vision. They fall into maintenance mode and stagnate. That is why it is so important for youth workers to start their ministries right by finding good leaders and learning to become a leader of leaders. If you are in a church that doesn't empower the congregation to do the work of the ministry, leadership development will be particularly difficult. Even ministries in churches that constantly challenge people to get involved struggle to find enough leaders.

> **Understaffed youth ministries are often overburdened, stressed, and too tired for new vision.**

This and the following chapter are based on three principles of leadership:

1. You can do it; you just can't do it alone (chapter 15).
2. God has the leaders; you just have to find them (chapter 15).
3. Students deserve leaders who minister, not simply chaperones who control crowds (chapter 16).

While these principles may seem simplistic, the amount of work that goes into quality leadership development never ends. It is a continuous cycle of finding leaders, training them, nurturing their spiritual growth, empowering them to do ministry, and motivating them to continue. The more quality leaders you have, the more your students will spiritually mature. As students grow spiritually, your ministry will grow numerically, and this growth will require additional leaders. Developing leaders is the best mix of blessing and burden I know of in the church. It is a *blessing* to watch adults minister to students, and it is a *burden* to find the adults, train them, and motivate them.

You Can't Do It Alone!

We see high turnover in youth ministry because many youth workers try to do everything themselves. Some youth workers tell me that they don't have enough time to find leaders; they don't have enough time because they are too busy doing everything themselves.

This is not a new problem. The famous leadership passage in Exodus 18 reveals that Moses tried to lead the people of Israel by himself until his father-in-law, Jethro, stepped in and said:

> What you are doing is not good. You and these people who come to you will only wear yourselves out. The work is too heavy for you; you cannot handle it alone. Listen now to me and I will give you some advice, and may God be with you. . . . select capable men from all the people—men who fear God, trustworthy men who hate dishonest gain—and appoint them as officials over thousands, hundreds, fifties and tens. . . . That will make your load lighter, because they will share it with you. If you do this and God so commands,

you will be able to stand the strain, and all these people will
go home satisfied. (vv. 17–23)

Go back through that passage and underline these important words:

- "What you are doing is not good"
- "You will only wear yourselves out"
- "The work is too heavy for you; you cannot handle it alone"
- "Select capable men [and, in our case, women] . . . who
  fear God"
- "Appoint them"
- "That will make your load lighter, because they will share
  it with you"
- "You will be able to stand the strain"
- "People will go home satisfied"

Jethro told Moses that people would go home satisfied because
they would be cared for and have their needs met. This advice is
thousands of years old but still applies to leadership today.

When I'm asked about the best student-to-leader ratio, I
often point to Jesus' example. He was God, and he had a twelve-
to-one ratio. Because of his relationship with Peter, James, and
John, I could even suggest that his ratio was more like three to
one. While I don't believe there is one answer for every youth
ministry setting, I do know the magic number is definitely less
than twelve. At Saddleback we try to set our goal at a five-to-one
ratio for our small groups, but most of our leaders still have a
difficult time trying to invest in and care for five students.

Both Jethro's words and Jesus' example show us our need for
assistance. With this imperative comes the greater obligation to
trust God for leaders. One of the promises I apply to finding leaders is Psalm 55:22: "Cast your cares on the LORD and he will sustain you; he will never let the righteous fall." This verse reminds
me that God is much more concerned about our youth ministry
than I am. I love our students deeply, but God cares more about
them than I can even imagine. Because he is concerned about

them, he watches out for our leadership more than I do. Students without leaders are like sheep without shepherds, and Jesus tells us to ask for workers to care for the sheep: "When he [Jesus] saw the crowds, he had compassion on them, because they were harassed and helpless, like sheep without a shepherd. Then he said to his disciples, 'The harvest is plentiful but the workers are few. Ask the Lord of the harvest, therefore, to send out workers into his harvest field'" (Matt. 9:36–39). These promises have made me confident that God has the leaders for our ministry; we just need to find them.

You Can Do It! A Five-Step Process for Finding Leaders

Our role is to be faithful doing the possible and to have faith that God will do the impossible. The steps that follow will help you do the possible in your search for good leaders. These steps make up an ongoing process. It is not realistic to finish the first step and never revisit it. As your ministry grows, you will never finish these steps; you will always be involved in the process.

Step 1: Think About Your Leadership Attitude

Your attitude about leaders will impact your methods of finding them. I prefer the word *leader* over *volunteer*. I like *leader* because it connotes action and affirms the value of the leader. *Volunteer* communicates that someone is needed to fill a slot no one else wants; it isn't as positive as *leader*. Your ability to find volunteer leaders begins with how you view them.

The "We Need Volunteers to Survive" Attitude

This attitude says, "I need someone to fill this slot, take over this responsibility, or teach this class." It is usually the result of being overwhelmed with ministry demands. This type of youth minister meets potential volunteers with desperate eyes and a pleading voice and settles for anyone instead of finding the right person for the job. Every youth pastor I know has horror stories of "I'll take anyone" volunteers who turn out to be a problem.

The "We Need Leaders to Thrive" Attitude

Youth ministers with this attitude are less overwhelmed by the tasks and are more concerned about nurturing students. They look at potential leaders as ministers and consider the unique way God has shaped them for ministry. These youth ministers are eager, but not desperate, to fill slots. They believe that the right people will flourish as leaders and that students will prosper because of their ministry.

Your attitude about potential leaders will affect your style of finding them and training them for ministry. A thrive attitude allows you to empower leaders to do ministry, because you really believe that God can and will work through them.

Step 2: Shatter Existing Stereotypes

We make the job of finding leaders more difficult when we perpetuate existing stereotypes of a youth worker profile. For years I have been asking people in the church how they would describe a good youth worker. Here are the top ten responses:

- young
- funny
- athletic
- good in front of crowds
- strong teacher
- has Bible knowledge
- outgoing personality
- charisma
- understands youth culture
- owns a van

When you look at this list, it is easy to understand why most people in our churches are reluctant to volunteer: They don't fit the description! These qualities represent a minuscule part of the body of Christ and only one type of youth worker—a rare one.

If you want to find leaders, give your congregation a new image of what a youth worker looks like. I tell the people in our church that we are looking for two qualities—a love for God and a heart for students. I say, "If you love God and care for students you can become a great youth worker. That's all it takes to start!" Then I show them a list of the types of leaders we're looking for:

senior citizens	college students
introverts	mechanics
young marrieds	single parents
musicians	accountants
high school dropouts	mature Christians
bowlers	people with rough pasts
bikers	computer nerds
new Christians	athletes
parents	entrepreneurs
ex-cheerleaders	busy people
blue collar workers	cooks
artists	administrators
old marrieds	professional wrestlers

We compiled this list to communicate that we need all types of leaders to minister to all types of students. I can't relate or minister to all the students in our ministry. I'm a flamboyant extrovert who greets and hugs everyone in the room. Some of our intensely introverted students think I'm scary. They need introverted leaders to sit next to them and have quiet conversations with them.

After working with hundreds of volunteers over the years, I've learned that the best leaders have not been the ones I would have picked out of a crowd. It may surprise you to know that some of the best volunteers are much older than the youth leader stereotype. I brought a man named Marv Ashford onto our volunteer team (at my previous church) when he was in his mid-seventies. I no longer pastor at that church, but Marv is well into his eighties and still working with students there today. He is a great youth worker! He is sensitive, consistent, encouraging, and passionate about students. He has a powerful ministry with parents because he has walked in their shoes and speaks the truth. Marv isn't flashy, and he doesn't know much about youth culture. He couldn't name one current band and probably doesn't know what MTV is. But he stands by the door as students walk into Sunday school class, and he gives them a grandpa hug and says, "You know Marv loves you, don't you?" They all do! These students are impressed with his genuine love, authentic expressions, and his aged wisdom. Youth ministries need to shatter their stereotypes and begin looking for candidates like Marv, who love God and have a heart for students.

> **I've learned that the best leaders have not been the ones I would have picked out of a crowd.**

Step 3: Simplify Your Serving Opportunities

Many of us lose potential leaders because we limit our serving opportunities to two positions—*All* or *Nothing*. Everyone in your church is a potential youth worker if you provide serving opportunities that are more simplified and less threatening than working directly with students.

The following diagram shows four different types of leadership teams. Notice the progression of the four teams within the church body. The more you move down the funnel, the more difficult it becomes to find this type of leader.

As we have seen, step one teaches that we should view leaders as ministers rather than as volunteer position-fillers. Step two teaches that a variety of people can minister to students. Step three is important because it

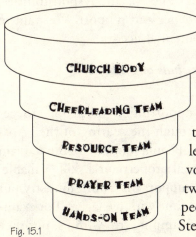

CHURCH BODY

CHEERLEADING TEAM

RESOURCE TEAM

PRAYER TEAM

HANDS-ON TEAM

Fig. 15.1

emphasizes that everyone in the church body can now be viewed as a potential candidate for youth ministry.

If you really believe that all Christians are called to do ministry, then every Christian should be seen as a potential youth worker. Your job isn't to tell people that it is God's will for them to be in youth ministry, but it is your job to make the church body aware of your needs and of the opportunities to serve in your ministry.

> **If you really believe that all Christians are called to do ministry, then every Christian should be seen as a potential youth worker.**

Gather Names for a Cheerleading Team

Our cheerleading team consists of people in our church body who show support for our youth ministry or for one of our leaders. Anytime someone says something positive about our ministry, our students, or our staff, we write his or her name down as someone who is friendly toward youth ministry. Then we occasionally call to gauge their interest in being involved in one of the other teams or in attending one of our special events. Cheerleaders have no specific responsibilities; they just shower us with confidence and support. We want to identify them for our future potential needs.

Gather People with Possessions or Skills for a Resource Team

This team provides an opportunity for people to get involved in youth ministry through the sharing of their possessions or specialized abilities. People join our resource team by making some of their personal property or a skill available. These are people who want to support our youth ministry but don't necessarily want to spend time with teenagers. For example, they don't want to go on a camping trip with us, but they are happy to let us borrow their tent. They don't want to direct our drama team, but they can build our sets.

Every church body has available resources which would be useful to those in youth ministry. One of the mistakes we generally make is to assign our hands-on leaders, who have limited time, to finding the resources we need for our events. By doing this, we waste their potential ministry time with students. For example, if Misha can give the youth ministry two hours a week, I want her spending that time with students and not wasting her two hours hunting down water coolers for our missions trip. I would rather have the church body make these resources available for us to borrow. Figure 15.2 shows a resource inventory sheet that we distribute to our congregation to find out resources they have that they might be willing to share. When church members turn in this sheet, they become part of our resource team. We organize their names by resources, and a resource team leader calls them when a need arises.

Gather Saints for a Prayer Team

The prayer team consists of men and women who participate in the youth ministry by gifting us with the support base of prayer. These are people who love God but who don't necessarily enjoy spending hands-on time with students. Their commitment is to pray through a list of prayer requests we send to them monthly. While they are praying for the youth ministry, we are praying that they will become part of the hands-on team. Over the years, we have had people begin on our prayer team, have their heart touched for the teenagers they were praying for, and become part of our hands-on team.

The cheerleading, resource, and prayer teams require little guidance and follow-up. Although they play significant roles in our ministry, they don't go through our interview process (see chapter 16). Since they are helping behind the scenes and not *working* directly with students, we keep our expectations simple. The main difference between these three teams and the hands-on team is that the latter *directly* ministers to and influences students.

RESOURCE INVENTORY

Name _____   Phone _____

Address _____

DO YOU HAVE . . .

Vehicles:

- ☐ van
- ☐ boat
- ☐ truck
- ☐ ski boat/Jet Ski
- ☐ motor home/camper
- ☐ other _____

Camping:

- ☐ tent
- ☐ stoves/lanterns
- ☐ sleeping bags/backpacks
- ☐ barbeque equipment
- ☐ water containers
- ☐ other _____

Sports Equipment:

- ☐ volleyball set
- ☐ badminton set
- ☐ Ping-Pong table
- ☐ football
- ☐ basketball
- ☐ pool table
- ☐ soccer ball
- ☐ Frisbees
- ☐ other _____

Miscellaneous:

- ☐ tables (card or other)
- ☐ chairs
- ☐ pool
- ☐ contacts with camps or retreat centers
- ☐ video equipment
- ☐ mountain cabin
- ☐ sound equipment
- ☐ big-screen TV
- ☐ beach house
- ☐ other _____

WOULD YOU BE WILLING TO . . .

- ☐ help coordinate special events
- ☐ chaperone special events
- ☐ buy/make food for events
- ☐ drive for activities
- ☐ help one weekend per month at the student ministry table
- ☐ provide office help prior to camps/retreats/events
- ☐ volunteer your home for special events
- ☐ host a Bible study in your home
- ☐ be involved with the Parents of Teens group
- ☐ other _____

WOULD YOU BE WILLING TO HELP WITH . . .

- ☐ sewing
- ☐ cooking
- ☐ typing
- ☐ band
- ☐ music
- ☐ computers
- ☐ art/graphics
- ☐ marketing
- ☐ design
- ☐ photography
- ☐ construction
- ☐ organization
- ☐ architecture
- ☐ other _____

Fig. 15.2

Find Leaders for a Hands-On Team

The hands-on team are people who work directly with and care for students. They are teachers, small-group leaders, and adults who go to campuses to watch students' games. Basically, these are the ministers, while the other three teams are made up of ministry supporters. Although we want to find people for the other teams, finding hands-on leaders is our ultimate goal. The more hands-on leaders we have, the larger the number of students who will receive personal attention and be nurtured.

Within the hands-on team, we have identified two types of leaders—*program-directed* leaders and *self-directed* leaders. These categories are determined by how much the leaders choose to invest in their ministry. The program-directed leaders love God and care for students, but they typically reserve their ministry time for a program. They don't pursue contact with students beyond the required time. These are often new leaders who are trying to find their place and fit in the youth ministry. Self-directed leaders are those who have caught the vision of caring for students. They minister to students beyond our definitive programs through letters, phone calls, visits, and outside activities. These leaders feel a sense of responsibility for their students' total spiritual development, and they express initiative to care for them.

If you are a leader of leaders, your goal is to see program-directed leaders mentored into becoming self-directed leaders. If a volunteer stays a program-directed leader for longer than a year, he or she may need some coaching, gentle confronting, or a change of responsibilities. The more a program-directed leader can observe a self-directed leader and hear about how to nurture students and how to minister outside of programs, the better. Program-directed leaders need self-directed leaders to model a ministry beyond the program boundaries.

By simplifying the opportunities to serve on the youth ministry teams (cheerleading, resource, prayer, and hands-on) you will have a much more attractive ministry. Giving those who are afraid to work with students less-threatening options will alleviate some of their fear. As they accept these less-intimidating roles, they will gradually become exposed to your ministry and be prepared for a hands-on position.

Step 4: Never Stop Looking for Potential Leaders

Searching for people to join your teams is a never-ending, top-priority task. Here are some ways to find leaders.

Expect Existing Leaders to Find New Ones

We ask our existing youth staff to find one other volunteer during the year. As a leader of leaders, I am ultimately accountable for developing a staff, but since I don't know everyone in the church and our hands-on leaders know different people than I do, they share in the responsibility of finding new leaders. For example, since Jeff is involved with the men's ministry, he looks at the men as potential youth leaders. And since Amanda is in the choir, she looks for choir members who love God and care about students. Our best new volunteers are those invited by our existing staff. They enter our ministry with a built-in trainer because of the relational connection with someone who is already serving.

Ask Students to Ask Adults

I met Patricia during our all-church camp. She was a sixty-year-old grandmother of six. I could tell that she cared for students because she always went out of her way to pass by the teenagers' dinner table and talk to them about their day. The students loved her! One day I said, "Patricia, have you ever considered that your ministry in our church could be youth work?" She laughed and told me that she was too old, couldn't relate to today's teenagers, and already had a ministry as an usher. I tried to persuade her by saying, "I can get the church another person to help people find seats, but I'm looking for ministers to usher students into God's presence." I knew I sounded godly, so I was shocked when my spiritual manipulation didn't work. I asked her three different times in three different ways and was rejected every time.

After the retreat, two students told Patricia that they thought she would be a great youth leader. They promised her that they would introduce her to their friends and help her feel comfortable. Patricia agreed. I couldn't believe it! These girls weren't seminary trained. They didn't know anything about developing leadership. Yet they were the key figures in bringing a great youth worker onto our staff. They had done a better job than I of relieving Patricia's fears.

Look to Parents As Leaders

Parents make great youth workers if they are brought on as volunteer staff in the right way. At the beginning of every school year, we make a big pitch for parents to join any of our three main teams (resource, prayer, hands-on). Prior to pursuing parents for our hands-on team, we talk to their teenagers to see how they feel about their parents' potential involvement. If a student is open to the idea, we "go after" the parent. If a student is adamantly opposed to parental involvement and is sensitive to wanting "space," we usually delay the parent's involvement until the student matures or until we can find a place in the ministry where they can "hide" from each other. We would rather keep the student involved in the ministry than add the parent to our leadership team. Most parents agree with this assessment and are willing to delay their involvement until the teenager is ready.

Before we bring parents aboard, we interview them as we do any potential hands-on leaders (see chapter 16) and attempt to discover their motives for serving in youth ministry. We don't need parents who are spying on their teenagers, are trying to appear saintly, are too controlling to let their teens go, or are desperate for teenage friendships.

Utilize Age-Appropriate Students

If you have a college ministry in your church, there are probably some students with leadership potential who can assist with high school ministry. Likewise, allow mature student leaders in your high school ministry to work with junior high students.

An effective way to keep your high school seniors involved is to allow them more responsibility within the ministry. I like the idea of having seniors work with seventh-grade students for one year. If these seniors don't move away to college, they will have the potential to disciple the same students for six years. By the way, we insist that all our leaders work with students of the same sex; this becomes even more important when the age difference is minimized.

Advertise at Christian Colleges

If your church is near a Christian college, you have a great opportunity to find young leaders. Most Christian-college students come from youth groups and have moved away from the comfort of their home churches. If you can be the first student ministry to advertise in their weekly college newsletter, you have a good chance of finding energetic and highly dedicated student leaders.

Also, most Christian colleges require their students to have practical training in ministry before they graduate. Contact a Christian college and make your church an available site for a mentoring or intern program where the college students can get experience while you oversee their progress.

Gather Names from Everyone

In addition to all the searching methods described above, I'm always asking adults and students if they know of anyone who fits our potential youth worker description. I say, "We're looking for all different types of people who love God and care about students. Do you know of anyone I should talk to?" If I'm given the name of someone I know, I call that person and explain our different teams and ask him or her to prayerfully consider joining one. I say something like, "Some of the students in our ministry picked you as one of their favorite adults." By telling them this, I break down their fear of "Will students like me?" If I don't know the adult who was recommended, I write a letter like the one in figure 15.3 and follow it up with a phone call.

Dear Dan,

I wanted to write you a quick letter to let you know that you won a popularity contest among some of the students at Saddleback Church. I recently asked a few junior highers if they knew of any adults in our church who would be good leaders in our youth ministry. Your name was given with enthusiastic support.

Would you please prayerfully consider joining our youth ministry team? We are always looking for adults who have a love for God and can get excited about spending time with students. If this describes you, I would love to tell you more about our ministry with students and the opportunities available to minister to the students at our church.

I will call you in a week and ask about your interest level. Thanks for taking the time to read this letter, to pray about the ministry, and for being the type of person students respect.

Blessings,

Doug Fields
Youth Pastor

P.S.: In case you are wondering, both Sarah Boyd and Amy Allen said you would be great!

Fig. 15.3

Step 5: Invite People to Join Your Hands-On Teams

As you invite people to join your teams, communicate your "thrive" attitude. The way you talk about your ministry begins the education process regarding youth ministry values, attitudes, and purposes.

Focus on the Word Invite

The word *recruit* is abrasive and evokes a military image. When we use the word *recruit* around the church, people hide. They're tired of being recruited. Instead of recruiting people, *invite* them. Which sounds better—"I want to recruit you" or "I want to invite you"? Invite people to be a part of your prayer team. Invite them to observe a Sunday school class and prayerfully consider if this might be a place for them to get involved in ministry. People don't mind being invited, but who likes to be recruited?

> ## The word RECRUIT is abrasive and evokes a military image.

Use a Promotional Flyer to Advertise Your Teams

It serves as a tangible reminder of their conversation with you. Note that our example in figure 15.4 refers to the resource, prayer, and hands-on teams. It gives people a quick overview of what we are looking for, as well as an opportunity to respond with their choice of interest. We also advertise in our church bulletin a few times a year.

Show Off Your Nonstereotypical Youth Workers

Marv shatters the stereotype of a youth worker. When I talked to potential leaders, at my former church, I often took him with me. He also shared his story in front of the congregation. When people heard about a senior citizen being effective in youth ministry, they said, "If he can do it, I can too."

Bring All Your Teams Together for a Celebration Party

One time during the year, throw a party to which you invite all of your teams. This could be a Christmas party or a summer picnic. One important reason for the party is to thank everyone for their support. Another realistic motive to have a party is for the hands-on team to get to know people from the prayer, resource, and cheerleading teams. They can share their experiences of in-the-trenches youth ministry and invite members from the

WHY ARE THESE GIRLS SO SAD?

a) they didn't make the cheerleading squad
b) they were cut from the volleyball team
c) they are forced to attend Saddleback's high school ministry
d) they don't have a small-group leader to care for them
e) all of the above

The answer is "D."

We're not looking for the "perfect" small-group leader; we're looking for youth workers who are . . .

senior citizens	blue collar workers	single parents	busy people
introverts	parents	accountants	cooks
young marrieds	ex-cheerleaders	old Christians	administrators
musicians	artists	people with rough	professional wrestlers
high school dropouts	old marrieds	pasts	butchers
bowlers	college students	computer nerds	bakers
bikers	mechanics	athletes	candlestick makers
van owners	Taco Bell executives	entrepreneurs	

If you love God and have a heart for students, take a minute and fill out a Communications Card with your name and phone number. Indicate the area in which you would be interested in serving (areas of need listed below).

Caring for students,
Doug Fields
Youth Pastor

WE'RE LOOKING FOR ADULTS TO JOIN OUR TEAM IN THREE AREAS:
1. Hands-On Team—Are you willing to invest in students and lead a small group? Students need relationships with adults—do you have one to offer? **2. Resource Team**—Do you have a tent? A boat? A van? Would you like to help with our special events? Do you have any special skills to offer? **3. Prayer Team**—We value the prayers of God's people! Can you pray for our students and our youth ministry needs?

Fig. 15.4

other teams to observe one of their small groups or sit at their table during a weekend worship service. For example, Nancy, one of our hands-on leaders, met Julie from the prayer team at our annual party and talked about our ministry. During their conversation, Nancy invited Julie to observe her small group. Their conversation went something like this:

Nancy: "Have you ever considered working with students or being a small-group leader?"

Julie: "Oh, no! I don't think I could do that. I like teenagers, but I'm pretty content just praying for the ministry."

Nancy: "I used to think I was too old to work with students. I love it now! I'd like to invite you to observe our small group for a week to see if you might be interested."

If the people from the other teams don't express interest in the hands-on team, don't consider the party a loss. You've just hosted an event that builds the credibility of the ministry by thanking people for their prayers, resources, and support. Regardless of their involvement, they need and deserve genuine appreciation.

Invite Potential Hands-On Team Leaders to Observe First Before They Commit

It's important to have your potential hands-on leaders observe your programs before they commit to them. You want to make sure they see the "big picture" of the ministry. Some people will enthusiastically respond to need without having a firsthand knowledge of what they are committing to. This isn't healthy. I prefer to move people onto the hands-on team slowly. I'm eager to develop leaders, but I want to make wise choices. Bringing someone into the ministry is easier than asking them to leave if they don't work out. Thus, leaders of leaders need to be selective.

The next chapter focuses on bringing potential hands-on leaders into your ministry and gives some specific safeguards so that new people benefit the ministry, not burden it.

MAKING IT PERSONAL

1. Why do you think so many youth ministries struggle to find leadership?

2. What do you see as a healthy doable student-to-leader ratio?

3. What has your volunteer attitude been: "We need volunteers to survive" or "We need leaders to thrive"?

4. Name someone in your church you could contact about being on your hands-on team.

5. List the names of some of your cheerleaders.

6. What resources do you find yourself continually looking for that you could ask your congregation to supply?

7. Name some people in your church who can be on the lookout for potential leaders.

8. What do you think of the promotional flyer in figure 15.4? Who could help you create an effective flyer?

9. Does your ministry have enough leaders right now? Are shepherding responsibilities shared by everyone on your staff, or do just a few care for the majority of the students?

10. Does your youth ministry team reflect an open and approachable atmosphere to potential leaders who are checking out your ministry?

Sixteen

Helping Potential Leaders Become Ministers

The preceding chapter encourages you to view everyone in your church body as a potential youth worker. *Potential* is a key word here. Not everyone who expresses interest or responds to your invitation should become a hands-on leader. Healthy youth ministries are careful about how they bring new leaders onto their team. Quality hands-on leaders become critical links for strong youth ministry, but the wrong hands-on leaders become problematic.

Some youth workers ask, "Why must I be selective about volunteers in the church? Isn't anyone who loves God and cares about students a qualified candidate?" No. We would be foolish not to show discernment with *all* potential hands-on leaders. If you are a leader of leaders, you must have a set procedure and criteria for selecting leaders. Your decisions in this area are far too important to your youth ministry to be made without a predetermined process.

> **Healthy youth ministries are careful about how they bring new leaders onto their team.**

Establish a Hands-on Involvement Process

At Saddleback Church we have a ten-step process that all potential leaders go through before they officially join our hands-on youth staff. (Remember, though, our resource and prayer team members don't go through this process.) This procedure ensures that we get to know applicants' strengths, weaknesses, motives, and attitudes. It also helps to develop committed leaders and builds longevity into their ministry involvement. Although this process is time-consuming, selecting quality leaders will, in the long run, mean less trouble and a more powerful ministry.

When I teach my PDYM seminar, I lose some youth workers at this point because they believe my selection structure is too rigid. It is usually the inexperienced ones who disagree. Experienced youth workers, who have had problems with inadequate leaders, are eager to learn. The process you are about to read shows concern for students and their families; it also protects the integrity of the church, minimizes conflict, and guarantees a higher quality of volunteer leadership.

Leaders with the "we need volunteers to survive" attitude mentioned in chapter 15 don't use a process. They drool with excitement over any warm body who volunteers. This sense of desperation can open the door to unlimited frustration. If this has been your approach (as it was mine for years), keep your eyes and ears open to the scores of churches that are paying the price for not being more selective about their leaders. It seems as though every other month another church makes the headlines because a student has been abused by a leader. The church gets sued, and the community brands the entire youth ministry leadership as abusive. While it may be an unfair label, it can stick for years; it is difficult for a youth ministry to recover from such a perception.

By establishing an involvement procedure, you do more than keep molesters at a distance; you also promote professionalism and communicate to potential leaders the importance of their youth ministry role. In addition, the involvement steps assure church families that the adults working in the youth ministry have been screened and, to the best of your knowledge, are people who can be trusted. Trust is an important message to send to families if you plan to develop a relational youth ministry in which adult leaders spend time with students outside of church programs.

> **Trust is an important message to send to families if you plan to develop a relational youth ministry in which adult leaders spend time with students outside of church programs.**

As a leader of leaders who had to learn this the hard way, I have avoided much painful conflict by following involvement steps. I have been spared the stress of constantly having to remove leaders, which is a much harder task than following a ten-step process to bring them on staff. The few times I had to ask people to leave were comparatively simple because the process had forewarned them—they weren't living up to their end of the covenant that was made during the involvement process. Clearly expressing our expectations in advance made for easier removal.

Now that you know the benefits of a formal involvement procedure, let's look at the steps.

1. Express Interest

Contact begins with potential leaders when they respond to the "Why Are These Girls so Sad" ad that we place in the church bulletin (see figure 15.4). Frankly though, not many people approach us through this method. Although we use this type of promotion, most people don't respond to our needs. They respond to vision and because of personal relationships. Most of the time we initiate contact by trying to find potential volunteers via the other methods discussed in chapter 15 (leader invitation, movement from resource team to hands-on team, annual thank-you party, and so on).

2. Have Initial Contact from Someone on the Youth Staff

Whether people come to us or we pursue them, we immediately let them know about the steps to becoming a hands-on leader. The steps allow them time to think and pray about the opportunity rather than making an impulsive decision. During this initial conversation, we provide a brief overview of our youth ministry and our needs, and we thank them for their willingness to walk through the steps. While we express sincere gratitude, we also clearly communicate that there will be a waiting period while we finish the process.

3. Receive the Youth Ministry Packet

After our verbal contact with potential leaders, we send them our youth ministry packet (see appendix F), which includes

- a welcome letter
- an overview of what students need in a leader
- our purpose statement and planned values
- a general job description for a leader's role in our ministry
- our involvement steps
- our application and request for references

This packet contains all of the information potential leaders need for an overview of our youth ministry. The welcome letter includes an invitation to visit and observe one of our programs. We suggest they do this before taking the time to fill out an application.

4. Observe Programs

It is important that potential leaders observe a program so they have a firsthand view of their future commitment. We can explain our ministry repeatedly, but until they see students and leaders interacting, they can't fully comprehend it. Although this observation time won't reveal the joy, intimacy, and rewards that come from leading a small group and investing in students, they can get a good idea of a leader's role.

We try hard to make sure we don't sabotage potential leaders during their observation time. For example, let's say Dave expresses some interest in becoming a leader. He shows some normal fear over facing the unexpected as well as some uncertainty as to what he might be able to offer. He enters our junior-high room on Sunday morning, where students are walking past him, talking to other leaders, and basically ignoring him. He stands against the wall pretending to be comfortable. The leaders in the room are too busy greeting other students to notice Dave. And there aren't any socially mature students who approach Dave and say, "Hi! Are you new? I'm a seventh grader, and I want to welcome you and make you feel comfortable." At the end of the meeting, Dave is the first to leave. Because of his discomfort, he is now more interested in the janitorial ministry than the youth ministry.

To keep this from happening, you should warn applicants that they will probably feel uncomfortable during their observation time and that this discomfort will most likely continue until they begin to connect with some students. By telling them that almost everyone feels uncomfortable in a new room with students, they won't be set up for failure.

5. Complete the Application

If potential leaders have observed our programs and are still interested in getting involved, we ask them to fill out the application so we can learn more about them. As you can see by looking at our application in appendix F, we ask personal questions about their faith, ministry, and lifestyle. Each series of questions gives us plenty to talk about during the interview.

If I sense too many "red flags" on the submitted application, I either slow down or stop the process and tell the applicant that I don't feel he or she is ready to get involved. When a major caution arises, I "first seek the counsel of the LORD" (1 Kings 22:5). Then, because I rarely make a major decision in isolation, I discuss the situation with my pastor and rely on his additional wisdom before acting. Proverbs says, "Plans fail for lack of counsel, but with many advisers they succeed" (15:22).

Telling someone that he or she can't get involved in youth ministry is not a mean-spirited act; it is an act of leadership. Although it is never an easy task, it is better done sooner than later. As much as I hate to tell someone that he or she isn't ready to be on our volunteer staff, I would hate it even more if that person became a problem in the ministry and I had failed to prevent it.

> **Telling someone that he or she can't get involved in youth ministry is not a mean-spirited act; it is an act of leadership.**

It is at this point in the process that your leadership will be tested. This is where some point people recognize they are not acting like a leader of leaders because they can't make the tough calls. Remember that God has appointed you to be the leader, and since God has entrusted you, you need to lead.

Some "red flags" to look for with potential volunteers might include

- a brand new Christian or a person new to your church
- a history of short-term commitments
- a critical spirit
- going through a major life crisis or transition (for example, death of a family member, divorce or separation, major career change)
- high expectation for staff to be best friends or for ministry to provide personal experiences (for example, a thirty-nine-year-old lonely, need-a-life single)
- hidden agendas—desires and expectations that are counter to your values or goals
- not committed to a lifestyle above reproach
- unsupportive spouse

6. Interview with Youth Pastor

We wait for a completed application before we have a face-to-face meeting so that we don't waste time interviewing people who don't follow through with the application. (One application is returned for every seven we hand out.) By this time, based on our initial contact, our observation, and the application, we usually have an accurate idea as to whether this person is going to be a good fit on our youth staff. If the person is obviously right for the position, the meeting becomes less of an interview and more of a time to talk through concerns and answer specific questions. At the end of the interview, we give the potential leader a copy of the commitment sheet (see appendix G) and thoroughly discuss each of the commitments.

7. Prayerfully Consider the Commitment

At the conclusion of the interview, we ask the applicant to spend time praying about the commitment, both individually and with his or her family. If we are confident of the applicant's place in our ministry, we ask him or her to return the commitment sheet whenever he or she is ready to begin.

If we are still unsure about the applicant after the interview, we ask the person to pray about the position for a specific length of time (for example, three weeks) so that we too can have some time to make a wise decision. This prayer time allows both parties to seek God's will.

8. Return the Signed Commitment Sheet

If you choose to modify any of these steps, I suggest that you do not delete the commitment sheet. This has been the best tool I have ever used in working with volunteers. When leaders sign a commitment sheet, it is our source of accountability. While I don't anticipate conflict, leaders give me permission to confront them if they don't follow through on their promises. For example, if a hands-on leader doesn't show up at our monthly mandatory staff meeting, he or she should expect a phone call. Or, if one of our leaders shows signs that he or she isn't growing, the commitment sheet serves as a basis for conversation and accountability. The commitment sheet is such a good tool that we ask all of our leaders to re-sign it at the start of every school year as a reminder of their commitments.[1]

9. Begin Ministry

Once we receive applicants' commitment sheets, they move from being applicants to hands-on leaders. They begin attending our weekend worship service (for crowd students) or an area Bible study small group (for congregation students). They can commit to both programs, but we don't insist on it. We would rather have our leaders committed to fewer programs and remain consistent than require them to attend every program and become inconsistent.

Make sure your leaders come into a role with clear expectations and directives. The goal is for their heart and passion to move them to self-directed ministry, and as discussed earlier, the novice youth leaders can look to self-directed leaders as role models to begin the journey.

10. Participate in a Thirty-Day Checkup and/or Evaluation Meeting

After new leaders have worked with students for four weeks, we get together privately with them to review their involvement. If new volunteers don't have contact from other staff members within the first few weeks, they will feel neglected. They need leadership and staff interaction; they need to hear that they are doing a good job; and they may need ideas for how to connect better with students. If they are doing well, we view the meeting as a checkup. If we observe warning signs, we refer to the meeting as an evaluation. During this time we informally review volunteers' attitudes, performance, and fit.

Attitude is more crucial than performance, because we can teach youth ministry skills but not proper attitude. Since we have a fairly good screening process, we are usually able to spot a negative attitude prior to a person joining our team. Fit, or teamwork, is easy to evaluate. We look at how new leaders fit with the personalities at their area Bible studies and determine whether they are team players or lone rangers.

Most reviews are positive and become an opportunity to affirm new leaders. If, however, we identify a problem, we try to correct it before it becomes exaggerated; and we set up another review within a month to see if things have improved. If they have, we monitor the situation. If not, we honestly express concern and reevaluate the leader's role. If we need to bring closure to the formal relationship, we do so privately, professionally, and empathetically. Removing a leader is difficult, but again, that's leadership. After the thirty-day evaluation, we have spontaneous checkup meetings, which are mostly motivational sessions.

> Take some time to make this process your own. Change the steps or add and subtract some, but whatever you do, be discerning in how you bring people onto your team.

How to Encourage Ongoing Ministry

Once you bring people onto your team, they must continue to grow. Quality leaders don't just evolve, so your job as a leader of leaders never ends. You must mentor your volunteers and motivate them to find ways to affirm and cherish students. Below are some action steps that will produce stronger ministers.

Quality leaders don't just evolve.

Assign Specific Responsibilities That Have Meaning and Purpose

Could you use ten hands-on volunteers immediately? How about twenty? If you answered yes, what would these leaders do in your ministry? Unless you can assign leaders specific responsibilities with meaning and purpose, they will lose interest and be ineffective. Good leaders don't want to waste their time standing around.

In chapter 15, I briefly mentioned two types of hands-on leaders—program-directed and self-directed. Self-directed leaders don't need as much guidance as program-directed leaders. When program-directed leaders ask me for ministry ideas, I challenge them to spend thirty minutes a week on ministry beyond their commitment to a program. Figure 16.1 offers suggestions for caring for students based on time availability.

Now, let's throw this principle into the equation: Your ideas may be explicit, but if you can't help leaders see a sense of meaning or purpose, the ideas will fall short of being powerful. For example, during our weekend worship services, students sit at round tables. We use tables instead of rows to create an environment for conversation and to give our hands-on leaders a designated place to care for students. Since our weekend worship services are student-run, there is little up-front responsibility for adult leaders. Leaders could easily feel as if their presence isn't needed during the weekend services, but this couldn't be further from the truth. Part of my job as a leader of leaders is to teach them that sitting at a table with students is ministry. To highlight the meaning and purpose behind the adults' presence, I made their responsibilities very definitive. The acronym M.I.N.I.S.T.R.Y. makes them easy to remember.

M EET all the students at your table

I NTERACT with the people at your table (get them talking)

N EW people: Make sure regulars meet them

I NVITE them to the next program: Class 101 and ABS small group

S IGN in the students at your table for accurate follow-up

T OUCH someone with a welcoming, gentle handshake or hug

R ESPOND to noise or distraction during the message in order to eliminate it

Y ES message: Communicate your excitement over a student's presence

MiNiSTRY iDEAS FOR THE TiME-CONSCiOUS VOLUNTeeR

If you have 15 minutes a week . . .

- write an encouraging note to a student
- make a phone call to a student
- drive a student home from a program
- initiate two 1-on-1 conversations before and after meetings

If you have 30 minutes a week . . .

- do two of the above ideas
- go to thirty minutes of a youth event (sports, drama, etc.)
- have a Coke with a student
- take a student on an errand
- write a letter to a parent

If you have 2 hours a week . . .

- have lunch with a parent
- visit a youth event (sports, drama, etc.)
- help someone with their homework
- start a small group
- help out in the church office

If you have 4 hours a week . . .

- organize a note-writing campaign for adult leaders
- volunteer to help a school or team or club
- volunteer to drive to student events
- create a videotape resource library for lessons and talks
- organize and lead one of our ministry teams

If you have 10 hours a week . . .

- read some youth ministry books
- take a Bible class
- wash & wax Doug's car

If you have 20 hours a week . . .

- get a life

Fig. 16.1

Our leaders realize that they are not just sitting at the tables as crowd control; they are ministering to students who need to feel loved and hear about God's love. One reason students return to a program and sit at a specific table is because the leader knows their names and is glad they are there.

Continually Communicate Your Expectations

Your leaders can't read your mind. If you are a leader of leaders, you have to communicate your expectations and update your leaders each time your expectations change. Your leaders won't mind hearing your expectations, but they will mind being held accountable for things they haven't been told.

I try to list a few expectations—written or spoken—for just about everything we do. It has been rewarding to watch our self-directed leaders do the same thing for the events they oversee. Recently, I showed up at an all-night event being run by some of our leaders, and they handed me a list of their expectations.

1. Spread out and meet all the new students.
2. Don't fall asleep with your mouth open; you never know what will make its way in.
3. Try to have at least one significant conversation with someone you don't know well.
4. Be a team player and support the other leaders.
5. See how many cups of coffee you can drink between trips to the bathroom. The biggest bladder wins a prize.
6. Have fun and generate a positive attitude toward everything. We mean "Everything!"
7. Count how many times you hear the word *totally* in one hour.
8. Be the first to follow directions; students will follow your lead.
9. Laugh at everything, even yourself.
10. Throughout the night, thank God that we only do this once a year.

> **Throughout the night, thank God that we only do this once a year.**

As a veteran youth pastor, I have learned the hard way about the value of continually stating my expectations. Once when I had not been clear, I upset one leader to the point of tears and another to the point of anger. Save your leaders some grief. Teach, tell, and remind them of your specific expectations regarding behavior and outcomes.

Be Liberal with Praise

I have never heard a leader say, "Don't encourage me anymore. I've had all I can handle. I can't take any more appreciation." Everyone I know values praise. Minister to your ministers by being liberal with kind words.

> **I have never heard a leader say, "Don't encourage me anymore. I've had all I can handle."**

Recognize and Appreciate the "Ordinary"

Recognition doesn't have to be saved for the spectacular. There is power in affirming people for their normal and ordinary acts of ministry. Your leaders probably aren't being shown much appreciation by students, so your kind words won't be easily forgotten. When you catch your leaders doing something good, praise them. You might say, "Matt, I really appreciate the way you make students feel so comfortable in our ministry." "Noelle, it means so much to me that you took time out of your schedule to go to Heather's soccer game. That's really good youth ministry!" Be specific with your praise.

Give Leader of the Month Awards

It may seem silly to give adults awards, but they really do like them! At our monthly staff meetings, we give a Leader of the Month certificate (see fig. 16.2). It is not an expensive, impressive award, but our leaders look bashful when they get one. They love the appreciation.

Occasionally I go to a thrift store and buy an old bowling or baseball trophy for a buck. Then I go to a trophy shop and get an engraved plate that reads "Leader of the Month" with the date and the leader's name on it. I stick the newly engraved plaque over the old one, and the result is an inexpensive but personalized award. The more outlandish the trophy, the more fun it is to give. Before our staff meeting I put a pillowcase over the trophy and place it by the door of our meeting room so that the leaders have to walk by it as they enter. It is entertaining to watch them gaze at the covered trophy and wonder if it's theirs. Receiving it becomes a treasured moment for a leader, because it is given with kind words and heartfelt appreciation.

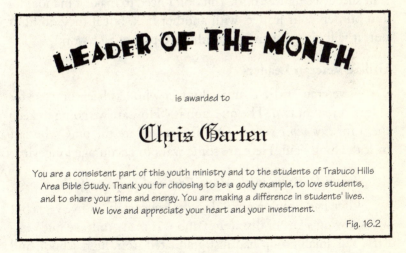

LEADER OF THE MONTH

is awarded to

Chris Garten

You are a consistent part of this youth ministry and to the students of Trabuco Hills Area Bible Study. Thank you for choosing to be a godly example, to love students, and to share your time and energy. You are making a difference in students' lives. We love and appreciate your heart and your investment.

Fig. 16.2

Provide Outside Encouragement

My leaders appreciate my praise but grow accustomed to it. Even more meaningful and motivating is when others thank them.

Occasionally, I ask my senior pastor to write an encouraging letter to someone on our youth staff. I don't do this often because he's so busy, but I do it when I really want to surprise someone with praise.

I also ask parents to write letters for me. For example, a mom recently told me she was thankful for our ministry and that her daughter, Lynne, loved it. She thanked me because I was the youth pastor, but I knew that I had very little to do with Lynne's growth. Lynne's growth was the result of Kathleen's small group and her gift for discipleship. I asked the mom if she would write Kathleen a letter thanking her. The mom was happy to do it, and Kathleen was blessed by the kindness. The words of Proverbs 25:11, "A word aptly spoken is like apples of gold in settings of silver," came alive in Kathleen's life.

Find Out How Your Leaders Are Ministering

A great deal of ministry takes place behind the scenes, and you'll never know about it unless you ask. Give your leaders an opportunity to brag about their ministry by filling out a monthly staff sheet (see figure 16.3). You don't need to make it mandatory and burden your leaders with another task, but if they do fill it out, it will give you an opportunity to praise their work.

Utilize Veteran Leaders

A veteran leader is any volunteer who has been on staff for at least a year or two. The question is, "How are we going to keep them for *two more* years?" Quality leaders are the ones who last over the long haul. Here are some ways to encourage longevity.

Provide Them with More Pastoral Responsibilities

Greg had been on our volunteer leader staff for five years but was showing signs of disinterest and was ready to leave our ministry. His small group had just graduated from high school, and he was feeling indifferent about youth ministry these days. As we talked about his feelings, we were able to create a new position for him. We moved his primary ministry from students to adults. I couldn't give quality time to our potential volunteer leaders and

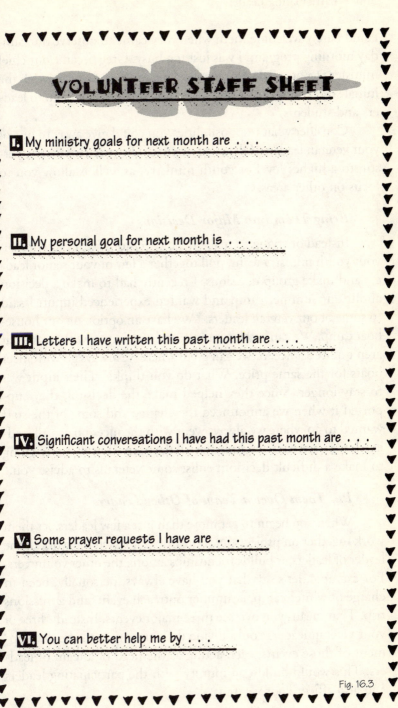

VOLUNTEER STAFF SHEET

I. My ministry goals for next month are . . .

II. My personal goal for next month is . . .

III. Letters I have written this past month are . . .

IV. Significant conversations I have had this past month are . . .

V. Some prayer requests I have are . . .

VI. You can better help me by . . .

Fig. 16.3

could barely welcome them when they came to observe our Sunday morning program. I was just too busy. Greg became our chief minister to potential volunteer leaders, walking them through the initial stages of our ten-step process and introducing them to leaders and students.

Consider what responsibilities you could give away to one of your veteran leaders. Advanced responsibility can empower a person to a higher level of youth ministry, as well as allow you to focus on other areas.

Bring Them into Major Decisions

Instead of trying to make major decisions with everyone on your youth ministry team, pull together a few of your senior leaders and make group decisions. I recently had to make a decision about our summer camp and wanted experienced input. I said to some of our veteran leaders, "We have an option on our houseboat camp. We can pay less money and stay longer with boats that aren't quite as nice, or we can go to where we always go with nicer boats for the same price. What do you think?" Their input was to stay longer. Since they helped make the decision, they supported it when we announced the change and some of the staff wanted to go where we always went with the nicer boats. All leaders don't need to be included in all decisions, but if you're going to make a difficult decision, enlist some veterans to advise you.

Put Them Over a Team of Other Leaders

When you begin to get more than just a few leaders, let them work together on projects. Not only does it lessen the work of the leader of leaders, it builds friendships among the other volunteers. For example, let's say that you have always, personally, been in charge of winter camp, a summer outreach event, and a missions trip. That means you oversee three major events. Instead, three of your veteran leaders could divide their time toward the development of those events, each acting as the head of a team of leaders. This would build community with the participating leaders and also affirm your veterans.

Take Them with You

If you are a leader of leaders, take your veteran youth workers with you when you go for youth ministry training. Tell them it is training geared for those who are serious about youth ministry and you want them to go. If you attend a seminar together, it will be easier for you to return and implement new ideas you embraced as a team.

Publicly Affirm Their Longevity

Long-term workers build more trust, confidence, and experience into ministry as the years go by. Let your volunteer leaders know that you value longevity by introducing your veteran youth workers as the backbone of your ministry. Tell them that you value their longevity because experience allows them to play a more substantial role in the ministry.

Exit Them with Appreciation

As seasons change in your leaders' lives, their commitment to youth ministry may end. Exiting these veterans with dignity communicates gratitude. Show them that they are valued for who they are, not just for what they accomplished in the ministry. If you have done your job well, you have trained them to succeed in any ministry. Although their departure is a loss for your ministry, it is a gain for another. Plus, they are joining your cheerleading team and will continue to be a source for scouting potential volunteers. Invite your exiting leaders to a staff meeting and publicly affirm them. Pray for them in their new direction of life.

Design Burdenless Staff Meetings

Most of our hands-on staff look forward to our monthly meetings. I couldn't say that about the staff at my previous church. They dreaded those meetings, and to be honest, I did too. It's a sad truth, but many of us don't change our style or our thinking until we change jobs. When we change positions, we need to evaluate our past in comparison with what we should be doing. Here are some things I have learned about staff meetings since changing churches.

Keep a Positive Agenda

At my previous church I gave the staff too much opportunity to complain. I would open our sharing time by saying, "What's on your mind? What do you want to talk about tonight?" As soon as one person would bring up a frustration or complaint, everyone seemed to jump in that direction. By the time "sharing" was over, I was depressed.

Now I start our sharing time with, "What has God been doing in your personal area of ministry?" or "What has been a ministry highlight for you this month?" These questions head us down a positive road. It's a simple change, but it has made a powerful difference in the spirit of our sharing.

Keep the business talk and decision-making to a minimum at volunteer staff meetings. Business issues are discussed and decisions are made during the course of any given day—especially at lunch, in rest rooms, and while driving to activities. Our volunteer staff meeting is more like a church service than a business meeting. Here is a simple agenda of what we do once a month in an evening meeting.

5:00–5:15	Devotional or Scripture reading that reminds us of the power of God working through passionate leaders with pure hearts. (We always start our meetings with a reminder of this first component of the PDYM: The Power of God.)
5:15–5:35	Personal highlights from the month: "How do you see God working in our ministry?"
5:35–5:50	Area Bible study small group reports
5:50–6:05	Some type of youth ministry training—for example, "Getting to Know Parents"
6:05–6:20	Planned values: Review them all and discuss one

6:20–6:40   Calendar items, upcoming events, and Leader of the Month award

6:40–7:00   Break into work teams to provide progress reports on current projects and to pray together. (Small prayer groups help to create intimacy and accountability.)

Tap into Their Initiative

If your leaders aren't contributing, it may be because you are always setting the agenda and telling them what to do. Instead, bring them into decisions and give them responsibility. Use teams to work on projects and events. Have the teams run by veteran leaders who can set the pace for getting involved and excited about a specific area of ministry.

Emphasize Spiritual Encouragement Over Training

At my previous church I felt a strong need for volunteers to be highly skilled. We would spend at least an hour of every meeting in some type of training. When I came to Saddleback, I minimized the training and maximized the sharing, spiritual encouragement, and input; godly leaders make better mentors, coaches, and role models. I now arrange skill training on an as-needed basis.

Play Together

Jesus said in John 13:35, "All men will know that you are my disciples if you love one another." Does your youth staff love one another? Have they deepened their relationships through experiences together outside of youth ministry programs? If not, you might consider spending some of your training time playing together.

At the end of our monthly staff meetings, we have an informal time of play. Since our baby-sitting ministry is available to watch our staff children, we take the opportunity to have fun together whether it's dinner or slick track racing cars. This time is optional, but most of the staff like being together and view it as mandatory to their mental health.

MAKING IT PERSONAL

1. What is your reaction to the ten-step volunteer involvement process?
2. What portion of the application packet can you see yourself using?
3. What are some "red flags" you should recognize when screening volunteer applicants?
4. What commitments should you expect from your volunteer leaders? What are some concerns you might express about lifestyle?
5. If twenty people expressed interest in being leaders, could you use them? Before you answer yes, what would they do? Do you have their roles and responsibilities written down? (Remember, volunteers won't last if they don't connect with students and see meaning in their responsibilities.)
6. If a leader can give you two hours a week, what do you want that person to do with his or her ministry time? Would your volunteers know the answer to this question?
7. What steps do you take to affirm your volunteers? What are some new ideas you can use?
8. Who could oversee a team of leaders to work on a project together?
9. How do leaders describe your staff meetings?

NOTES

1. At this point in the process, we ask our potential leaders to get fingerprinted. I didn't include this as part of the process because I recognize that it is probably too intense a requirement for many churches. At Saddleback we believe it is our responsibility to seek adults who are able to provide healthy, safe, and nurturing relationships with students. Any ministry working with minors has the potential to attract unhealthy adults who could cause harm to students and to the ministry. This additional precautionary step informs us of any criminal convictions an applicant may have and tends to discourage deviant individuals from getting involved in the first place. At the time of this writing, California legislators are considering writing legislation requiring all nonprofit organizations to fingerprint anyone working with minors.

COMPONENT NINE

PERSEVERANCE

SeveNTeeN

Handling Pressure, Projects, and Time Demands

A youth worker's job never ends! There is always another student to visit, another event to plan, another lesson to prepare, another family to help, another campus to visit, and another book to apply. Can it all be done?

Not only can it be done, it can be done well and with enthusiasm and longevity. How? By using survival techniques. *Survival* may seem to be a strong word, but it is appropriate for youth ministry. Persevering, or finishing the race well, through the strain of youth ministry, is a serious responsibility. Many youth workers start off resolutely but quickly exhaust themselves. They burn out, leaving the church and students in a dismal situation. Students need leaders who are stable and balanced—leaders they can trust to be there for them long-term. If your church has a way of attracting and then losing leaders, students will begin to mistrust every leader who comes their way. Why develop a relationship with an adult who, in all likelihood, will flame out like the previous leaders?

Give yourself time to read this chapter. Slow down long enough to apply the anti-burnout principles to your situation. After reading it, look for people who can help bring balance to your life.

How to Keep from Burning Out

It's unfortunate, but many people view busyness as a virtue. We ask one another, "Keeping busy?" We interpret a yes answer as good. Instead, we ought to ask, "Keeping balanced?" Any youth worker can be busy, but only a few are able to balance ministry demands, personal needs, and family time. A balanced life is a healthy life.

> We ask one another, "Keeping busy?" Instead, we ought to ask, "Keeping balanced?"

The demands on a youth worker don't start at 9:00 A.M. and stop at 5:00 P.M. They are constant. I have often joked about changing careers and getting a nine-to-five job flipping burgers at McDonalds. Why? Because when I left work I would actually be finished! No one would call me at home and ask me how to save a Big Mac that had fallen on the floor. I could emotionally disconnect when I left work. Ministry-minded people can't do this; caring hearts don't detach easily. Since youth ministry doesn't begin and end at convenient hours, we must learn to survive the trials and struggles of an emotional job so that we don't burn out.

God has wired me with the ability to keep a fast pace, and I am comfortable with that. I have juggled college, seminary, writing, speaking, and full-time ministry since 1979. (Somehow I even managed to get married and have three kids!) The main reason I have been able to manage is that I had a youth ministry mentor who modeled a balanced life. Although he never sat me down and gave me his list of ten ways to keep from turning my back on youth ministry, I saw him live out perseverance techniques. I have slowed down long enough to learn the strategies and develop the disciplines that help me run the race at a pace I can manage.

For me, finishing strong has much more to do with maintaining emotional energy than physical energy. When I'm emotionally tired, I become physically and spiritually weak as well. I have never experienced emotional burnout, but at times I have been extremely tired, frustrated, angry, disappointed, hurt, or lonely.

Numerous situations in the church cause emotional "withdrawals," and too many withdrawals can result in emotional bankruptcy. Below are some suggestions for keeping your emotional level high and burnout factor low.

Remember the "Act Your Age" Principle

When I was chasing my little sister around the backyard with a rake dipped in dog droppings, I was doing something my mom didn't believe was age-appropriate for the developmental temperament of an eleven-year-old, prepubescent boy. I can still hear her: "Douglas Montgomery Fields, act your age!" I had let her down because I wasn't acting like she wanted me to act.

I have seen many youth workers emotionally defeated because one of their star Christian students let them down. They get disappointed and believe they're not making any difference in that student's life. I remember a major letdown with a student I had been discipling for three years. His name was Rand, and he showed up drunk at our New Year's party. I took his sin quite personally. I remember questioning my call to youth ministry and wondering if I was making any difference. Eight years later I received this letter from Rand:

Dear Doug,

My time in Chicago has turned out to be a real blessing. I am placed in the midst of a great mix of training, school, and ministry. I have been praying, thinking, and planning for what is ahead. I finish the Barnabas Training program and graduate from Trinity Evangelical Divinity School in June. As you know, I've been preparing to plant a church. I would appreciate your prayers as I seek God for his clear direction. I just wanted to write and say thank you for your love, your prayers, and your support that started so many years ago. Thank you for investing in my life.

Love,

Rand

I'm not saying you should let your students drink. I'm reminding you that students will act their age at appropriate times (a water balloon fight in the summer) and at inappropriate times (a water balloon fight during Sunday school).

Don't place your adult expectations on a fourteen-year-old; it is not fair to you or to the student. I can't expect a teenager who has been a Christian for two years to display the same type of Christian maturity I display as a believer of twenty-five years. Students will act *their* spiritual age, not yours. One minute they will be caught up in worship, singing praises to God or taking communion, and twenty minutes later they will be arguing with a friend about sitting in the front seat of your car. That's age-appropriate behavior. You can and should paint your students a picture of spiritual maturity, but do expect some disappointments.

> ### Students will act THEIR spiritual age, not yours.

Don't Feel the Need to Be Liked by Everyone

Many youth workers I know are people-pleasers. This presents a big struggle for them, because a person can't be a good leader and be liked by everyone. Leaders sometimes have to make unpopular decisions.

I don't intentionally try to make people angry, but I have sometimes been the source of people's disappointment and anger. Leaders must learn to accept this reality, or they will become emotionally drained (I still don't enjoy it, but I accept it).

Practice Saying No

At some point you have to become comfortable saying no to some of the wonderful ministry-related opportunities vying for your time. You just can't do everything! When you love God and people, every request seems like a *special* request. To keep from burning out and sacrificing your health, you must establish boundaries, even though doing so will upset some people.

A word to married-with-children youth workers: Every time you say yes to overload, you are saying no to your family. Even though it is easier to disappoint your family, it is not wiser. In the long run your church will respect you for having a healthy family.

> Every time you say yes to overload, you are saying no to your family.

Learn to Confront

There is nothing more emotionally draining for me than an unresolved conflict. I never have liked conflict, but in my development as a leader, I've had to learn to confront. It's part of being a leader and working with people. Even Jesus wasn't without conflict in his ministry.

Personally, I believe quick confrontation with an attitude of grace and truth is a solid approach when dealing with people. Grace says, "I care about you," and truth says, "Let me be honest with you and share how I'm feeling."

For me, learning to manage conflict resulted from the pain of living with too many unresolved issues—with students, staff, coworkers, and parents. When I ignored issues I became bitter. The bitterness ate at me and didn't go away until I talked with the person. Most of the time, the other person didn't know my feelings. I'd be in emotional turmoil, and the other person was clueless and unbothered. I learned that the sooner I confronted an issue, the sooner I experienced emotional healing.

Talk to Other Youth Workers

It is important to talk about some of your ministry-related frustrations so that you don't feel alone and think you're the only youth worker on the planet who struggles with such things as unproductive quiet times, uncooperative parents of students, or deficient teaching skills. Share with a person you can trust to keep your conversations confidential, or with other youth workers with whom you can be honest without trying to impress one another.

Have Accountable Friendships Outside the Ministry

Most of my social interaction and friendships come from our youth staff. Because of this and my passion for youth ministry, I'm always talking about our ministry, our students, and our future. Several times I have caught myself being more eager to talk about youth ministry than about God. Not only do I need an occasional break, but my family also needs a break from my youth ministry addiction.

It is refreshing to have some friendships with people who care about you but aren't familiar with your youth ministry. I have a few friends who love me but aren't interested in our new area Bible study curriculum or my clever evangelism ideas. If I tell them I bombed while teaching a message, they nod and grunt, "Bummer." They love me no matter what happens in our youth ministry. These relationships are healthy to my long-term emotional stability.

Find a Caring Mentor

As a leader, you are always giving to other people. This constant outflow is draining and must be replenished. A caring mentor will make nourishing deposits into your emotional bank account. This type of confidant/coach is not easy to find. People may agree to counsel you, but they stay too busy to personally get involved in your life. A caring mentor will give you what you can't get from acquaintances—unconditional love, personal attention, and advice.

My chief mentor is Jim Burns. Although he is a busy man in constant demand, he has made me a priority in his life. He has challenged my thinking, and his youth ministry influence is reflected throughout the pages of this book. He has modeled life, faith, marriage, and fathering for me. When we get together, we talk about life, marriage, our spiritual disciplines, and our joys and frustrations. The time flies and I never want it to end. When it does end I feel renewed, challenged, and understood. If you don't have someone like Jim in your life, put a request for such a mentor at the top of your prayer list.

Block Out a Day Off

Unless you have a twenty-four-hour period of time each week when you don't work, you are a prime candidate for burnout. If I were to ask you if you have a consistent day off, what would you say? If your answer is, "I *try* to take Mondays off," that's not consistency. I have found that lack of a day off tends to be one of the common denominators in the lives of youth workers who don't last.

You should have one day off every week. It's biblical. Make it the same day each week and protect it adamantly. Don't do any ministry-related tasks on that day. Don't schedule a quick meeting; don't say yes to a brief appearance or a short prayer at a banquet. Say no. Furthermore, unplug your phone. If you want to keep from burning out, keep your day off sacred.

If you're a married youth worker, this day off is essential for your family. If you're single, you should also develop the habit, because single youth workers need to live balanced lives too; and if you do get married, you won't have to undo your workaholic tendencies.

Make good use of your day off and schedule times that will bring

- personal restoration—reading a book for fun, taking a nap, anything that gives you something to look forward to;
- physical restoration—an extended run, an hour at the gym, a hike, any type of exercise that pushes you a little;
- family restoration—lunch with your kids, a date with your spouse, anything he/she/they will look forward to enjoying with you;
- spiritual restoration—you might try to plan an extended quiet time every fourth day off. Get up early so that you don't cut too deeply into your family time. Go away for three or four hours to journal, read, and pray. Get recharged by an extended time with the King.

Block Out Your Vacation

There is never a good time for a full-time youth worker to take a vacation. Summer is full; fall is busy; winter is hectic; and spring is spent gearing up for summer. There never seems to be a "downtime" in youth ministry. If you wait until life slows down, you'll never get away. Find a time in your family calendar (or if you're single—in your personal calendar) for a vacation and block it out several months in advance. Then stick to the dates and view them as nonnegotiable. When something comes up during those days on the youth ministry or church calendar—and it will—make it known that you won't be available.

Let Your Family Have Input into Your Youth Ministry Calendar

If you're married, it's wise to allow your spouse to have input regarding your youth ministry calendar. I want Cathy to be fully supportive of all youth ministry events that take me away from the family; therefore, we work together when planning the calendar. Cathy maintains our family calendar, so I have to check out potential church-related dates with her; I don't want to plan a youth ministry event on the night one of my children has a school program. My wife thus becomes a source of accountability for maintaining a healthy balance in my schedule. And when the inevitable "goof ups" do happen, we try hard to honor our top priorities anyway.

In addition to long-term planning, we spend time every week looking at our family calendar and upcoming youth ministry events so that we know how our home life is going to be affected. Family-friendly youth ministry includes ministering to our own families.

> **Family-friendly youth ministry includes ministering to our own families.**

Ask for a Job Description and a Review

I'm convinced that more youth workers don't have a written job description than do. If you are one of those people who don't, how are you being evaluated? A problem arises when you're not doing what your superiors think you should be doing. If you don't have a job description, write your own and ask your supervisor to approve it or modify it.

Once you get a job description, ask for a review. A semiannual review will highlight areas that need improvement and keep you from being caught off guard. Everyone has weak areas. When someone points out one of mine, I view it as an opportunity for growth. I talk to youth workers all the time who say, "I was fired, and I never saw it coming." Don't let this happen to you. Ask for a job description and regular reviews.

Control Your Time or Others Will Control It for You

Too many youth workers allow other people to control their time. If you give people the opportunity to take advantage of your time, they will. They're not malicious; they're needy. There is always someone who wants to talk "right now" or needs your attention immediately. No one will be as protective of your time as you are. If you don't guard it, no one will. I am not suggesting that you become callous to people's requests, but I am suggesting that you give some serious thought to where your time goes.

If someone calls, for example, and says they "must" (the words *need* or *have to* are also good clues) see me right away, and I am in the middle of preparing my weekend message, I ask them how much time they think they will need. Most people say, "About an hour." Depending on the tone of their voice and the nature of the crisis, I might say, "I don't have an hour today. I can give you ten minutes right now over the phone or we can spend an hour together next week." I find that most people take me up on the immediate ten minutes and honor my time.

I went through this scenario just the other day. One of our leaders called and told my secretary that he had a crisis and needed an appointment that day. She knows my methods of handling such calls, so instead of scheduling an appointment, she put me on the phone with him. I discovered that his crisis didn't really require an hour of my time. He did need, however, some material on cults because he was meeting with a student who needed help in that area in the afternoon. I prayed with him over the phone, and I set some books out (notice that I set the books *out*) for him to pick up. He was pleased with this. If I had said yes to that appointment, I would have said no to dinner with my family. If the youth worker had called with a severe crisis, I would have asked how, when, and where I could help.

Some people may view me as insensitive. The truth is that I am deeply sensitive and extremely busy. I have learned to be realistic about with whom and how I spend my time. Leaders must decide what is important; not everything is of equal value, especially in kingdom-building.

> **Leaders must decide what is important; not everything is of equal value, especially in kingdom-building.**

Keep Track of Your Time

It is critical for paid youth workers to keep track of their hours. I keep a time diary in case I'm ever asked to account for my time. To the nine-to-five office worker, I look like a "flake." Some days I arrive at the office late. Some days I leave at mid-morning and don't return for four hours. Other days I head home early. What some secretaries, elders, and parents don't realize is that I arrive later in the morning because I was either out doing ministry the night before or will be out late that night. I leave many days at 11:00 A.M. and don't return until 3:00 P.M. Why? Because I have a tough time preparing my message at the church office. I'm constantly interrupted. I work best at my other office—Taco Bell—where my phone doesn't ring and I can have my soda refilled.

The nature of youth ministry requires flexible office hours. Track your hours in case a question arises. If you follow the time-management plan in the remainder of this chapter, you will have clear documentation of what you do with your time. Inform your supervisor of your schedule so that you don't have to live in emotional fear for the hours you keep. Don't try to please a secretary or anyone else with your office hours: You are working for God, and he is calling you to be effective. If you're most effective outside the office, get permission for your schedule, keep track of your time, and quit trying to please everyone.

Balancing the Demands on Your Time

"I can never figure out where to start." "I can never get anything done." "I go home at the end of the day and wonder what I did with my time." "I'm always taking work home with me just to catch up." "I want to spend time with students, but I can't find the time." "My to-do list is unmanageable." Can you relate to any of these comments? Do any of them describe you or your current circumstances?

If so, you're not alone. I've heard these comments, and I've made them myself. Ministry tasks never end, and there never seems to be enough time to complete them. If you feel like your schedule is out of control, you're a typical relational youth worker. But if you don't learn to manage your time, you will continue to live in frustration.

Anyone who has ever worked with me could tell you that I'm not a time-management guru, but they would tell you that I live a fairly balanced life for the pace I keep. Below are the steps I have gleaned from several time management experts and have adapted to fit my lifestyle.

Determine Your Roles

The first step toward managing your time is identifying what roles you play. I have six primary ones:

1. child of God
2. husband
3. father
4. friend and relative
5. owner
6. employee

I combine the first four roles into one category, which I refer to as my *personal* role. This relates to my inner life and my family life. The role of owner refers to my small company called Making Young Lives Count, which handles the sale of my books and youth ministry resources, and speaking engagements. While this company isn't a huge demand on my time, it still occupies a priority in my life. My role of employee refers to being a youth pastor at Saddleback Church, for which I have identified five subroles—teacher, pastor, administrator, developer, and leader.

As an employee of Saddleback Church, I try to spend ten hours per week within each of these subroles.

- As a *teacher,* I prepare my weekend message and write or edit our area Bible study curriculum.
- As a *pastor,* I spend time with students, families, and people at programs.
- As an *administrator,* I plan programs, oversee the budget, return phone calls, write letters, attend meetings, and dream about doing less administrative work and more pastoral care.
- As a *developer,* I create our discipleship tools (chapter 9).
- As a *leader,* I attend staff meetings, spend time with volunteers, work on communicating the purposes, and study to grow as a leader.

What are your subroles? Once you establish your roles clearly in your mind, you will be ready to work off a time sheet like the one on page 386 in Appendix H. Using it will allow you to be intentional about your projects instead of responding to the situation that clamors loudest for your time.

Block Out Your Nonnegotiables and Your Weekly Meetings and Appointments

On page 387 you will see that I blocked out my nonnegotiable family times and weekly meetings. After this, I wrote down any appointments I made prior to the week. Once these time commitments were written in, I had a better idea of how many hours I had left in the week to accomplish my tasks. You can follow this procedure on your own time sheet.

List Your Weekly Tasks Under Your Roles

Now you can begin to transfer your tasks from your to-do list by writing them under the appropriate roles as shown in the example on page 388. For example, if one of the items on the to-do list is "write parent letter," transfer it to the role of administrator.

Block Out Realistic Amounts of Time to Accomplish Your Tasks

For each item listed, record a realistic amount of time needed for completion (see p. 389). When I first started doing this, I would give myself an hour for a project that I assumed would take an hour. My problem was that I didn't plan for little things like bathroom breaks, stretching, killing the ants in my office, and other interruptions. The hour-long project would take an hour and a half, and I would fall behind in my schedule. Then I would get frustrated because I wasn't able to accomplish everything I had planned. Now, to give myself a little breathing room, I schedule more time for a task than I need. If I end up having extra time (I rarely do), I use it to catch up on my endless list of phone calls and encouragement notes.

Take Time to Save Time

When I first started using this system, it took me about an hour to plan my week. The more I did it, the faster I became. One hour of planning saved me several hours during the week, because planning increased my productivity time. I'm now more flexible for the "it will only take a minute" meetings. This system also serves as a work diary for keeping track of my hours. When more responsibilities arise, I simply pencil them in—for the following week. If I gain a new top priority, I move a lesser priority to the next week.

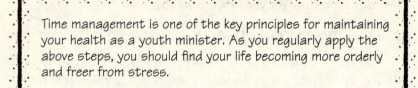

Time management is one of the key principles for maintaining your health as a youth minister. As you regularly apply the above steps, you should find your life becoming more orderly and freer from stress.

MAKING IT PERSONAL

1. Are there signs in your life that show you are weakening emotionally?
2. Of the thirteen suggestions for keeping your emotional bank account high, which three do you struggle with the most?
3. Where can you go for help and accountability in these areas?
4. Define *balance* for your life.
5. Is your present style of time management working? How would your spouse or best friend answer that question about you?
6. How would you rate your ability to resolve conflict (1 = low; 10 = high)? Do you avoid conflict in order to be liked by others?
7. Who is someone in your life who can help you with conflict management and confrontation?
8. What are some of your current youth ministry frustrations? How might God be using these situations to help you grow as a leader?

EIGHTEEN

Disciplining Positively

"Either get these students under control or shut down the program!"

That was the emphatic bottom line on a memo I once received concerning behavior problems at our midweek program. The week before, about a dozen students never made it into our meeting. Instead, they formed a pack to pillage the church property. It was typical student stuff—some stolen toilet paper, a smoke bomb tossed in the general direction of the children's program—but it was enough to irritate some people and set off a chain of letters and meetings that resulted in the above ultimatum.

My first reaction was, "If they only knew!" Was last Wednesday night a worst-case scenario in their minds? I guess they weren't around when a student with a knife showed up looking for a fight. Or when a student pepper-sprayed a visitor. Or when a group decided to smoke pot in a church drainage ditch instead of attending our meeting. Or when a guy in the back of the camp bus shot aerosol spray through the flame of his Bic lighter and caught someone's hair on fire. Some toilet paper and a smoke bomb? Nobody was killed! Sounds like a pretty tame night to me.

> **Some toilet paper and a smoke bomb? Nobody was killed! Sounds like a pretty tame night to me.**

But my second thought was a little more understanding. The normally patient children's workers had had an abnormally rough time with this group. As I probed, I found that the problem wasn't the students' *misdemeanors;* it was more their *demeanor*—profanity, disrespect, and general belligerence. We all know that "attitude" is part of adolescent life, but the force of it took these adults by surprise. And it should have. The day we stop expecting appropriate behavior is the day the good guys lose.

There is not a youth worker with a "lock-in's worth of experience" who hasn't had to deal with discipline problems. Most are merely annoying, but some are absolutely heartbreaking as students we truly care about persist in driving us nuts. Not many of us have been wired to confront misbehavior and then move on. We find confrontation uncomfortable and emotionally draining.

Fortunately, shutting down the program is not an option, regardless of what some militant elder may think. Neither is your resignation, whether that means giving up on decent behavior or giving up on the ministry altogether. The fact that so many students lack self-discipline points to the need for people like us to help develop it in them.

Understanding the Big Picture of Discipline

A Biblical Perspective of Discipline

Biblically speaking, discipline is not a necessary evil. It is a necessary good because of evil. Discipline is a virtue, a positive promoter of spirituality, morality, and relational integrity, which the Bible refers to as "righteousness."

Discipline comes from the same root as *disciple,* which means "follower" or "learner." There is no such thing as an undisciplined disciple. Since our mission is to go into all of the world and make disciples (self-disciplined followers) of Jesus who obey his ways and honor him, having a strategy for discipline is virtually synonymous with having a strategy for discipleship.

> **Having a strategy for discipline is virtually synonymous with having a strategy for discipleship.**

In Deuteronomy 4:36 the word *discipline* is used within the context of God's revelation to the Israelites at Mount Sinai. The very act of God speaking in love to his children is called discipline. And what did the Israelites hear? They received the Law, summarized by the Ten Commandments—nonnegotiable guidelines for a blessed life. Communicating and setting boundaries in love are elements of biblical discipline.

Hebrews 12, a classic New Testament passage on discipline, echoes the words of Deuteronomy. Notice that the chapter opens with a statement of God's provision. It says that he has surrounded us with a great cloud of witnesses, and Jesus himself has gone before us blazing the path of salvation. This calls for a response of self-discipline. We are to train for the race, overcome hindrances, and run with joy and perseverance. Then we are reminded of the purpose of punishment: "The Lord disciplines those he loves, and he punishes everyone he accepts as a son" (v. 6). Both provision and punishment are evidence of belonging to God's family.

So we see that provision and punishment stand as pillars of good discipline. Of course, those words aren't exactly twenty-first-century-friendly. We might prefer packaging like

- love and limits
- grace and truth
- affirmation and correction
- support and boundaries

Regardless of how we describe it, self-discipline, which is equivalent to discipleship, is predicated on both hugs and hurts. Without a rich mix of kisses on the cheek and "kicks to the cheeks," we just don't mature.

A Sociological Perspective of Discipline

Sociological studies have borne out the value of providing positive discipline through both support and control. In college I remember learning about a classic study that evaluated the effectiveness of parenting in light of control and support. Four styles of parenting were identified. The first was *authoritarian,* which is high in control (rules and consequences) and low in support (love and affirmation). In this situation, rules take priority regardless of the cost to people. *Democratic* parenting was just the opposite—high in support and low in control. These families operated on a "one-person, one-vote" system in which children had as much say as parents. *Laissez faire* described something that was low in both control and support. In effect, these parents said, "We don't care what you do because we don't care about you." Finally, those parents who maintained a high level of both control and support were described as *authoritative.* They didn't shrink from enforcing the rules, but they enforced them with love and understanding. Figure 18.1 charts the four styles.

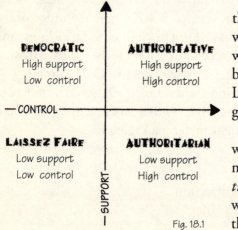

DEMOCRATIC
High support
Low control

AUTHORITATIVE
High support
High control

— CONTROL —

LAISSEZ FAIRE
Low support
Low control

AUTHORITARIAN
Low support
High control

— SUPPORT —

Fig. 18.1

As we would expect, the young people who were most successful and well adjusted were raised by *authoritative* parents. Love and limits bore good fruit in their lives.

But the second most well-adjusted group were not raised by *democratic* parents, though we would tend to reason that if you're going to err, err on the side of love and affection. Actually, the second most successful group were those raised in a *laissez faire* environment. Apparently, when people are neither supported nor controlled, they go elsewhere to find what they need—to friends, gangs, clubs, teams, and so on.

Finally, more or less tied for last, were those who were skewed one way or another. Too much support or too much control without the counterbalance of the other did tremendous damage. Unfortunately, in the decades since this study, people have learned little. The romantic, democratic notion of allowing students to bloom with few controls and unconditional affirmation continues to be standard practice today.

Consider the ramifications of this study for youth ministry. In effect, the second most successful parents weren't parents at all; they were people like us in pastoral care. If children raised without love or limits are driven to surrogates who will give them what they need, then youth workers can fill a strategic void and powerfully influence them.

I have often wished that parents would just do their job so I could do mine. But I have come to realize the selfishness of that attitude: it is nothing more than feeling that our ministry would run more smoothly if we didn't have so many messed-up students to deal with. But ministry and discipling messed-up students are not two different directions. They are the same journey. We are building disciples through love and limits, grace and truth, affirmation and correction, support and control. As more unloved, boundary-free students show up in our youth ministry, greater opportunity knocks.

A Youth Ministry Perspective on Discipline

Seeing discipline positively from a theological and sociological perspective can give us the incentive we need for disciplining as we should. My changing perspective over the years has been accompanied by a stronger willingness—even a desire—to discipline positively. I have seen mounting evidence that discipline is serving students and families well over the long haul.

On the other hand, I am convinced that insecure youth workers miss out on molding young lives because of their own desire to be liked. They have some fun, teach some good truths, and make some memories. But they don't have as much life-shaping impact as they could if they just sat down one-to-one with undisciplined students to talk about their lives or spoke to parents more pointedly about the needs of their children. Often the greatest problems are exposed and the greatest needs met when we talk about what some people have called "the last ten percent"—the bottom-line truths, the uncomfortable and painful things we dance around or leave unsaid in most serious conversations.

The courage to say these things and the love to say them well are the marks of a good leader. John 1 describes Jesus as full of grace *and* truth. He never danced around the hard truths in his conversations. Nicodemus, Peter, the woman at the well, the rich young ruler, and just about everyone else with whom he spoke felt the sting of truth but always with the stroke of grace. And which of them—including the ones who refused to follow—weren't indelibly marked by him? That is the kind of disciple-maker we have the potential to become.

Obviously, it is not easy trying to be like Jesus. But we are called to follow him as we exercise leadership in our groups. And if it gives you any hope, remember that misbehavior was hurtful and frustrating to Jesus too. We hear it in his voice as he asks, "How long shall I put up with you?" We see it in his eyes when he looks around and says, "Weren't ten healed? Where are the nine others?" And we see it in his tears when he says to Jerusalem, the city that killed and rejected God's messengers, "How I have longed to gather you like a mother hen does her chicks, but you would have none of it."

Again, discipline is hard and confrontation is painful, but both come with the leadership role.

Stacy and the Final Ten Percent

Stacy is a new freshman. She was one of the most difficult junior highers with whom our staff had ever dealt. She insisted on doing her own thing and was absolutely cold to anyone in authority, especially men. When confronted she responded with dramatic emotions, tears, and accusations that she was picked on and hated. Because of this, leaders would soft-shoe their way around Stacy, gingerly trying to guide her behavior without detonating any emotional explosions. Whenever her insecurity and narcissism surfaced, leaders scrambled to squelch them with multiplied reaffirmations that she really was liked. Behind her back they just threw up their hands and prayed for the high school staff's patience. Last summer ended her stay in the junior high ministry. That staff was eager to say good-bye, and Stacy was happy to go.

During Stacy's last week at junior high camp, the tension mounted. Everyone avoided her, just hanging on until she would graduate into another ministry. But when things blew up at camp, threatening to drag down a whole cabin, it was time to say the last ten percent. Stacy was confronted with stinging truth about who she really was and why everyone was frightened of her and for her. Cornered, she spit back with the strongest venom she could muster. Afterward it seemed that the relationship was completely severed. Stacy moved out of her cabin and everyone sighed in relief.

But three months later Stacy wrote our junior high director this letter:

> Dear Greg,
>
> I thought I would write to you because I wanted to let you know how I feel. I know last year I wasn't on the right track with God. But even though that was true, God kept me from doing anything I would really regret later. Camp made me realize I needed to be closer to him again. I began to think that if my leaders from church really saw me this way and had this many problems with me, then my lifestyle needed to change. I talked to some people who helped me realize that God is always going to be there for me. I wanted then to be the kind of girl that the Bible talks about in Proverbs 31. Basically, I wrote this note to say I'm sorry.
>
> Love in Christ,
> Stacy

Stacy has grown tremendously this year because she heard the truth and came to a realization of God's grace.

There is no discipleship without discipline; no purpose-driven youth ministry without the pillars of grace and truth. We read this truth in Scripture, and it is borne out in life. What remains is to appropriate it into our ministry style.

How to Balance Your Boundaries

Imagine that you hire a fence builder to enclose your property. He makes an initial visit to your home, says he will begin on Monday, but then disappears for weeks. You make several phone calls to find out when the work on your fence will begin, and each time the company reassures you everything is right on schedule. Finally, after six months, you receive a bill for $3 million. Shaking your head in amusement, you call the fence company.

The builder explains that the bill is no joke. You have a fence all right—it encloses one square mile, encircles your subdivision, and has your home precisely in the center of the area it surrounds. He says that you told him you planned to have a large family, so he wanted to give you plenty of space for your kids. "Too many boundaries aren't good for kids," he says. "Healthy children need plenty of room to explore and experiment."

Following successful litigation, you call a second fence builder and explain your need for safety, security, and well-defined boundaries for your children. He hears your concerns and promises to do a much better job. In fact, he'll start tomorrow.

Sure enough, he pulls up just as you leave for work. But when you return home, you can hardly believe your eyes. A tall barbed-wire fence has been erected around your house precisely twelve inches from each wall. Several TV cameras are mounted on the poles, trained on every inch of your home. The invoice taped to your gate explains that your home and family are the most important things you have. Children aren't safe near streets, and even lawns present serious health risks, so your fence has been designed to protect what is most valuable. You begin to wonder if a reasonable fence builder resides on this planet.

Where do we place our fences? If the fence is a mile away so that a student has to kill someone before we notice, our boundaries are meaningless. But if everywhere you look there is an armed guard and a list of rules, our boundaries are stifling. Where do we put a fence that is useful for our ministry? How do we keep it anchored in love?

Below are some "fence posts" we have found to be well placed in our youth ministry at Saddleback. They aren't specific rules; rather, they are principles our staff is encouraged to incorporate into ministry situations. When these are in place, we are on our way to discipling students with love and limits.

Expect Good Behavior

Students rise and fall to our levels of expectation. Therefore, in our youth ministry we always anticipate that students will participate in, cooperate with, and enjoy our programs. We expect students to like our programs and to consider our leaders desirable people who are worth knowing. We are genuinely surprised when that doesn't happen, and we try to communicate that when a student gets out of line.

Have a Few Simple Rules

Don't waste rules; students will only follow a few. If you die trying to keep chewing gum out of the youth room or forcing everyone to stand up and sing like good Christians, you'll miss out in other areas that need the strategic help of rules. Choose rules carefully based on your values and use them to shape behaviors that are critical to life and the cause of the ministry.

We tell our students that we have two goals and therefore two rules. Our goals are to have fun and to think. So when it is time to have fun, have fun; when it is time to think, get a little more serious and think.

State Rules Positively and Explain Their Purpose

Few things are more irritating than unreasonable rules, so if you're asking for conformity in some area, explain why.

When I first came to Saddleback, I wanted to set a tone of respect during my teaching time, so I stated a rule: "During our last set of songs, while people are standing, you're all free to go. I'm not going to make you sit and listen to me teach the Bible if you don't want to be here. No one will take names or get mad or catch you on video. But I believe in the Bible with all of my heart and I believe in what I have to say about it. So if you stay, I am taking that as a commitment from you to hear me out and participate by listening." As you might expect, few ever left, and an amazing amount of respect quickly ensued.

Make the Consequences Appropriate and Known Ahead of Time

It is not fair to surprise students by disciplining them with measures of which they were unaware. Usually our consequence is removal from the meeting if actions are too far out of bounds. At camps we use KP duty or loss of free time—if we have made students aware of those disciplines ahead of time. Figure 18.2 is a contract that students and parents sign prior to our summer camp. It clearly lays out the ground rules as well as the consequences. Thus, no one is surprised when discipline is enforced.

Know the Difference Between Annoying and Inappropriate

Students do annoying things; that's part of adolescence. But these irritations often call for understanding, not discipline. Talking, rude body noises, muffled laughter during prayer time—these often fall into the category of annoyances rather than malicious wrongs. Don't lower the boom on teens unless their behavior is truly destructive and inappropriate.

Moreover, we are all likely to have students with whom, from time to time, we just don't get along. Our personalities clash, and they bug us. These annoying students probably require extra grace and space (not to mention another leader to get close to them) rather than extra disciplinary measures.

HOUSEBOAT TRIP COMMUNITY COVENANT

Because of the potential dangers regarding a houseboat trip (i.e., propellers, ski boats, Sea Doos, etc. . . .) I understand the need to be responsible on this trip and follow these specific guidelines. I realize my actions may affect the safety and the community of this trip.

Guidelines

1. I understand I can't push people off the top of the houseboat even though it's really tempting.

2. I understand that I need to limit my public display of affection (PDA) if I'm not married.

3. I understand and I will honor the established music guidelines. I will not bring a Walkman on this trip.

4. I understand that there's no unsupervised night swimming.

5. I understand the need for separated sleeping arrangements and I will honor this.

6. I understand the following skiing rules:
   - No spraying other boats
   - No skiing close to boats, land, or other skiers

7. I understand the following Sea Doo rules:
   - No wild driving or dumping of passengers
   - No driving close to boats, land, skiers, or other Sea Doos
   - No close racing of other Sea Doos

8. I understand that I'm not allowed to POSSESS or USE tobacco, alcohol, or any other type of drugs.

Consequences

1–3 These actions will be confronted once and ski time and Sea Doo time will be taken away if repeated.

4–8 These actions will result in being sent home at my family's expense.

HOUSEBOAT TRIP
COMMUNITY COVENANT con't.

Commitment

I will follow the above guidelines and respect Saddleback's leadership. I understand the consequences if I choose not to follow the rules.

_____   _____
Student's Signature   Print Name

I/We understand all of the guidelines and safety procedures and the potential consequences. If my/our son/daughter chooses to not honor the guidelines 4 through 8, I realize that they will be sent home at my/our expense. I/We have discussed these guidelines with my/our child, and am/are confident he/she will honor these guidelines and Saddleback's leadership.

_____   _____
Parent's Signature(s)

Fig. 18.2

Minimize Your Warnings for Misbehavior

Minimize the number of warnings, especially with younger students in small-group settings. How many Bible studies have been ruined by disruptions despite repeated warnings from the leader? Repeated warnings that call for control only show that you don't have it. Disruptive students need to be removed, especially from Bible studies and prayer times. So give two warnings, then follow through with removal.

In my experience, removal is the most underused punitive measure in youth ministry. We put up with incessant interruptions, offer innumerable pleas and warnings, and then scratch our heads when we don't accomplish anything worthwhile. Remove the problem! Unruly students will never get the lessons you are trying to teach, anyway, until they first learn to manage their behavior in your ministry setting. Don't allow one student's behavior to ruin a meeting for the others.

Avoid Defining Students as Discipline Problems

We all know the prophetic power of words. Quite literally, they create the realities they describe. Stigmatized students tend to live down to the names we call them. Maybe that's what happened with "problem twins" Brad and Roger the year before camp (see their story on page 341). We hadn't called them the problem twins to their face, but that label was probably reflected in the way we treated them. It took some extra work and divine intervention to overcome our negative labels. When we finally spelled out to them the behavior we desired, they showed another side of themselves.

Enforce Rules Without Anger

Enforcing rules without anger is really two principles: First, *enforce rules.* They are worthless if not enforced. Because we like students and want to be liked ourselves, our tendency is to shrink away from painful disciplinary measures. I agonized over the decision to put a student on a bus and send her home, three hundred miles from summer camp. It hurt me to discipline her even when she unquestionably deserved it. Besides, there were the logistics, the uncomfortable phone calls, and the potentially ugly follow-up to deal with when I returned home.

At times like these, we need to remember that enforcement is anchored deeply in love. Proverbs 13:24 says, "He who spares the rod hates his son, but he who loves him is careful to discipline him." For the sake of the individual, we must let her or him experience the consequences. In the aforementioned case, sending the student home clearly paid off. The parents were supportive and understanding; the student stayed in our ministry and turned around within a few months. The story of that one act of enforcement has made its rounds camp after camp, deterring numerous other problems! I'm sure!

The second principle is to enforce rules *without anger*. Most people use discipline *because* they are angry. Rather, we should discipline *before* we get angry. Some behaviors may legitimately make you mad, but in the case of mild offenses, don't wait until you are fed up to respond. Stop the problem before it gets on your nerves. At first, students will be puzzled when they get kicked out with a smile, but they will soon get used to your style, and others will appreciate it. I tell students, "I love you, but I won't allow you to ruin this program."

> I tell students, "I love you, but I won't allow you to ruin this program."

Don't Embarrass the Students You Discipline

We want students to lose their misbehavior, not lose face. Removal won't make a student leave your youth group but humiliation will. Listen to the difference when discipline is seasoned with grace. Say, "Hey, you're out of line for the third time; I've got to ask you to step outside," not, "Listen, jerk, get your punklike body out of this room before I tear your lips off."

Speak Privately to Students
About Their Behavior Problems

If failing to remove problem students is the greatest discipline mistake in youth ministry, then failing to follow up is second. Follow-up brings further grace and balance to the use of rules. Emphasize the rules when disciplining a student, then reaffirm your love and forgiveness in a follow-up conversation. Talk through the situation; explain again why you did what you did; and tell the student you like him or her and that you consider the misbehavior part of the past.

Even better, use private conversations as preventive measures. We all have students who push us, then masterfully back off just before they send us over the edge. "Getting away with it" is their sport of choice. These students must be confronted personally. In PDYM seminars youth workers often ask me how to handle unmanageable students. I am amazed at how many haven't actually talked to the problem students.

By the way, when facing a potentially volatile confrontation, meet privately in a public place. The presence of other people in the nearby area will help keep emotions under control. And for your own protection, take notes. If the circle of conflict is ever broadened to include parents, pastors, or others, your careful record of statements and events may prove valuable.

Brad and Roger were the problem twins of their class last year. Their constant obnoxious acts were always just short of removal-level offenses. To make matters worse, they wouldn't let any of our leaders in emotionally. We couldn't get to know them or even get straight answers to simple questions.

Yet in the spring, to my horror, these two signed up for summer camp. I couldn't believe it. How could they stand to be with us for a week? I was tempted to book their return bus tickets ahead of time.

Sitting down face-to-face, I told them that I didn't want them to go to camp because I didn't think they would last. I reminded them that all year we had problems with them and that it would be a miserable week for all of us. They assured me that they sincerely wanted to go. So I told them that I expected to see a major breakthrough in their attitudes. If they were going, they needed to be part of the group. I told them that I would be watching them with the expectation of being amazed. Camp was going to be a time of change.

The *problem twins* became the *dynamite duo,* the stars of the camp. Not only did they not cause problems, they were actually major contributors to our drama team, wowing us with talent and humor we didn't know they had. I am convinced that God used the transforming power of a well-timed conversation to touch their hearts.

Don't Be Afraid to Involve Parents

We all want to be confidants whom students can trust with any secret. But I have observed a dangerous tendency among youth workers to maintain confidentiality at almost any cost. Remember, you are not a lawyer or psychiatrist; you are a shepherd. And those who shepherd people's children are accountable to both parents and their teens.

When several reliable people told me that Rob was dealing drugs, I had a strong sense in my heart that it was true. As expected, when I first confronted him, he acted like he had no idea what I was talking about. But within a few minutes, I elicited a confession. He hadn't *dealt* drugs; he had only delivered them; and he had only done it a couple of times. As we talked, he seemed genuinely repentant. He assured me that he thought taking drugs was stupid and that, in fact, he had already ended his involvement with those "friends."

That was wonderful to hear. I even believed him (sort of). Regardless of his sincerity, though, it was not my responsibility to absolve him of guilt or hold him accountable for his actions. Since Rob was a minor, his parents had responsibility for him.

I told Rob—as I tell all students in this kind of situation— that he had the weekend to tell his parents. I informed him that on Monday evening I would call them to make sure they knew. If he wanted, I would go with him for moral support as he broke the news. But his parents were going to know about this issue, either from him, me, or the two of us. Rob told his folks on Sunday night.

> Discipline is like a root canal. It isn't fun, but it is good for you. Both are simple but decisive procedures that keep decay from destroying a whole structure, whether it be a tooth, a person, or an entire ministry. Once done, the weak and painful is restored to a state of strength and usefulness.

MAKING IT PERSONAL

1. Is disciplining students easy or difficult for you? Why?
2. What are some constructive ways to handle a student who needs discipline?
3. What do your current methods of discipline communicate to your students?
4. What are some major discipline problems that may require an individual consultation with the parent(s)?
5. What was the most difficult discipline situation you have had to handle?
6. Do students know the behavior and discipline boundaries you have set for them?
7. Do your leaders know how to handle a tough discipline situation?
8. Of the ideas listed, which three do you need to work on in order to provide students with better guidance?

NiNeTeeN

Initiating
Purpose-Driven Change

From the very first chapter it has been my intention to encourage, challenge, and inspire you. If you desire to move forward and build a purpose-driven youth ministry, I am sincerely thrilled. I look forward to hearing reports of your success in establishing a healthy youth ministry. To become purpose driven, you may need to initiate some significant changes, so this final chapter helps you to build a support base for making structural adjustments.

Since we are creatures of habit and comfort, change is disruptive and challenging for us. Inviting new ideas into your youth ministry requires an adventure of faith. Like any true adventure, this one will be full of uncertainties and will prompt many questions:

Where will the changes lead our ministry?
What will we encounter along the way?
How will we handle opposition and adversity?
What resources will we need?
Will our innovations be successful?

Questions like these can cause doubt and choke out faith. My prayer is that the long-lasting value of your change will outweigh your doubt and fear. Be inspired by the words of the apostle Paul in 1 Timothy 4:10: "This is why we've thrown ourselves into this venture so totally. We're banking on the living God" (THE MESSAGE). When you "bank" on God for your ministry modifications, you will be in good hands.

Actions for Wise Change

Change is never easy and it is rarely fun, but there are some steps you can take to ease the pain of a complete paradigm shift or, even, just slight adjustments to your current strategy.

Evaluate Your Motives for Change

Before you activate your plans for a new direction, it is wise to evaluate your motives. If they are impure or inappropriate, the value of your change will diminish. Just as the means should complement the end, so should your motives be in holy harmony with the final decisions made for your ministry. If your personal motives are ego-driven, they're wrong. Don't seek ego advancement in youth ministry. Your primary motivation for change should be faithful obedience to Christ. If your motivation for change relates to how success will position you for future advancement, beware. Upward mobility is the world's vocational standard. In the end, the test is not how great you became, but rather how faithfully you served.

Be in Prayer

From the beginning, spend time with God and find out if your desires for changes within your ministry are consistent with his. Ask God's will for all your proposed ideas. Proverbs 2:3–6 says, "If you call out for insight and cry aloud for understanding, and if you look for it as for silver and search for it as for hidden treasure, then you will understand the fear of the LORD and find the knowledge of God. For the LORD gives wisdom, and from his mouth come knowledge and understanding." Now go back through that passage and circle the words "call out," "cry aloud," "look for it," and "search." These actions reflect an attitude of prayer and result in receiving wisdom far greater than your own. Significant shifts require mighty doses of God's wisdom.

Evaluate Honestly, Listing Specific Pros and Cons

To honestly evaluate your proposed changes, make a detailed list of the pluses and minuses they will create. This will show you and others that you have thought through your plans. Beware that the thrill of the change hasn't limited your vision to only the pros. You may need to ask others if you are being accurate and honest in your assessment.

Seek Counsel and Support from Your Supervisor

Proverbs 27:9 says, "Perfume and incense bring joy to the heart, and the pleasantness of one's friend springs from his earnest counsel." Discuss your pro and con list with your supervisor. Show him or her that you have thought issues through from all possible angles. Anticipate the questions and be prepared with sensible answers. This discussion session would be a good time to solicit support for the intended change; the better prepared you are, the easier it will be to get support. Make sure you get your supervisor's advice on the new idea so that he or she will be inclined to give genuine support and maybe even champion the cause.

Spend Time with Your Most Supportive Volunteer, Parent, and Student

When we switched the structure of our Tuesday night program from one large youth group meeting to area Bible study small groups, I knew I was going to "get flak." I was smart enough to know that I wanted the positive people to be the first to hear about our intended experiment. I knew they would ask questions without attacking me. I needed a positive audience before whom I could practice explaining the new idea.

Spend Time with Your Most Negative Volunteer, Parent, and Student

Negative people aren't usually as opposing and reactionary when you meet them one-to-one as they are in a group. Meeting alone with them allows you to hear their concerns without them trying to influence others to their position. Many times this type of person just wants to be heard. Negative people are typically insecure, critical, and in need of more time and love than others. I am not suggesting that all negative people will respond kindly to your changes, but they will appreciate the special attention and explanation.

> **Negative people are typically insecure, critical, and in need of more time and love than others.**

Refer to Your Changes as "Experiments"

One of the many leadership principles I have learned from my pastor is to communicate changes as experiments. Doing this makes changes less "risky." If the experiment works, people are predisposed to fully implement the plan. If the experiment doesn't work, it is no big deal; it was just a trial.

Prepare for People to Be Hurt

The old phrase "We've always done it that way" is a testimony to the discomfort that transformation creates. Most people don't like change—period. Often, it isn't instituting the change that is difficult; it is motivating and leading others to accept it. People who are willing to settle for mediocrity or who see no value in the new proposed direction are difficult to convince.

Change forces people to move beyond their comfort zone and develop new behaviors. It can easily hurt those who have an invested interest in what is being revamped. Some will be hurt by you, the change agent, because you are out to make their lives uncomfortable. Nevertheless, their anxiety should not be an excuse that keeps you from embracing purposeful progress.

Be Wise in Your Timing

Wise timing makes changes appear more strategic. Three good times to make significant youth ministry face-lifts are January, after Christmas break; June, right after graduation; and August/September, at the beginning of the school year.

Realize That People Adjust Over Time

When we switched from sitting in rows at our services and programs to sitting at round tables, our students complained for several weeks. Now they have forgotten about it. When I asked a few hardened volunteers to resign, people complained. Now the complaints have passed. When we moved our midweek program from Wednesday to Tuesday, I "took heat" for such an outrageous heretical suggestion. Now I would be criticized if we moved it back to Wednesday. People do adjust over time.

Thank Your Change Agents

I was asked a while ago by our church leadership to increase the number of our weekend services for youth ministry from two to three. This single change caused great alarm among students who were being nudged to attend the new Saturday night service instead of their usual Sunday mornings. We faced comments ranging from, "But that cute new guy goes on Sunday mornings!" to "We can't eat donuts on Saturday night—it's just not traditional!"

Some staff members stood aghast at the news with a look of "Please don't do this to me!" and "Are you sure you mean *every* Saturday night?" Their concerns included, "How will we promote it, sustain it, and equip it with musicians, a drama team, and volunteers?"

We finally reached the bottom line, and our ministry staff rallied around the cause to create another quality program. I can't stop thanking the volunteer leaders who have made Saturday night a success. (Wait till they find out we may be adding a fourth service!)

> Making people comfortable with change takes time. This comfort level is often contingent on the strength of your position, and the strength of your position is often dependent on your support. When I have solid support, changes come easily. When my support is waning, change is difficult.

The Deposits of Change:
Planning, Politics, and Prayer

Three primary factors influence my support. I like to refer to these three factors as "deposits" in my support-account. They are planning, politics, and prayer.

Once you define, understand, and develop these three deposits, your position of support will be enhanced. Individually, these three elements are valid and important, but collectively, they form a synergistic base for successful restructuring or redesigning of your youth ministry process or programs.

The Deposit of Planning

Many youth workers are accused (and rightly so) of "flying by the seat of their pants." I empathize because I fell into that category for years. Although I have been praised many times for my spontaneity and relational skills, I have been criticized just as often for my lack of administrating and planning abilities.

As your ministry grows, so must your willingness to organize. The reason is simple: As your impact increases, more people (both within and outside your ministry) are depending on you to "get it right." The further in advance programs are planned, rooms reserved, the budget established, and the camp secured, the more time you will have to walk alongside students and their parents at events.

Many of the decision makers in the church are business oriented. These people feel comfortable with order and structure and possess strong administrative skills. They aren't the type of people who try to plan a camp the week before the campers arrive. They plan it a year in advance and have five quotes for every expense. Whether or not you like their style, they are in positions to influence your budget, and often, your future. If you aren't organized yourself find a helper who enjoys planning; it is essential to your success and future support.

At my previous church, I had an organizational volunteer. This dad didn't want to work with students, but he did want a quality ministry for his son. He was God's special gift to me. In addition to getting us organized, he taught me how to plan events and activities using the O.A.R. method of planning:

Outcome
Actions
Resources

Outcome

Start with an image of the end in mind. Ask yourself, "What will a successful event look like?" Your answer may include numbers of students, budget parameters, and parents' responses. The clearer you can conceptualize the desired outcome, the easier the next two factors become.

Actions

What actions must be taken to reach your outcome? Your list of action steps becomes your game plan. The more time you spend thinking through your intended outcome, the more articulate your list of actions will become. Listing all the action steps will give you a better idea of the time required to accomplish your outcome.

Resources

In creating a game plan, consider what resources are needed to accomplish your outcome. An unrealistic appraisal of your resources, be they personal, physical, or financial, can doom your plans to failure and become a source of frustration.

The Deposit of Politics

If you are surprised that I am mentioning church politics, you must be new to ministry. If you are thankful that I am addressing the issue, you are probably a veteran. And if you think politics isn't an issue in the church, you are probably a Disney character with a Fantasyland address.

If you think politics isn't an issue in the church, you are probably a Disney character with a Fantasyland address.

The fears and frustrations associated with church politics are many and varied. Over the years I have heard and had more than my share of horror stories, so I am well educated in the power of politics. I have watched well-intentioned and gifted youth workers get burned by inappropriate use of politics. Thus, I can relate to and sympathize with all the reasons to fear church politics, but I conclude that any attempt to ignore them is foolish and futile.

Behind our fears and frustrations with church politics is a misunderstanding of their definition. To help defang this beast, let me offer a new definition of church politics that isn't scary: *The ability to gain support for the ministry God has entrusted to you.*

My responsibility within this definition is to trust God, remain faithful to my calling, and nurture support for the youth ministry in our church. If I submit to our church's leadership and build support for our youth ministry, God will take care of the rest. As humans, we require a facilitating structure and system to assist us with our work. Without such, there is chaos. The apostle Paul describes the church as a body having many individual parts but functioning as a whole (see 1 Corinthians 12:12–31). For smooth operation there must be order, organization, and coordinating systems. As it is in the human body, so it must be in the corporate body of Christ. Here are six suggestions designed to build political staying power for your youth ministry.

Learn the Systems

Every church has its own unique structure of organizational leadership. Whether it is bound by tradition, denomination, or personalities, the system forms the avenues for decisions. An understanding of the systems will strengthen your ministry's political base, so if you are new to a church, find a trustworthy member who is willing to school you.

Discover What Is Valuable

It is imperative that you understand and sincerely appreciate the values of your church. As you are discerning these, be sure to look beneath the surface of the "happy" church. You, as an enthusiastic youth worker may appear critical and unappreciative of a congregation's "sacred cow" and thereby offend longtime church members. If, after careful consideration, you conclude that you understand the values correctly but cannot support them, it is probably time for a change of venue.

Become a Team Player

The quickest way to destroy support is to think and act as if youth ministry is the only ministry in the church. You are not leading a separate entity; you are leading one part of the overall mission of the church. Your commitment to other church leaders and members of the congregation will enhance your church's success, and in turn, your own.

Enthusiastically Support Your Church Leadership, Especially Your Senior Pastor

If you want to get support from others, you need to give it as well. The best way to do this is by wholeheartedly supporting the leadership of your church, especially the senior pastor. Here are a few suggestions for developing these relationships:

- Respect their time.
- Invite them to your programs, but tell them they don't need to attend.
- Submit to their leadership.
- Care for their families.
- Take work away from them.
- Support them publicly and privately.
- Serve them.

If your motives are authentic, one of the wonderful benefits will be lifelong friendships. Another by-product of your support will be the example you model for the students in your church. You see, these quality relationships with your church leaders and senior pastor can, when observed by students, have powerful, long-term benefits for the church. In addition, these are important investments that will pay large dividends in your attempt to win support and succeed in ministry.

Know How to Measure and Communicate Success

It is vital that you can measure your youth ministry's successes and communicate them to the church. Whatever the measures may be (numerical, degrees of involvement, spiritual maturity of students, and so on), don't assume that the church staff and church body will be aware of them. A significant role of the youth minister is to carefully showcase the ministry. No one is better positioned—and no one should be more impassioned—to spread the good news about what God is doing in your midst. As you herald results, always be *honest* (don't inflate numbers or results) and be *humble* (don't take credit for what God or others have accomplished). Both qualities will attract support.

Pick Your Battles Wisely

It is inevitable, if you stay at a church for any significant length of time, that you will encounter issues, problems, and people who cause conflict. Whenever possible, resolve the conflict amicably and without undue confrontation. But if reason or God's Word demands confrontation, answer these questions first.

- Does the confrontation have potential positive results?
- Have I sought the wisdom and advice of a trusted (older/wiser) friend?
- Have I worked hard to understand and appreciate the difference(s)?
- Is the difference reconcilable without confrontation?
- Am I absolutely sure I am not wrong, misinformed, or myopic?
- Have I humbly sought and sensed God's leading?

If you pray diligently over each of your answers to these questions, and if you obey God's leading, you can be confident, irrespective of the outcome, that you have done the right thing. Hopefully, for Christ's sake and yours, the results will honor God, his people, and his purposes.

One last thought regarding battles: Make sure you are aware that the real battle is with Satan, not with members or leaders in your own church or other churches. The Enemy would love to turn God's people against one another for his purposes, so do everything in your power to thwart Satan's plan and maintain a loving unity within churches. The only real battle worth fighting is the one Christ is leading against the Prince of Darkness.

The Deposit of Prayer

This book began by positing the belief that anything we do of value in youth ministry must be powered by God. I'm sure that you wholeheartedly agree. It is fitting that the conclusion brings us full-circle back to the power of God.

If the power of God is the indispensable source of energy for building a purpose-driven youth ministry, then it is only logical that we will want to connect to that source and remain dependent on its life-giving nature. As we all know, our connection to God comes most appropriately through prayer. I am sure you believe that prayer is important to effective youth ministry, but are you convinced that it is essential? Are you bold enough to say that you and your ministry can't survive without it? Do you love to pray for your ministry? Do you crave being in God's presence?

I have no problem admitting that I am codependent. Prayer is what keeps me connected to and dependent on God. Practice witnessing the presence of God through prayer and you will recognize his power.

> I am sure you believe that prayer is important to effective youth ministry, but are you convinced that it is essential?

The Purpose of Prayer

God is not in need of new purposes or new plans. He has made his purposes plain. The purpose of prayer, therefore, is not to inform God of anything new. He is already aware of everything we do every moment of every day. The purpose of prayer is to keep us dependent on and in relationship with the One who gives life. Through prayer, we can thank God for what he is doing, and we can cry out to him with our requests, hopes, and desires.

> **Youth ministry doesn't need more creative, gifted, or winsome leaders, but it is desperate for renewed leaders.**

The Person of Prayer

Prayer is the backbone of a godly person. People who delight themselves in God and seek to honor and serve him are people who also love to spend time with him. As in any other relationship, we tend to become like those with whom we spend time; therefore, godly people spend time—both in quality and quantity—with God. Youth ministry doesn't need more creative, gifted, or winsome leaders, but it is desperate for renewed leaders.

The Priority of Prayer

For many, prayer is something we tag on (intentionally or habitually) to the end of our plans and discussions about ministry. We use our minds and methods first, then seek God's blessing for what we have already created. I have made this mistake more times than I want to admit. It is a great temptation to dive in and trust our own tendencies, desires, abilities, and plans before checking in with God and seeking his heart and mind for our ministry.

When we make prayer a priority as Jesus did, we will begin and end all we do in dialogue with the Father so that we might know his mind and experience his blessing.

The Potential Power of Prayer

If we believe that the Word of God is true, then we must also believe

- all things are possible through Christ
- if we ask in faith, God will work on our behalf
- God hears our every prayer and petition
- the prayers of a person living right with God can accomplish much
- God is eager to hear our prayers and answer our cries for help
- he who is in us is greater than he who is in the world
- we will do even greater things

If we know these things to be true, we must put them into practice. As Jesus said, "If you know these things ... blessed are you if you do them." He has inspired us through his model prayer by showing us that through prayer we can be part of his kingdom on earth as it is in heaven. What a privilege! Better yet, what a potential!

Take God at his word and trust him to do what he has promised. As we pray, he will lead us as purpose-driven agents of change, significant change that will allow the kingdom of God to come fully into the lives of the students with whom we are honored to share life—here, now, and hopefully forever.

It is fitting to conclude with this prayer of St. Francis of Assisi. May the courage, serenity, and wisdom it speaks of be yours to help make young lives count. May it also serve as a benediction and encouragement as you press on to build a purpose-driven youth ministry for our Lord Jesus Christ.

Lord, grant me the courage to change the things I can,
The serenity to accept the things I cannot,
And the wisdom to know the difference.

MAKING IT PERSONAL

1. What are your three biggest hurdles for implementing change?
2. Who is an objective friend who will listen to your ideas and ask hard questions?
3. Who will be hurt the most by the changes you are anticipating?
4. What are the best times to make changes in your ministry?
5. Why is planning a crucial element of change?
6. How do you respond to this definition of politics: "the ability to gain support for the ministry God has entrusted to you"?
7. What steps can you take to be a stronger team player?
8. What are three things you can do in the next month to support your pastor?
9. This book comes full circle. It starts with the power of God and closes with an emphasis on prayer. What can you do to remind yourself daily of those critical truths for fruitful youth ministry?

Your First Two Years

If you are new to youth ministry, this book may seem overwhelming. But broad concepts can be narrowed down to manageable principles. The following list will help you take the first steps as you begin your ministry:

1. *Go before God.* Ask for God's wisdom with your life, your family, your ministry, your dreams, and your questions. He will not disappoint you. (See chapter 1.)

2. *Focus on relationships.* Spend a great deal of time getting to know the students, leaders, and parents. Ask some friends to hold you accountable to living a balanced life. (See chapters 11, 17.)

3. *Communicate your desire to help families.* From the very beginning, let people know that you desire to create a family-friendly youth ministry. (See chapter 14.)

4. *Identify your personal values.* Ask yourself what you are passionate about and what you want to communicate through your leadership. (See chapter 13.)

5. *Teach on the purposes.* Spend a significant amount of time making sure everyone understands the five purposes of the church. (See chapter 2.)

6. *Pursue leaders.* Strategically pursue both adult and student leaders to help you. Your survival and the health of the ministry is dependent on leaders. (See chapters 10, 15, 16.)

7. *Develop a purpose statement.* After you teach on the topic of *purpose* and embrace some new leaders, ask them to help you craft a statement that communicates why your ministry exists. (See chapter 3.)

8. *Evaluate your current programs.* Teach your staff to evaluate all current programs and their intended audience. Make necessary changes through the eyes of evangelism, worship, fellowship, discipleship, and ministry. (See chapter 5.)

9. *Create programs to reach your target audience and fulfill the purposes.* You and your staff may need to create new programs, evaluate them, and fine tune them in order to become more purpose driven. (See chapters 6–10, 12, 19.)

10. *Communicate clearly.* Cast the vision. Inspire people to see the reasoning behind your program strategy and to understand the changes. (See chapters 4, 11, 12.)

Differences Between Junior High and High School Ministries at Saddleback Church

Because I spend most of my time in high school ministry, I use high school examples and anecdotes as the frame of reference for *Purpose-Driven Youth Ministry*.

But if you are a junior high minister, this book is still applicable for you. At Saddleback Church our junior and senior high school ministries are under separate leadership but similar in all nine components. We agree on all key principles and even use the same purpose statement. All that to say, it's very applicable!

The only minor difference is with our program strategy. Both ministries use the same primary purpose for the community, crowd, congregation, committed, and core, with the following slight modifications for junior high programs:

Potential Audience	Purpose	
Community	Evangelism	Junior high relies more heavily on occasional evangelistic events while the high school ministry relies on friendship evangelism (see chapter 6).

Potential Audience	Purpose	
Crowd	Worship	Junior high and high school are separated for our weekend worship services, but they are essentially the same format (see chapter 7).
Congregation	Fellowship	The junior high meets at the church property in small groups scattered throughout the church property, while the high school meets in homes throughout the community, with each home hosting several small groups (see chapter 8).
Committed	Discipleship	The junior high ministry focuses their discipleship effort at an additional small group that meets with an assigned leader, while the high school ministry utilizes the discipleship tools addressed in chapter 9.
Core	Ministry	The junior high ministry focuses on getting students involved in ministry teams for their core students (much like the high school secondary program called ministry teams, see page 121). The high school ministry has a student leadership group as their primary program which is discussed in chapter 10.

Appendix C

Getting Students Into the Bible

One major frustration for youth workers is trying to get students to develop an appetite and discipline for God's Word. We know that regularly reading the Bible is a vital element of the discipleship process, but we also know that most students have only good intentions, at best, of keeping a regular reading schedule. The reality is that we are ministering to a biblically illiterate generation.

Every year several new, user-friendly, student Bibles are published in an attempt to make the Bible an easier read. I have come to the conclusion that new Bibles aren't the answer. Teenagers need tools to guide them through the Scriptures and help them understand God's Word. Part of the problem is that students don't know how to begin reading the Bible. Typically, they start at the beginning and work their way through Genesis. If they are real eager and disciplined, they may make it through Exodus. Then around Leviticus they scowl and raise their eyebrows as they try to discern what Moses did when it says in 8:16–17, "Moses also took all the fat around the inner parts, the covering of the liver, and both kidneys and their fat, and burned it on the altar. But the bull with its hide and its flesh and its offal he burned up outside the camp, as the LORD commanded Moses." After a few chapters of blood, animal sacrifice, and anointing oil, students become confused, and they often abandon their quest to read the Bible. They say, "I tried!"

Another stumbling block to better discipline in reading the Bible is that students become overwhelmed by the idea that they should be able to read through the entire Bible in a year. A program that requires them to read three chapters a day can be intimidating. Sure, it's empowering and exhilarating for the first few days of January. Then the student misses two days and has to read nine chapters to catch up! That can be discouraging. There is no reason to recommend such a difficult, high-pressure reading plan for the average student when our real goal is to nurture Christian disciplines for spiritual growth.

A most effective tool for getting students into God's Word is *The One-Minute Bible for Students.* This book has 365 days of passages and takes away the mystery of what a student should read. Each day's reading requires only about one minute.* At the end of one year, the student will have read an overview of the entire Bible. The Scripture readings were chosen by John R. Kohlenberger III, an internationally recognized expert in biblical reference works and Bible translation. In addition to the daily Bible reading, a "one-minute extra" application written by myself shows how the Scripture can be applied in a student's life. (To order, see phone number page 389.)

The One-Minute Bible for Students isn't intended to replace the Bible; it is a tool geared to help students develop an appetite and discipline for reading God's Word. (I have even found that non-Christians will read the Bible a minute a day.) If your students need help in reading God's Word and you want to arm them with a sense of victory, this is the best resource I know. It will give them direction for their reading and confidence with the development of the discipline. Ease of reading begets confidence, which begets more intense study—which leads to life change.

For those of you who prefer charts to paragraphs, what follows in appendix D is an overview of our programs and key information for a quick reference guide.

---

*Of course I would love for every student to spend an hour a day in the Word. Since that is unlikely, I have chosen to focus not on the amount of time a student spends reading, but rather on helping them feel victorious in the effort they've made.

Guide to Programs

Program	FRIENDSHIP EVANGELISM CHALLENGE	HOT-NIGHT EVENTS	WEEKEND WORSHIP SERVICES	NEW BELIEVERS' CLASS	DINNER FOR 10
Church Purpose	mission	mission	magnification	maturity	membership
Youth Ministry Purpose	reach	reach	honor	grow	connect
Target Audience	community	community	crowd	crowd	crowd
Key Terms	• relationships • ongoing evangelism • "earning" the right to be heard • non-programmatic • 5 steps • everyone can participate • challenging	• big and fun • safe environment • accepting • stereotype of "boring church" broken • help community • pre-evangelistic	• laughter • celebration • drama and video • aligns with "big church" philosophy • open door to ministry • student involvement • 3 identical services	• foundational • assurance • God's love • prayer • Bible • quiet times • questions and answers	• intimate • fun • make the "big group" feel small • connection with leaders • no agenda • at Doug and Cathy's house • for new or unconnected
Process Number	1	2	3	4	5
Time	ongoing	3 times a year	weekly	monthly	monthly

Program	TEENS 'N TEMPTATION TNT	MINISTRY TEAMS	CLASS 101	AREA BIBLE STUDY SMALL GROUPS	CLASS 201
Church Purpose	membership	ministry	membership	membership	maturity
Youth Ministry Purpose	connect	discover	connect	connect	grow
Target Audience	crowd	crowd	crowd	congregation	congregation
Key Terms	• "recovery" • shared experiences • safe • accepting • small groups • honesty • recovery leaders	• student involvement • 30+ ministries • experiential • open to everyone to participate • impact the health of the ministry	class includes: • plan of salvation • what we believe • all about Saddleback Church	• small groups • several convenient locations • Bible study • life-on-life • discussion oriented • volunteer ownership	class includes: • spiritual disciplines (H.A.B.I.T.S.)
Process Number	6	7	8	9	10
Time	weekly	varies	monthly	weekly	monthly

Program	DISCIPLESHIP TOOLS: QUIET-TIME JOURNAL	DISCIPLESHIP TOOLS: S.A.G. FIVE	DISCIPLESHIP TOOLS: HIDDEN TREASURES	DISCIPLESHIP TOOLS: BANK OF BLESSINGS	DISCIPLESHIP TOOLS: ROOTWORKS
Church Purpose	maturity	maturity	maturity	maturity	maturity
Youth Ministry Purpose	grow	grow	grow	grow	grow
Target Audience	committed	committed	committed	committed	committed
Key Terms	• quiet-time assistant • measurable results • self-initiative • prayer requests	• **S**tudent **A**ccountability **G**roups • 5 minutes a week • prayer partner • on campus	• self-directed memorization • self-initiative • work at own pace • 3-5 verses at a time	• self-study • tithing • bank • envelopes	• self-directed Bible study • inductive • self-initiative • practical application • work at own pace
Process Number	11	11	11	11	11
Time	on their own	on their own	on their own	on their own	on their own

Program	PRAISE AND WORSHIP	MISSIONS MONTHLY	BIBLE INSTITUTE	CLASS 301	MINISTRY TEAM LEADER	STUDENT LEADERSHIP	CLASS 401
Church Purpose	magnification	missions	maturity	ministry	ministry	ministry	missions
Youth Ministry Purpose	honor	discover	grow	discover	discover	discover	reach
Target Audience	committed	committed	committed	committed	core	core	core
Key Terms	• a lot of singing • Bible teaching • mature believer "feel" • families invited	• experiential • local community • Mexico • Third World	• section 1: 12 Bible classes • section 2: 6 theology classes • section 3: 6 apologetics classes	class includes: • spiritual gifts study • detailed study of S.H.A.P.E.	• 301 graduate • encourager • pastors participating students • organizes ministry team • keeps it running	• "leadership" attitude • lifestyle covenant • dedicated to ministry • high requirement, high reward • servant	class includes: • missions awareness • evangelistic training • life purpose
Process Number	12	13	14	15	16	17	18
Time	weekly	monthly	monthly	monthly	varies	monthly	monthly

Appendix E

Finding Your S.H.A.P.E. in Student Ministries

Personal Information

Name: _____

Address: _____ City: _____ Zip: _____

Home Phone: _____ School: _____ Grade: ___

Spiritual Gifts

". . . Each one has his own gift from God; one has this gift, another has that."
(1 Corinthians 7:7)

Spiritual gifts I believe I have: (see below)

1.

2.

3.

I feel I may have these gifts because:

1.

2.

3.

Spiritual gifts that COMMUNICATE God's Word:
preaching   evangelism   apostle   missions   leadership
Spiritual gifts that EDUCATE God's People:
teaching   encouragement (exhortation)   wisdom   knowledge
Spiritual gifts that DEMONSTRATE God's Love:
serving mercy hospitality pastoring giving helping faith administering
Spiritual gifts that CELEBRATE God's Presence:
healing   miracles   tongues   interpretation of tongues   prophecy

Heart

> *"God has put it into their hearts to accomplish his purpose . . ."*
> (Revelation 17:17)

> *"Delight yourself in the Lord and he will give you the desires of your heart."*
> (Psalm 37:4)

List some things you're good at and love doing:

1.

2.

3.

People compliment me when:

Abilities

> *"There are different abilities to perform service . . ."* (1 Corinthians 12:6)

The following are my strongest abilities:

1.

2.

3.

Other skills and/or abilities I'm learning and/or working on are:

1.

2.

3.

A few examples include:
drama, writing, speaking, artistic, photography, video, counseling, fixing, designing, computers, accounting, music, memory, tutoring/explaining, athletics, etc.

Personality

"No one can really know what anyone else is thinking or what he is really like, except that person himself." (1 Corinthians 2:11)

This is how I see myself: (circle one of the two words for each comment)

1. Around others I am more:

RESERVED or OUTGOING

2. My decisions are based more on:

FACTS/THINKING or FEELINGS

3. In my relationships I tend to be more:

DEPENDENT ON OTHERS or INDEPENDENT

4. My use of time is more:

DETERMINED or SPONTANEOUS

One example of why I circled each of the above is:

1.

2.

3.

4.

Experience

"And we know that in all things God works for the good of those who love him, who have been called according to his purpose." (Romans 8:28)

My spiritual experience is (or how I became a Christian):

Some painful experiences that I've had:

A past experience I've learned from is:

S.H.A.P.E.

If I could design a specific way to serve God around my personal SHAPE, and I knew I couldn't fail, it might be:

Volunteer Application Packet

Welcome Letter

Dear Potential Volunteer Leader,

I'M GLAD YOU'RE INTERESTED IN WORKING WITH OUR STUDENT MINISTRY!

Our church is always looking for volunteer leaders to serve on our team in the student ministry. We believe that solid ministry is built on relationships between adult staff and students. Relationships are key to students feeling loved and understanding God's love in practical ways. This is when real spiritual growth takes place in a student's life.

The quality of our staff is very important. We are looking for men and women who have a commitment to Christ and a desire to care for students. With the aid of prayer and consideration, read the enclosed material. I encourage you to observe one of our weekend services or midweek programs before making your decision. Then fill out the application. Because we place great value on this ministry, we place great value on our staff.

Once I have received your application, I will call you to schedule an appointment. All information will be kept strictly confidential. In the meantime, please feel free to observe one of our weekend services or midweek programs.

Youth ministry is a great way to invest your time and serve the Lord! I'm looking forward to meeting with you and spending some time talking about your hopes and desires for ministry. If you have any need to reach me, please feel free to call.

Blessings,

Doug Fields
Youth Pastor

WHAT STUDENTS NEED FROM CARING ADULTS

Changing the youth world happens one student at a time. Students do not connect to programs; they connect to people. The most effective way to influence students is through significant relationships with key people in their lives. Our goal is to develop leaders who minister to students.

Students need adults who will

- love God and live for him
- be interested in their lives
- take initiative to spend time with them
- pray for them
- be real
- say encouraging words
- believe in them
- laugh
- go to "their world"
- remember their names and care for them
- share God's love through personal experience
- be consistent to the programs
- be patient
- enjoy life

HOW TO BE INVOLVED IN STUDENTS' LIVES

We will later explain the application process, but first it is important for you to understand what commitment we ask from our staff. For effective ministry with students, you need to:

1. *Understand the Purpose and Planned Values of our Ministry.* Take a look at the values and goals that make our youth ministry effective in reaching and caring for students.
2. *Commit to a Program.* Consider the role for which God has SHAPED you in order to build relationships with students.
3. *Grow as a Minister.* Develop your personal ministry, which will ultimately influence students.

UNDERSTAND THE PURPOSE AND PLANNED VALUES OF OUR MINISTRY

Purpose Statement

Our youth ministry exists to **REACH** nonbelieving students, to **CONNECT** them with other Christians, to help them **GROW** in their faith, and to challenge the growing to **DISCOVER** their ministry and **HONOR** God with their life.

Planned Values

Planned values are descriptive words that reflect our values, attitudes, styles, and beliefs that "influence" our purpose. We try to incorporate these key elements into our programs and our lives. It is all built on RELATIONSHIPS.

R.E.L.A.T.I.O.N.S.H.I.P.S.

R elational approach
E ncouragement
L aughter and celebration
A cceptance
T ransparency
I nvolvement of students
O utreach oriented
N umerical growth
S piritual growth
H ome-like
I ntimacy
P rofessionalism
S trategic follow-up

Commit to a Program

Program Option: Weekend Services—Saturday, 5:00 P.M.; Sunday, 8:45 A.M. & 11:00 A.M.

This is our large-group meeting that is designed to have a friendly, fun, challenging, and exciting atmosphere. This program shatters the "church is boring" stereotype and helps students celebrate life. It is filled with laughter, antics, videos, singing, dramas, and a message that moves students toward spiritual maturity.

Volunteer Role: Weekend Service Greeter/Table Leader

We need adults to greet, learn names, talk to students at tables, encourage students to attend other programs, and help create an accepting atmosphere.

Program Option: Area Bible Study Small Groups—Various nights, 7:00–9:00 p.m.

This is a key program for making our big group small. We divide into midweek Bible study groups. These groups meet in homes for Bible study and then break into small groups for interaction, prayer requests, and accountability. It is very powerful for students who are being cared for on a small-group basis.

Volunteer Role: A.B.S. Teacher, Pastor, or Small-Group Leader

In general, most of our new volunteers start as small-group leaders. This is your opportunity to go deeper with a group of students you can care for, encourage, pray with, and follow up on during the week.

Program Option: Ministry Teams—Meeting times vary

Ministry teams are filled with students who are involved in an area of ministry based on their desires, gifts, and/or S.H.A.P.E. We'd love to have all our students committed to having a ministry where they serve God. Examples of these teams include drama, music, greeting, missions trips, organizing special events, surfing, video, computers— the options are limitless and the ministry experience is invaluable.

Volunteer Role: Ministry Team Coordinator/Overseer

Oversee the organizing and implementation of one of the several ministries. Most teams are started by students but function best when an adult leader walks alongside for coaching, strategy, and encouragement.

There are many other opportunities to get involved in our ministry. The three listed above are the best places to start. If you have a specific gift and desire, I would love to talk with you about how you might express it in the context of our youth ministry.

WHAT AM I COMMITTING TO?

- Consistent attendance at a program (We ask that you arrive at least 15 minutes early and stay at least 15 minutes late. These extra minutes become key relational times with students)
- Relational ministry with students during the week (one-half hour additional time commitment for follow-up with students through notes, phone calls, meetings, etc. . . .)
- Attendance at a monthly staff meeting
- Growing as a minister

Our goal is to help volunteer leaders move from program-directed ministry (dependent on the program) to self-directed ministry (independent minister). A few keys to help you develop as a minister are:

- Time: Be patient; feeling comfortable and connecting with students takes time.
- Participation: Going on special events and camps will help intensify and solidify your relationships with students.
- Initiative: The more you invest, the more you will get out of it. Your relationships will grow deeper as you invest your time.

HOW TO BECOME A YOUTH MINISTRY VOLUNTEER: THE APPLICATION PROCESS

1. Express Interest

You may have an interest in serving God by loving students but are unsure as to where you can help. We will help you with this. Some of the most "unlikely people" make the greatest youth workers, so take the next step as you prayerfully consider this ministry.

2. Initial Contact by Church Staff

This is an opportunity for us to briefly connect and hear your desire to be involved in ministry. We will also give you a general overview of the ministry and arrange for you to visit and observe our programs.

3. Receive Youth Ministry Material

This packet gives you the basic information that will help you make decisions about our ministry. We have tried to explain as much as we can, but the clear picture happens when you observe a program.

4. Observe Programs

Before you fill out the application, we encourage you to observe a program. This is a good opportunity to get a better feel for the ministry without having expectations or responsibilities placed on you. You will have a chance to meet students, other staff, and write questions for our future meeting. It will be natural for you to feel uncomfortable while observing a program (students won't typically go out of their way to make you feel welcome until you get to know them).

5. Complete Application Packet

This application packet was developed to obtain appropriate information for our screening process. We request two references. You can choose a (1) pastor, (2) close friend, and/or (3) an employer within the past year.

6. Interview with Youth Pastor

This is an opportunity for you to share thoughts from your observations, describe your spiritual journey, and communicate your gifts and desires for working in student ministry. We will discuss a more specific job description that fits your S.H.A.P.E.

7. Prayerfully Consider Your Commitment

We want you to take time to pray and think through this commitment. We also encourage you to seek the counsel of family and/or friends regarding your commitment.

8. Return the Signed Commitment Sheet

After you have decided you want to make a commitment, sign the commitment sheet and return it to us.

9. Begin Ministry

We will discuss the beginning date when you turn in the commitment sheet. This date may vary depending on your intended involvement.

10. Evaluation Meeting

At your one-month mark, we will meet to evaluate your feelings and perceptions regarding your involvement. We will continue to evaluate throughout the year and adjust your role to better fit your style, personality, and strengths.

WHAT YOU CAN EXPECT FROM OUR CHURCH

- structure and leadership
- encouraging words
- training and learning opportunities
- letters of support and direction
- prayer and accountability
- challenge to develop your ministry

Congratulations, you have almost made it through this packet. I know it seems like a lot of material, but through this "process" you will learn valuable information to make your transition into our youth ministry much easier. Now, please complete the application and send out your reference forms. Again, if you have questions or need additional assistance, please feel free to contact me.

YOUTH MINISTRY VOLUNTEER APPLICATION

GENERAL INFORMATION

name   today's date

address

date of birth   phone day

occupation   phone night

employer

Work Status

☐ part time   ☐ full time   ☐ student

Marital Status

☐ single   ☐ married   ☐ divorced

Education

high school   year graduated

college/trade school   year graduated

degree   minor

other education   year graduated

PERSONAL AND SPIRITUAL HISTORY

Write a brief testimony about how you became a Christian (include date).

Write briefly about significant events in your life that have impacted you spiritually.

Describe three major ways in which you have grown in your spiritual journey since you became a Christian.

How would you describe your spiritual journey now?

What accountability do you currently have in your spiritual journey?

What do you do when you have a conflict with someone? How do you handle confrontation?

Are there any special issues or concerns happening in your life right now that would have an impact in your commitment and involvement in the youth ministry? (e.g., relationships, other commitments, etc.)

In caring for students, we believe it is our responsibility to seek an adult staff that is able to provide healthy, safe, and nurturing relationships. Please answer the following questions accordingly. Any special concerns can be discussed individually with the pastoral staff.

Are you using illegal drugs?   ❏ yes ❏ no

Have you ever gone through treatment for alcohol or drug abuse?
                                                      ❏ yes ❏ no
If yes, please describe.

What is your view on drinking alcohol?

Have you ever had sexual relations with any minor after you became
an adult?   □ yes   □ no

Have you ever been accused or convicted of any form of child abuse?
                                                         □ yes   □ no
If yes, please describe.

Have you ever been a victim of any form of child abuse? □ yes   □ no
If yes, would you like to speak to a counselor or pastor? □ yes   □ no

Are you willing to be fingerprinted for State Criminal Conviction
Clearing?   □ yes   □ no

How long have you attended Saddleback Church? _____

Are you a member?   □ yes   □ no

List the date and activities of other ministry experiences here at Saddleback
Church, and the reasons for ending that ministry.

DATE STARTED MINISTRY/ACTIVITY   DATED ENDED   REASON

Describe any other ministry/church experience you have been involved with.

What spiritual gifts do you feel you have, and how would you like to use them in youth ministry?

Why do you want to do youth ministry?

What are some of your expectations of the youth ministry staff?

The information contained in this application is correct to the best of my knowledge. I, the undersigned, give my authorization to Saddleback Valley Community Church or its representatives to release any and all records or information relating to working with minors. Saddleback Church may contact my references and appropriate government agencies as deemed necessary in order to verify my suitability as a youth worker. I understand that the personal information in this application will be held confidential by the professional church staff.

_____   _____
signature   today's date

SADDLEBACK CHURCH
Youth Ministry Reference

_____ is applying to become a volunteer youth worker with the youth ministry at Saddleback Church and has given your name as a personal reference.

The person in this staff position will be in close contact with students, and we want to ensure that these relationships will be healthy ones. Please complete the form below and use the enclosed envelope to send us your evaluation of this person's character and integrity. Your response will remain confidential.

1. Describe your relationship with this person:

2. How long have you known this person?

Please use the following scale to respond to questions 3 through 8:

1—low   2—below average   3—average   4—very good
5—excellent

How would you rate his/her ability in the following:

3. Involvement in peer relationships?

4. Emotional maturity?

5. Resolving conflict?

6. Following through with commitments?

7. Ability to relate to students?

8. Spiritual maturity?

9. What are this applicant's greatest strengths?

10. Do you have concerns regarding this person working with students? If so, please explain.

Thank you for taking the time to fill this out. If you have any questions regarding this reference, please contact the Student Ministry Department.

_____

Your name   Date

_____

Phone

YOUTH MINISTRY STAFF COMMITMENTS

After observing the ministry, spending time in prayer, and discussing with my family the commitment involved with being on youth staff, I choose to commit to the following:

☐ I acknowledge the lordship of Jesus Christ in my life and have a personal relationship with him.

☐ I am committed toward growing and maturing my relationship with God through quiet times, active attendance at church, and involvement in accountable relationships.

☐ I am committed to choices and a lifestyle that are both godly and "above reproach," knowing that my lifestyle is a model for students.

☐ I am making a commitment to the youth ministry for at least the full school year.

☐ I will attend the monthly staff meetings.

☐ I will make a committed attempt to help find at least one other adult volunteer for our growing need in the youth ministry.

☐ I understand the five purposes of the church as well as the strategy of the youth ministry and commit to help fulfill the purposes and care for the students God brings in my ministry.

☐ Because I am making a significant commitment and my presence is important, I agree to be consistent and on-time to the program(s) I commit myself to.

I am making a commitment to at least one of the following programs:
    ☐ Weekend Services ☐ 5 p.m. ☐ 8:45 a.m. ☐ 11:00 a.m.
    ☐ Area Bible Study Small Group
    ☐ Ministry Team Coordinator – Ministry: _____
    ☐ Recovery (Divorce, TNT, Eating Disorder)
    ☐ Special Events

_____   _____
Signature   Date

Appendix H

DOUG FIELDS Roles • Goals		Month: Week of:		MONDAY	TUESDAY	WEDNESDAY	THURSDAY	FRIDAY	SATURDAY	SUNDAY
Personal		Developer		7:00	7:00	7:00	7:00	7:00	7:00	7:00
				8:00	8:00	8:00	8:00	8:00	8:00	8:00
				9:00	9:00	9:00	9:00	9:00	9:00	9:00
				10:00	10:00	10:00	10:00	10:00	10:00	10:00
				11:00	11:00	11:00	11:00	11:00	11:00	11:00
Teacher		Leader		12:00	12:00	12:00	12:00	12:00	12:00	12:00
				1:00	1:00	1:00	1:00	1:00	1:00	1:00
				2:00	2:00	2:00	2:00	2:00	2:00	2:00
				3:00	3:00	3:00	3:00	3:00	3:00	3:00
				4:00	4:00	4:00	4:00	4:00	4:00	4:00
Pastor		MYLC		5:00	5:00	5:00	5:00	5:00	5:00	5:00
				6:00	6:00	6:00	6:00	6:00	6:00	6:00
				7:00	7:00	7:00	7:00	7:00	7:00	7:00
Admin		Other		8:00	8:00	8:00	8:00	8:00	8:00	8:00
				9:00	9:00	9:00	9:00	9:00	9:00	9:00

*Permission is granted by the author to copy this page for personal use.

DOUG FIELDS — Roles • Goals: Personal, Teacher, Pastor, Admin

Month: March **Week of:** 6–12

Categories: Developer, Leader, MYLC, Other

Time	MONDAY 6	TUESDAY 7	WEDNESDAY 8	THURSDAY 9	FRIDAY 10	SATURDAY 11	SUNDAY 12
7:00	F			J. BURNS @DENNY'S			CHURCH #2
8:00	A			LIFE DEV MEETING			
9:00	M	CHURCH STAFF				CODY SOCCER	
10:00	I						CHURCH #3
11:00	L		AARON	KURT	KATHLEEN		
12:00	Y	TED	MATT	J.	LYNNE		STAFF LUNCH
1:00							
2:00							
3:00		YOUTH STAFF	CAMPUS LHHS		CAMPUS ETHS		
4:00			B-BALL DAN/STEVE	HOME	WRESTLING DAVID/BILL		
5:00						CHURCH #1	
6:00			TORIES GAME	AREA BIBLE STUDY	CATHY		
7:00							
8:00							
9:00							

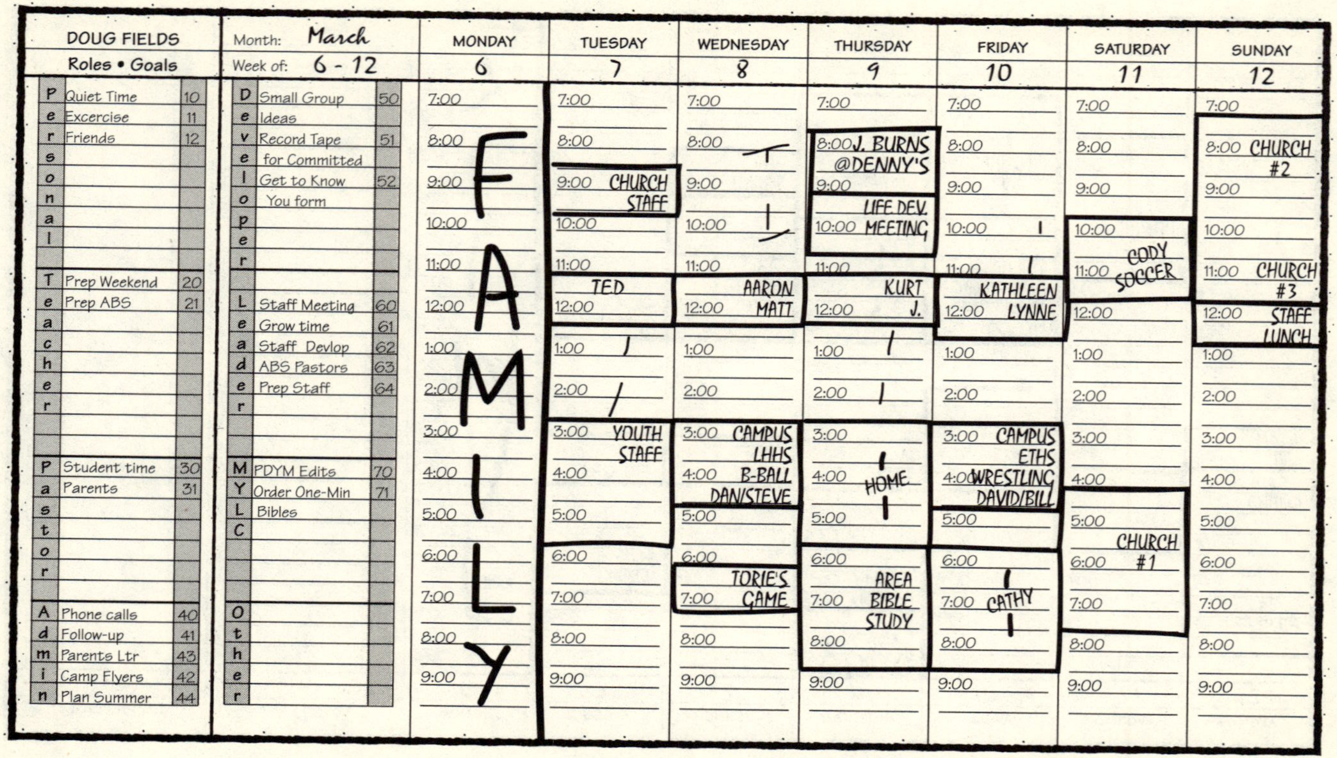

DOUG FIELDS Roles • Goals			Month: _March_ Week of: 6 – 12			MONDAY 6	TUESDAY 7	WEDNESDAY 8	THURSDAY 9	FRIDAY 10	SATURDAY 11	SUNDAY 12
P	Quiet Time	10	D	Small Group	50	7:00	7:00	7:00	7:00	7:00	7:00	7:00
e	Exercise	11	e	Ideas		8:00	8:00	8:00	8:00 J. BURNS @DENNY'S	8:00	8:00 CHURCH #2
r	Friends	12	v	Record Tape	51	9:00	9:00 CHURCH STAFF	9:00	9:00 LIFE DEV. MEETING	9:00	9:00	9:00
s			e	for Committed							CODY SOCCER	
o			i	Get to Know	52	10:00	10:00	10:00	10:00	10:00	10:00	10:00
n			o	You form						KATHLEEN		CHURCH #3
a			P			11:00	11:00 TED	11:00 AARON	11:00 KURT	11:00	11:00	11:00
l			e					MATT	J.	LYNNE		
			r			12:00	12:00	12:00	12:00	12:00	12:00	12:00 STAFF LUNCH
T	Prep Weekend	20	L	Staff Meeting	60	1:00	1:00	1:00	1:00	1:00	1:00	1:00
e	Prep ABS	21	e	Grow time	61				HOME			
a			a	Staff Devlop	62	2:00	2:00	2:00	2:00	2:00	2:00	2:00
c			d	ABS Pastors	63							
h			e	Prep Staff	64	3:00	3:00 YOUTH STAFF	3:00 CAMPUS LHHS	3:00	3:00 CAMPUS ETHS	3:00	3:00
e			r			4:00	4:00	4:00 B-BALL DAN/STEVE	4:00	4:00 WRESTLING DAVID/BILL	4:00	4:00
r												
P	Student time	30	M	PDYM Edits	70	5:00	5:00	5:00	5:00	5:00	5:00 CHURCH #1	5:00
a	Parents	31	Y	Order One-Min	71	6:00	6:00	6:00 TORIES GAME	6:00 AREA BIBLE STUDY	6:00 CATHY	6:00	6:00
s			L	Bibles								
t			C			7:00	7:00	7:00	7:00	7:00	7:00	7:00
o			O									
r			t			8:00	8:00	8:00	8:00	8:00	8:00	8:00
A	Phone calls	40	h									
d	Follow-up	41	e			9:00	9:00	9:00	9:00	9:00	9:00	9:00
m	Parents Ltr	43	r									
i	Camp Flyers	42											
n	Plan Summer	44											

(Large handwritten letters spelling "FAMILY" across the MONDAY column)

DOUG FIELDS — Roles • Goals		Month: March — Week of: 6–12	
P Quiet Time	10	D Small Group	50
e Exercise	11	e Ideas	51
r Friends	12	v Record Tape	51
s		e for Committed	52
o		l Get to Know	52
n		o You form	
a		p	
l		e	
T Prep Weekend	20	r	
e Prep ABS	21	L Staff Meeting	60
a		e Grow time	61
c		a Staff Devlop	62
h		d ABS Pastors	63
e		e Prep Staff	64
r		r	
P Student time	30	M PDYM Edits	70
a Parents	31	Y Order One-Min	71
s		L Bibles	
t		C	
o			
r			
A Phone calls	40	O	
d Follow-up	41	t	
m Parents Ltr	43	h	
i Camp Flyers	42	e	
n Plan Summer	44	r	

Weekly Schedule

Time	MONDAY 6	TUESDAY 7	WEDNESDAY 8	THURSDAY 9	FRIDAY 10	SATURDAY 11	SUNDAY 12
7:00	F	(10)(11)	(10)(11)	(10)	(10)(11)	(10)	(11)
8:00		(64)		J. BURNS @ DENNY'S	(61)		CHURCH #2
9:00		CHURCH STAFF	(20)	LIFE DEV MEETING (12)	(42)		
10:00	A	(41)		(63)	(43)	CODY SOCCER	
11:00			(40)	(40)	KATHLEEN LYNNE		CHURCH #3
12:00	M	TED (62)	AARON (62) MATT	KURT J.	(31)		STAFF LUNCH
1:00		(51)	(50)	(44)			
2:00	I		(52)		(21)		
3:00		YOUTH STAFF	CAMPUS I/HHS B-BALL DAN/STEVE	HOME	CAMPUS ETHS WRESTLING DAVID/BILL		
4:00	L	(60)					
5:00			(40)			CHURCH #1	
6:00		(40)	TODIES GAME	AREA BIBLE STUDY	CATHY		
7:00	Y						
8:00							
9:00							

Further Resources

Two elements of youth ministry not discussed in this book are adolescent development and adolescent culture. Volumes have already been written on adolescent development and culture and many excellent bibliographies on youth ministries already exist. It would be more logical, then, to direct you to the existing works.

For more information on adolescent development, see *Introduction to Youth Ministry* by John Dettoni (Zondervan, 1995). It includes a forty-page bibliography with dozens of adolescent development sources.

Walt Mueller from the Center for Parent/Youth Understanding (CPYU) has written an excellent book titled *Understanding Today's Youth Culture* (Tyndale, 1994). CPYU also publishes a newsletter to make parents and youth workers aware of current cultural trends and of resources on the World Wide Web. You can get more information about CPYU's ministry at http://www.cpyu.org/index.html.

For the most up-to-date bibliography of youth ministry works, check the compilation of *Youth Worker Journal* at:

http://www.youthspecialties.com.

Subject Index

Doug's Resources

For information on:

Purpose-Driven Youth Ministry Seminars (audio or video)
Class 101, 201, 301, 401 student version
The One-Minute Bible for Students and its curriculum
Tape series
Ideas Library
The Bible Institute curriculum
Bible study curriculum
Discipleship tools (H.A.B.I.T.S.)
Volunteer training tapes
Other books by Doug Fields
New Believer's workbooks
Youth ministry internships
at Saddleback Church contact:

MAKING YOUNG LIVES COUNT
21612 Plano Trabuco Q-30
Trabuco Canyon, CA 92679
Phone: 949-459-9517
Fax: 949-459-6303

All resources can be viewed and ordered at:
http://www.dougfields.com

We want to hear from you. Please send your comments about
this book to us in care of the address below. Thank you.

ZondervanPublishingHouse
Grand Rapids, Michigan 49530
http://www.zondervan.com